BOUGHT AND PAID FOR

Charles Gasparino, an award-winning journalist, is currently a senior correspondent for Fox Business Network and a columnist for the *New York Post*. He previously wrote for *Newsweek* and *The Wall Street Journal* and reported breaking news for CNBC. His books include *The Sellout*, *King of the Club*, and *Blood on the Street*. He is currently writing his next book on the government's insider trading investigation of prominent hedge funds. He lives in New York City.

Bought
and
Paid For

THE HIDDEN RELATIONSHIP BETWEEN
WALL STREET AND WASHINGTON

CHARLES GASPARINO

PORTFOLIO / PENGUIN

PORTFOLIO / PENGUIN
Published by the Penguin Group
Penguin Group (USA) Inc., 375 Hudson Street,
New York, New York 10014, U.S.A.
Penguin Group (Canada), 90 Eglinton Avenue East, Suite 700,
Toronto, Ontario, Canada M4P 2Y3
(a division of Pearson Penguin Canada Inc.)
Penguin Books Ltd, 80 Strand, London WC2R 0RL, England
Penguin Ireland, 25 St. Stephen's Green, Dublin 2, Ireland
(a division of Penguin Books Ltd)
Penguin Books Australia Ltd, 250 Camberwell Road, Camberwell,
Victoria 3124, Australia
(a division of Pearson Australia Group Pty Ltd)
Penguin Books India Pvt Ltd, 11 Community Centre, Panchsheel Park,
New Delhi – 110 017, India
Penguin Group (NZ), 67 Apollo Drive, Rosedale, Auckland 0632,
New Zealand (a division of Pearson New Zealand Ltd)
Penguin Books (South Africa) (Pty) Ltd, 24 Sturdee Avenue,
Rosebank, Johannesburg 2196, South Africa

Penguin Books Ltd, Registered Offices:
80 Strand, London WC2R 0RL, England

First published in the United States of America by Sentinel, a member of Penguin Group (USA) Inc. 2010
This paperback edition with a new epilogue published by Portfolio / Penguin 2012

1   3   5   7   9   10   8   6   4   2

THE LIBRARY OF CONGRESS HAS CATALOGED THE HARDCOVER EDITION AS FOLLOWS:
Gasparino, Charles.
Bought and paid for : the unholy alliance between Barack Obama and Wall Street / Charles Gasparino.
p. cm.
Includes bibliographical references and index.
ISBN 978-1-59523-071-3 (hc.)
ISBN 978-1-59184-536-2 (pbk.)
1. United States—Economic policy—2009–   2. United States–Politics and government—2009–   3. Business
and politics—United States.   4. Global Financial Crisis, 2008–2009.   5. Finance—Government policy—United
States.   6. Obama, Barack.   I. Title.
HC106.84.G37 2010
330.973—dc22
2010026888

Printed in the United States of America
Set in Adobe Garamond Regular
Designed by Spring Hoteling

To Austin Koenen:
A man of many talents, including not being afraid to speak his mind

Contents

7

Fat Cats and Fat Bonuses

8

Money Well Spent

A Partial List of Wall Street Firms and Executives Who Made Donations to Political Candidates Since 2008

Note: The dollar amounts given here do not reflect amounts raised from friends and family, and so understate the true size of the contributions; sums shown are total amounts from January 1, 2007, to June 2010. Note that the limit for personal contributions to a Presidential campaign is $2,400 but by giving to national committees and political action committees (PACs) as well as other organizations, that amount can be vastly exceeded.

Amount donated to Republicans	Wall Street executive or firm	Amount donated to Democrats
$432,824	American International Group	$783,574
$1,903,861	Bank of America	$2,083,740
$34,000	Bear Stearns	$50,000
$2,400	Lloyd Blankfein	$37,900
$2,191,040	Citigroup	$3,431,508
$2,400	Gary Cohn	$76,500 (incl. $2,300 to Obama)

Continued . . .

Amount donated to Republicans	Wall Street executive or firm	Amount donated to Democrats
$116,000	Countrywide Financial	$82,000
$1,483,449	Credit Suisse	$1,588,705
$4,250	James (Jamie) Dimon	$37,850
$0	Laurence (Larry) Fink	$9,500 (incl. $2,300 to Obama)
$1,000	Gregory (Greg) Fleming	$31,800 (incl. $2,300 to Obama)
$2,300	Richard (Dick) Fuld	$12,000
$0	Mark Gallogly	$176,900 (incl. $2,300 to Obama)
$1,821,563	Goldman Sachs	$5,047,913
$1,000	James Gorman	$11,600
$0	Alan (Ace) Greenberg	$7,000 (incl. $2,300 to Obama)
$20,300	Maurice (Hank) Greenberg	$10,000
$2,256,856	JPMorgan Chase	$2,256,856
$13,000	Lehman Brothers	$38,400
$6,800	John Mack	$14,400
$1,530,669	Merrill Lynch	$1,399,377
$2,036,022	Morgan Stanley	$2,494,874
$10,300	Angelo Mozillo	$6,100

Continued . . .

Amount donated to Republicans	Wall Street executive or firm	Amount donated to Democrats
$4,400	Stanley (Stan) O'Neal	$7,800 (incl. $2,300 to Obama)
$2,400	Vikram Pandit	$0
$81,000	Henry (Hank) Paulson	$0
$13,950	John Paulson	$77,400
$4,600	Charles (Chuck) Prince	$21,900 (incl. $2,300 to Obama)
$0	Robert Rubin	$74,000 (incl. $5,000 to Obama)
$0	George Soros	$203,690 (incl. $4,400 to Obama)
$0	Warren Spector	$23,500 (incl. $2,300 to Obama)
$0	Lawrence (Larry) Summers	$7,900 (incl. $2,300 to Obama)
$0	David Viniar	$2,300 to Obama
$1,000	Sanford (Sandy) Weill	$8,600
$13,977,384	**GRAND TOTAL**	**$20,115,587**

INTRODUCTION

Lloyd Blankfein was exhausted. It was May of 2010, and the American public was furious at him for his role in the credit crisis currently plaguing the economy. After taking over Goldman Sachs as its CEO in 2006, Blankfein had transformed one of America's largest investment banks into a Darwinian trading enterprise—generating billions of dollars in trading profits with little regard for competitors or even its own clients—and shepherded it through the recession relatively unscathed. Yet despite his and Goldman's success, he had come to be viewed by many as nothing more than a greedy, deceitful, and manipulative traitor—out to make a buck no matter the consequences.

To make matters worse, the Securities and Exchange Commission (SEC) was threatening to charge the company with fraud involving its dealings in the lead-up to the financial crisis. Prior to the crisis, Goldman had made a fortune selling products known as "synthetic CDOs," one of which was called Abacus. The SEC was alleging that Goldman had misrepresented Abacus to potential purchasers, telling them that ACA Management, an independent bond insurer, had reviewed the mortgages packed within the product, even though Goldman had failed to disclose to ACA (and to investors) that the hedge fund Paulson & Co., led by billionaire investor John Paulson, was trying to bet against (short sell) the product at the same time Goldman was encouraging clients to buy it.

Being hit with even a civil fraud charge (the SEC can't put people in jail) could be a serious blow to any firm, and Blankfein was well aware of the potentially severe consequences he was facing as well. If the charges held up, Goldman would be forced to admit it had committed fraud—an act that usually serves as the kiss of death for a bank when important pieces of business are on the line. Not only would future business be lost; according to people close to the firm, Blankfein could be forced to resign.

But despite his trials, Blankfein had taken time out of his grueling schedule to help a firm that wasn't a Goldman client, not even a prospective one. The firm was ShoreBank Corporation, a small community bank located in Chicago that lent money to inner-city businesses and was exploring the possibility of financing nascent and as-yet-unprofitable "green" businesses through so-called conservation loans and environmental banking, according to the bank's Web site. The bank's self-described mission was to "change the world." And yet despite its seemingly good intentions, the bank's urban commercial borrowers were suffering greatly from the lower property values and high unemployment that stemmed from post–financial crisis recession. Without Blankfein's help (and the help of other major Wall Street firms) ShoreBank would follow the fate of dozens of other banks during the great recession and face almost certain collapse and government liquidation.

To be sure, helping out a struggling bank that wasn't even a client was a most un-Goldman-like thing to do. Goldman dealt with only the biggest companies in corporate America or with superwealthy individuals (typically, those with $10 million or more to invest with the firm). More than that, this was a firm that had a reputation for screwing just about any company, clients included, when business was on the line. Goldman, of course, would deny that assertion. Even so, in the normal course of business, a bank like ShoreBank, with its modest funds and do-gooder reputation, wouldn't even appear on Goldman's radar as a potential customer.

Yet for some seemingly inexplicable reason, Lloyd Blankfein—who had a net worth close to $500 million and until recently had never heard of ShoreBank—started imploring his friends at other firms, like Morgan Stanley, GE Capital, and others, to help this little bank. Not that Blankfein suggested there was money to be made here. Quite the contrary; it was simply the right thing to do.

To any casual observer, this puzzling scenario raises the question: Why would Blankfein possibly want to save ShoreBank?

- - - - - - - - - - - - -

First a little background. For Blankfein, it had been a good year—at least on paper. Goldman earned more than $13.4 billion in 2009, and now, nearly midway through 2010, the firm was well on its way to a repeat performance. But with success came a lot of controversy. Goldman, the most profitable firm on Wall Street, and among the most profitable firms in corporate America, had become the poster child for the inequalities of the American economy that followed the financial collapse of 2008.

That collapse was the result of a combination of government policies, reckless risk taking, and sheer greed. The big financial firms, including Goldman, created literally trillions of dollars' worth of debt products based on mortgages that were given to people who couldn't afford them, for houses that were way overpriced. When the housing market collapsed, the firms were left with tons of toxic housing debt on their balance sheets. One by one, they started to go under: First, Bear Stearns was rescued by the government, and then Lehman Brothers was allowed to fail. Following Lehman, the other firms (including Goldman), which had been in relatively better shape (but were by no means healthy), were now in the market's crosshairs.

At that point the government, which at the time was being run by Republican president George W. Bush but would shift entirely to the Democrats when Barack Obama was elected president the following year, realized a true collapse of the entire financial system was a distinct possibility and stepped in to bail out the remaining firms.

Like the rest of Wall Street, Goldman had benefited from a bailout, funded entirely by taxpayer dollars, to survive. Yet since then, it had used a number of special privileges created by the Bush administration to help the big banks in the aftermath of the financial crisis to make more money than ever before. The profits of the big banks began rolling in just weeks after the 2008 bailout, yet the government support continued through 2009 and into 2010 as the programs remained firmly in place under the Obama administration. These included, among other perks, guarantees on the firms' debt, superlow interest rates set and then left untouched by the Fed, changes in accounting rules that allowed the firms to create profits out of losses, and maybe most of all, the notion that the remaining banks, backed up as they were by the federal government, were too big to fail. In a desperate attempt to save the economy from total collapse, the government did for a handful of banks what the mob does for its highest, most important criminals: It made them, in effect, made men. This policy, known as too big to fail, asserted that some firms—including many of those responsible for the credit crisis—should not be allowed to collapse for fear that, if they did, the entire economy would follow.

It was an unprecedented assortment of government goodies that allowed Wall Street to survive and, after the initial threat of collapse had waned, thrive. They all made out like, for lack of a better word, bandits; even lowly Citigroup, after two rounds of federal bailouts, was profitable early in 2009, so much so that its CEO, Vikram Pandit, who was nearly pushed out as head of the firm a few months later, found job security and a second chance.

But Goldman was the most adept at gaming this no-lose system, executing a business plan based on government support that made it the envy of every other firm on the Street. Goldman, probably more than any other firm, was able to use its status as a government-protected business to gain access to billions of dollars of borrowed money at rock-bottom borrowing rates and then use those funds to buy bonds—many of which were the same as those that had helped cause the financial crisis but were now trading at just pennies on the dollar.

Thanks to new government guarantees, these once risky investments became sure bets because of another government program in which the Federal Reserve was snapping up mortgage-backed securities in the open market to help prop up their prices. According to the Fed's Web site, the program is designed to "provide support to mortgage and housing markets," the theory being that if the mortgage-bond market stabilizes, banks will increase their lending and housing prices will rise. But the biggest beneficiary of this program hasn't been the average American homeowner (the housing market remains pitifully soft in many parts of the country) but the average big-bank bond trader, who profited by buying debt on the cheap and sitting back and watching his investments pay off thanks to a government payout.

And what about the men, including Blankfein, who ran these firms? They saw no problem with reaping profits at the expense of the American taxpayer. In their minds, they were doing "God's work" (a phrase Blankfein would later make famous) simply by funneling billions of dollars each year throughout the markets in an effort to churn out trading profits and thus, in the end, fuel the economy. In their eyes, if they won, everyone won; and thus, if they failed, as they nearly all did in late 2008, everyone failed.

But as the economy stagnated and companies continued to lay off employees, only Wall Street seemed to be winning. While the banks that had been largely responsible for the recession were saved, the taxpayers who had funded these bailouts and government initiatives were suffering. The national unemployment rate was hovering at close to 10 percent; in fact, the only sector seeming to fare well was state, local, and federal government (which faced an estimated 3 percent unemployment) and the bailed-out Wall Street firms, which began hiring again just months after receiving the bailout money. With Wall Street benefitting from this unequal redistribution of wealth, the public wanted blood. And with Goldman benefitting the most, the firm and its CEO, Lloyd Blankfein, became public enemy number one.

Goldman, which enjoyed a pristine reputation with the national media as the firm that government turned to for advice and counsel, was suddenly portrayed as a villain or, as Matt Taibbi of *Rolling Stone* put it, "the great vampire squid wrapped around the face of humanity, relentlessly jamming its blood funnel into anything that smells like money." The article crystallized America's burgeoning hatred of Wall Street and deep-seated suspicion that the financial service industry was just out to screw regular people.

Even President Obama, who had supported the bank bailouts and the subsequent federal policies (e.g., super-low interest rates) that led to the banks' resurgence, had started changing his tune in the face of the public outrage. Just as Goldman was getting ready to celebrate the accumulation of some $25 billion in bonus money for 2009 (one report had Blankfein set to receive $100 million in compensation), Obama referred to the bailed-out bankers as "fat cats" enriching themselves at the public's expense, even if his polices were mostly to blame.

Of course, the fattest of those fat cats, Lloyd Blankfein, took the focus on Goldman, and him, particularly hard.

It wasn't just the insurmountable press attacks that had Blankfein telling people he felt like crap all the time (or as one friend told me at the time, "Lloyd always looks like shit"). It was also the notion that he, a man who had fought his way out of a Brooklyn, New York, housing project and up the ladder to the very pinnacle of high finance, was a greedy businessman feasting on taxpayers' hard-earned money. Some polls showed that Wall Street had an approval rating lower than that of House Speaker Nancy Pelosi, who was unpopular with an amazing 80 percent of all Americans. In fact, Wall Street would have been happy with Pelosi's lousy numbers; one poll conducted in the spring of 2010 gave it an unpopularity rating closer to *94 percent.*

And now those low poll numbers, just as they would doom any political candidate, began to doom Blankfein and Goldman. In early May 2010, the Securities and Exchange Commission, led by Obama appointee Mary Schapiro, filed a civil fraud case against Goldman. The charge was the most serious regulatory attack on any Wall Street firm stemming from the financial crisis; it accused the firm of failing to disclose to its clients key pieces of information regarding an investment Goldman had sold back in 2007.

According to some of his acquaintances, Blankfein was outraged. His already long days at the office got considerably longer as he began marshaling all the firm's resources to fight the charges, or at the very least whittle them down so the firm could settle in a palatable manner.

Blankfein's problems were compounded because Goldman wasn't completely out of the woods in terms of criminal inquiries, either; the U.S. attorney for the Southern District of New York, as well as New York attorney general Andrew Cuomo, were launching investigations at the same time that British regulators and even the securities industry's self-regulator, the Financial Industry Regulatory Authority (FINRA) launched their own probes into the firm.

With Goldman enmeshed in a huge PR and legal debacle, Blankfein knew he needed a game changer, something that put the firm back in the good graces of the government and, most important, of the man who controls the government, President Obama. For the most part, Obama had been good to the banks—really good. They'd gotten everything they wanted in terms of bailouts and handouts and reaped enormous profits because of it. But now, realizing the public's increasing anger, Obama came to the conclusion that he needed to change his tune or risk appearing completely out of touch with the national mood. So he and his fellow Democrats made banker bashing their pet project.

Amid this assault, ShoreBank's demise presented a unique opportunity for Wall Street's battered CEOs. After all, Obama hailed from Chicago, where the bank was based. He had earned his political chops there serving in local government and later as a senator. Obama had even once touted ShoreBank as doing God's work, even though according to independent analysts I spoke to it hasn't generated a profit in years. Judging by its financial troubles and unprofitability, the bank seemed to exist to lend money to poor people or investors who tried to spur economic growth in the inner cities, even if that growth didn't really work out as planned. But it kept lending anyway and also began to pursue so-called green investing, or investing in businesses that are environmentally friendly even if those businesses lose money and generate few jobs.

Blankfein knew all of this and more, namely that ShoreBank had direct ties to senior administration officials: Presidential senior adviser Valerie Jarrett sat on the board of Chicago Metropolis 2020, a civic organization run by Adele Simmons, one of ShoreBank's directors; Obama's own controversial green czar, Van Jones (who later resigned after reports linked him to controversial remarks about the September 11 terrorist attacks), was involved in one of ShoreBank's many projects. Eugene Ludwig, the former comptroller of the currency under President Bill Clinton who was a former ShoreBank director, had called many top Wall Street executives, including Blankfein, and explained all the societal "good" they could accomplish if they helped bail out the struggling, civic-minded bank.

Another layer of pressure came from Sheila Bair, the head of the Federal Deposit Insurance Corporation (FDIC), the federal agency in charge of taking over and liquidating failed banks. A Republican who was reappointed by the new president, Bair made it clear in her calls to various Wall Street executives that despite taking over more than two hundred banks since the financial crisis began, she didn't want to liquidate this one.

It didn't take Blankfein long to put together the pieces. Blankfein may be brutal in front of the press of congressional committees (check out his public appearances), but he knows that in politics, sometimes it pays to play nice. In fact, one of the first things he did as the regulatory noose began to tighten was hire former Obama counsel Greg Craig as a senior adviser. Craig knows better than anyone on Wall Street whom to cozy up to in the administration.

Knowing what he could gain from an investment in ShoreBank, Blankfein pledged $20 million of Goldman money to the troubled bank to help rescue it, and called around to his friends in corporate America to do the same. And it worked. GE Capital, the giant finance arm of General Electric Company, came up with $20 million, and Morgan Stanley threw in $10 million on top of the tens of millions already donated by JPMorgan Chase, Bank of America, and Citigroup.

Blankfein—who by some accounts was fighting for his job as he struggled against multiple regulatory probes, mounting shareholder lawsuits over the company's problems, and growing dissatisfaction inside Goldman over his management—had just fought to save a small bank in Chicago that had had a history of unprofitability and no signs of turning itself around. These weren't exactly the kind of maneuvers that had helped Goldman earn $12 billion in 2009.

But what if they were? What if the ShoreBank bailout, disguised as an act of charity at best and a desperate attempt to save Goldman's public image at worst, actually represents just one more example of how Wall Street and the government, namely Big Government, really work?

The fact of the matter is, when you strip away the name-calling and class warfare coming from the Obama administration, and when you ignore Wall Street's gripes about the new financial reform legislation that will put a crimp in some of its profits, these two entities are far more aligned than meets the casual eye. They coexist to help each other—in an unholy alliance against the American taxpayer.

This is why I decided to write *Bought and Paid For*. I've spent much of my career covering Wall Street, and I've always had a particular interest in the intersection of Wall Street and politics. My first big story, back in the early to mid-1990s, focused on the major scandal of that era, involving the issuance of municipal bonds, and showed how Wall Street used politically connected consultants, such as the young political operative turned senior White House chief of staff Rahm Emanuel, to win municipal bond business from their friends in government and induce municipalities to take on greater degrees of public indebtedness. (Emanuel left Goldman in the early 1990s to work in the Clinton White House.)

In the mid-1990s I covered the research scandals, where, according to the SEC, the big firms and their analysts, like Henry Blodget, then of Merrill Lynch and now a business journalist, routinely supplied high ratings to companies so that their firms could win large and lucrative investment-banking assignments that increased their year-end bonuses. These research scandals were the subject of my first book, *Blood on the Street*. I later reported extensively on the politically motivated prosecution of former New York Stock Exchange chief Richard "Dick" Grasso by then New York attorney general (and later governor) Eliot Spitzer, the subject of my second book, *King of the Club*. In the fall of 2009, I published my third book, *The Sellout*, about the financial crisis and how it came to be.

But now I've found a new, perhaps even more urgent topic. This book won't dwell on the collapse of the big firms, which began with the fall of

Bear Stearns and ended with the liquidation of Lehman Brothers, or on how the remaining Wall Street titans survived the 2008 financial collapse through an unprecedented taxpayer-financed bailout. It will, however, dwell on how these same taxpayers suffered the fallout from Wall Street's demise: persistently high unemployment, massive amounts of debt, and a shrinking currency thanks to the Federal Reserve's unprecedented policy of keeping interest rates near zero, while Wall Street prospered.

As I discovered in the course of writing *The Sellout*, these issues are part of a bigger story: While the unbridled greed and lack of morals of many on the Street played a huge role (as legendary financier Teddy Forstmann told me, "Wall Street *never* had principles"), a critical part of the story, and one that the left-leaning mainstream media has generally chosen to ignore, was the role that government played in bringing about the downfall of the American economy and the propping up of the one business that caused the trouble in the first place.

Without that in mind, it's easy to see why Wall Street, even in its beaten-down and broken state, spared almost no expense to elect Barack Obama, who, as we shall see, promised a partnership with the Wall Street money men. Wall Street certainly got what it paid for: It has benefited disproportionately from that support in the two years since Obama became president. The big multibillion-dollar firms of Manhattan have been given guarantees no small businesses (the linchpins of our economy) would get, including but not limited to support from the Federal Reserve to keep interest rates near zero—a policy that President Obama fully endorses—which virtually guarantees titanic profits at places like Goldman Sachs even as small businesses are denied loans and unemployment remains close to 10 percent.

And of course, the same bias that causes so many in the mainstream media to ignore the negative side of government often causes many of the best reporters to miss Big Government's warped relationship with Big Business and Wall Street.

For decades government has been enriching the thousands of white-collar Wall Street bankers at the expense of millions of ordinary Americans.

It began in the 1970s, with the transformation of Wall Street from a musty advisory-driven business focused on matching up those with money to invest with those who needed it into a wild, risk-taking, anything-goes world where twentysomething recent college graduates were risking tens, even hundreds of millions of dollars each on increasingly exotic and difficult-to-understand bets.

And there was no better investment to bet on than the mortgage bond. It not only allowed more people to get access to credit, but it also became Wall Street's way of fueling Big Government's desire to extend homeownership to almost everyone by giving banks the opportunity to extend mortgages to more and more people, regardless of whether they could afford them. The banks could make these loans and sell them to government-backed mortgage corporations, who would in turn sell them to Wall Street and then to investors. The invester demand was so great for the products that Wall Street invented increasingly risky and complicated new forms of mortgage bonds so they could make even more money. And the harder it was to understand a product, the more the bankers could charge for them.

Despite their complexity, the mortgage bonds (and their more exotic cousins) were considered supersafe. Rating agencies slapped their much desired triple-A ratings on them and presto, investors had a supersafe bond. Yet mortgage bonds periodically did what other high-risk bonds do—they blew up. And each time, as we'll see, government stepped in to lend a hand.

When it all came crashing down, all the blame in the mainstream, left-leaning media came down on the bankers—the ones who took helicopters to their weekend houses in the Hamptons, soaring over thousands of homes bought by investors without the money to pay back their loans—loans whose fat fees paid for the helicopter rides. But what the liberal media ignored was the other half of the story: that these bankers' destructive risk taking was encouraged, enabled, and funded by politicians in Washington, politicians who had been bought and paid for by fat campaign checks from Lower Manhattan.

To be fair, this wasn't just a Democratic Party thing—politicians on both sides of the fence happily took Wall Street's cash and ignored the broader interests of their voters in favor of keeping the money spigot wide open and flowing. But it was a Big Government thing: Wall Street made bundles off its role in fulfilling the dreams and desires of Big Government, even if those dreams became a nightmare and sent the nation into the worst recession since the Great Depression.

This cozy relationship continues today, and as this book will demonstrate, it's thriving more than ever before. It's why Lloyd Blankfein will go out of his way to help ShoreBank, which for all intents and purposes would be a failed institution without the help of the Wall Street firms and a dose of government bailout money (sound familiar?) and it still may; as this book goes to press, the Federal Reserve has raised concerns about whether the Goldman-led bailout provides enough capital to maintain ShoreBank's long-term viability. Even if ShoreBank does indeed die, as it should, the entire sordid episode underscores a larger point: Other small banks—hundreds of them since the financial collapse sparked the great recession—have been allowed to fail, as they should. But like the big Wall Street firms, ShoreBank has friends in high places, including a friend in the highest of places— Barack Obama—whom Blankfein knows, fears, and, maybe most important of all, ultimately respects. And with that, ShoreBank got a second chance.

For all the rhetoric and apparent abuse Obama and his fellow Democrats heap on the big Wall Street firms, they're still receiving money from the fat cats. In other words, despite the name-calling, the banks' contributions to Obama have been money well spent. Elected on a message of change, a message of reversing the (supposedly) destructive policies of George W. Bush, Obama in fact has given Wall Street a free ride, while doing little more to help the broader economy.

Of course, as I write this book, the economy, at least according to gross domestic product (GDP) and economic statistics, is improving. But how could it not, with the Fed pumping astronomical amounts of new money into it for the past two years?

But even these modestly encouraging numbers can't hide the fact that

Obama and his political team have mismanaged the nation's finances time and again, so much so that even as the economy is improving, businesses continue to refuse to hire back workers in sufficient numbers and unemployment remains high. And it's clear that more than a year into his presidency, Obama's twin policies of largely coddling the banks (despite the new financial reform legislation, which I will describe in more detail later) while running up massive deficits through huge entitlement programs won't solve the problem anytime soon.

The administration has instituted new spending programs of extraordinary magnitude (the ill-fated stimulus package, Obamacare, and planned climate-control legislation) that require the issuance of titanic amounts of new government debt (again, filling the coffers of the bankers, who earn fees from selling the debt) but little reason for businesses to begin hiring again.

At the urging of Obama's friends on Wall Street, the administration has left in place many of the same corrosive structures that led the financial system to near collapse in the first place, again (you get the picture) to the benefit of the bankers who've made fortunes—and continue to do so—while ordinary Americans have struggled.

Even the president's "financial reform" bill, which became established law in the summer of 2010, does little of the sort; sure, it makes grand gestures toward regulating the financial industry, including a new rule (the "Volcker rule"), created by presidential adviser Paul Volcker, that is supposed to root out the risky practices that led to the 2008 financial meltdown. But in practice it leaves firmly in place a landscape of policies that allow banks to play roulette with taxpayers' money because in the end they are all "too big to fail." The massive banks, like Citigroup, that mixed risk taking and safeguarding the deposits of average Americans haven't been forced to break up, even though this very same business model (once outlawed because it opened taxpayers up to tremendous risk) was one of the main contributing factors to the financial meltdown in the first place.

In these pages, I'm going to lay out the roots of Big Government's relationship with Wall Street and how Wall Street views Barack Obama, despite his plans for even bigger government, as someone who will ensure their survival and profitability even if they have to endure a little name-calling along the way.

But before I begin, I want to dedicate this book to the man who first alerted me to the unholy alliance between Big Government and Wall Street. I first met Austin Koenen in the early days of my journalism career, when I was a young reporter at the *Bond Buyer*, a newspaper that covered the market in bonds sold by cities and states allegedly to finance infrastructure. At least that's what I was told by nearly every government official and banker I met during those formative years in my journalism career; together Wall Street and government were doing good things like helping the public get clean water, new bridges, and good highways.

To borrow a phrase from a more contemporary executive, Lloyd Blankfein himself, these banks believed they were doing "God's work."

But not Austin Koenen. He was an investment banker at Morgan Stanley who made his living brokering bonds issued by cities and states, and he saw the seedy side of the business about as often as he saw all the good things that municipal bonds allegedly did. And he wasn't afraid to talk about it, particularly to reporters who wanted to listen. I was one of the few who did, a fact that I can only attribute to my own political bias against Big Government.

Austin was hardly an ardent, small-government right-winger, but he did teach me how the connivance of Big Government and Wall Street really worked: In order for a firm to be considered to underwrite one of the municipal-bond sales, it must first contribute significant amounts of money to the politicians orchestrating the programs.

This is how I discovered that Wall Street really didn't have a conservative Republican political agenda, despite its media image as a bastion of right-wing free-market capitalism; it supported the candidates—on the left (e.g., far-left New York City mayor David Dinkins) or the right (e.g., his right-of-center successor, Rudy Giuliani)—who were good for business.

During his long career on Wall Street, Austin would watch as the municipal bond business, created to help the American people by creating jobs building and repairing the nation's infrastructure, morphed into a debt-creating monster, one that pushed for more and more spending on the part of government so that the banks could make more money. It was a never-ending cycle—the big banks donated oodles of money to the favored candidates, and in turn, the politicians threw business their way.

Like a quick dose of heroin, debt makes Big Government feel good for a moment—until it wears off and the pain sets in later in even larger degrees. The problem Austin had was that many of his colleagues, men and women he had worked with for years and had once admired, really had no problem with being the financial equivalent of dope pushers.

Austin would eventually leave the municipal bond business; it had changed radically over his long career, so much so, in fact, I think he felt that he had sold out a bit by staying in it as long as he had. New York City was the ultimate prize for any bond underwriter, and I recall one conversation I had with Austin where he told me he didn't want to be part of the process that forced him to collect checks from his fellow bankers who lived in New Jersey to elect the mayor of New York, who was slowly bankrupting the city.

So he took a job representing Morgan Stanley's investment-banking business in China and became one of the first American bankers to set up shop over there. Austin described it as a "challenge," and he loved challenges. Morgan created a partnership with the Chinese government to build infrastructure and make investments in the mainland. Austin laughed at one point that his "business partner is some general from the People's Army." Still, I always thought it was an odd fit for someone who wasn't particularly fond of traveling and didn't speak a word of Chinese. For all the money he made during his long career on Wall Street, he lived modestly in the same home for decades and loved to spend time with his wife and three kids.

But more than that, he was Austin Koenen, the investment banker who couldn't keep his mouth shut about the sins of investment banking and Big Government. So how could he keep his mouth shut while working with the Chinese Communists?

He couldn't, of course. "You know China will never have a real free market until it allows religious expression," he sniped to me one afternoon, calling me long distance from Beijing to complain about the brutal repression of the government he was now forced to work with. I had since moved to the *Wall Street Journal,* and that made Austin proud. I covered many of the same issues I had while at the *Bond Buyer,* but on a much bigger platform.

"You're having impact," he would say one day after I wrote a page-one story about the sleazy New York State bond issue to bail out the Shoreham nuclear plant. Even the *New York Times* was forced to follow the piece, both on its news pages and in an editorial. Before he hung up, Austin said he would be traveling back and forth a lot from China and we'd catch up over dinner. Then Austin reminded me about how important it was to stay on the story.

That was the last time I spoke with Austin Koenen. He died in his sleep a few days later of a heart attack. He was fifty-five years old.

But if Austin Koenen were here today, he would tell me I haven't done enough to explain how Wall Street and Big Government work so beautifully together; how, despite the notion that these alleged free-market capitalists really despise modern liberalism, Wall Street makes a mint when these pols get into office and how the American people get screwed by this unholy alliance.

And he would be right, and that's why I'm writing this book.

Charles Gasparino
July 2010

1

A SECRETIVE MEETING

In June 2007, the credit crisis was starting to shake the foundations of Wall Street. Two hedge funds at Bear Stearns had imploded, their investment portfolios packed with esoteric bonds, igniting the first stirrings of what would become a massive financial panic unlike any since the Great Depression, a panic that would directly lead to the demise of two of the most historic American financial firms, Bear Stearns and Lehman Brothers. The rest of the country's biggest commercial and investment banks, firms like Citigroup, Morgan Stanley, JPMorgan, Goldman Sachs, Merrill Lynch, barely survived and then only after an unprecedented government bailout.

And yet astonishingly, the heads of some of these same institutions—people like then Lehman Brothers CEO Dick Fuld; Greg Fleming, the number two executive at Merrill Lynch, the nation's largest brokerage firm; Larry Fink, the head of money-management powerhouse BlackRock; former Federal Reserve chairman Paul Volcker; Gary Cohn, one of the top executives at megabank Goldman Sachs; and mortgage-bond whiz Warren Spector, one of the heads of Bear Stearns—all seemed to be in a good mood. They were assembled around a large table in a private dining room at the Washington DC restaurant Johnny's Half Shell to meet with an inexperienced but charismatic senator from Illinois: a then relatively unknown man named Barack Obama, who wanted their help in becoming the next president of the United States.

Like most meetings at which the heads of the biggest banks assemble all in one place, this one was conducted in private. No press was allowed in, and it's unclear if any of the men present even told their press departments that they would be at the meeting. But what wasn't so private was the reason for the meeting. During the last presidential election, Wall Street had largely divided its support between the incumbent, George W. Bush, and his Democratic challenger, John Kerry. But the coming election, the heads of the Wall Street firms had told one another, would probably be different. All the polling showed the Democrats in the lead for both Congress and the presidency.

And Wall Street loves a winner. But Hillary Clinton, the odds-on Democratic favorite at this point and the wife of former president Bill Clinton, wasn't the winner the men at Johnny's Half Shell were looking for. To be sure, most of the senior executives at the top firms were committed Democrats—despite the mainstream-media cliché that Wall Street is a bastion of country-club Republicans. A more accurate cliché would be that the executive suites of the big firms house some of the most rabid limousine liberals in corporate America, and Hillary Clinton made the most of the Street's Democratic Party bias. Her Wall Street support included the CEOs of Wall Street's most prestigious investment banks, Lloyd Blankfein of Goldman Sachs and a former Republican, John Mack of Morgan Stanley, and she was on her way to collecting nearly $750,000 in donations from Wall Street executives during the next three months, while Obama would pick up less than $200,000 during the initial stages of the campaign.

Yet change was in the air, as the attendance at this restaurant showed. Many of Wall Street's limousine liberals might have given money to Hillary Clinton out of a combination of ideology and convenience (2008, by all accounts, was supposed to be a big Democratic year given President Bush's low poll numbers, the unpopular war in Iraq, and the burgeoning financial crisis), yet they weren't crazy about supporting another Clinton for president. They had several reasons, but the primary one they shared with me back in 2007 had to do with her sense of conviction: Simply put, Hillary

Clinton was considered too independent and ready to turn her back on Wall Street as soon as it became politically expedient.

In fact, as the financial crisis grew in intensity throughout 2007, she began to lay the blame squarely at the feet of her Wall Street supporters. "Wall Street shifted risk away from the people who knew what was going on and onto the people who did not," she said in a speech at the NASDAQ market headquarters in Midtown Manhattan.

It didn't matter that the financial crisis (rooted in the housing bubble, in which average Americans took out loans they couldn't afford) began with policies instituted by her husband, who had prodded banks and the federal housing agencies Fannie Mae and Freddie Mac to expand mortgage lending to poor communities. It didn't even matter that Wall Street was one of her biggest contributors. Hillary Clinton was one of the first national politicians to believe bashing Wall Street was a vote getter.

Barack Obama, on the other hand, turned up the charm.

The Wall Street liberals may say they favor leftist causes like gun control, abortion rights, the so-called green agenda, and higher taxes on the rich and on businesses (except, of course, their own). JPMorgan Chase CEO Jamie Dimon has told me repeatedly that he believes the "rich" need to pay their fair share of taxes, even when "rich" constitutes a family of four living in New York and earning $200,000 a year (a sum that doesn't go far in New York, with its sky-high taxes, and that amounts to a sliver of Dimon's own 2009 compensation of more than $17 million).

But in fact, what the liberals on Wall Street love more than anything else are friends in very high places and the profits that they derive from managing those friendships—a function of the largesse of Big Government. Why else did big Wall Street firms whose bankers live in New Jersey make campaign contributions to help elect city and state officials in California? Every time one of these politicians approves a bond issue, the bankers collect a fee. Likewise, every time the federal government goes into debt to fund another entitlement, the big firms "underwriting" that debt (buying it from the government and selling it to investors) get rich. The presumed bastions of free-market capitalism—the heads of the firms who are responsible for ensuring the free flow of capital throughout the economy—love feasting on the government as much as the laziest civil servant.

But Hillary Clinton, with her shrill voice, her oversexed husband, and, most of all, her vaunting political ambitions ever since her ill-fated and unwieldy attempt to remake health care early in her husband's presidency, made the bankers all think twice. Could she really be trusted to deliver for them?

The Wall Street fat cats of the Left certainly weren't ready to fully endorse the Republican Party, either. Of the two men likely to win the GOP nomination, the longtime U.S. senator and self-proclaimed "maverick" John McCain was far too testy and independent for the control freaks running Wall Street, and Mitt Romney, the former private-equity tycoon who had become Massachusetts governor, hadn't been able to gain much traction among voters.

McCain would ultimately become the Republican presidential candidate, and his speeches during the campaign would prove the bankers' early concern justified. He publicly supported the bailouts of the big banks during the darkest days of the financial crisis, but he would more than match Hillary Clinton in antibank rhetoric, proclaiming on the campaign trail that "Wall Street is the villain"; that if elected, he and his running mate, Sarah Palin, would "put an end to the reckless conduct, corruption, and unbridled greed that have caused a crisis on Wall Street"; and, perhaps most alarming for the Wall Street elite, that "we need to change the way Washington and Wall Street does business."

No, they were on the prowl for someone else: a breath of fresh air. They were looking for someone of intellect but also a voice of moderation. This would have to be a person who, if not an active part of the tight-knit Wall Street–Washington club, wouldn't want to do anything to rock the boat. For decades, Wall Street's interests had been safeguarded by the coterie of bureaucrats who survived administrations, passing back and forth from Wall Street to Washington, and who always seemed to work with the

Street's best interests at heart—even if those interests were at the expense of the country's larger needs. What the bankers wanted in a new president was someone who would keep this system safely intact.

These bureaucrats were people like Robert Rubin, the former Treasury secretary and now a top figure at Citigroup; Hank Paulson, George Bush's Treasury secretary and former CEO of Goldman Sachs; and Rahm Emanuel, a former Clinton administration official and Wall Street "political consultant" (whose main political advice for Goldman Sachs in the late 1980s and early 1990s had been how best to win underwriting assignments from municipalities in Illinois, like his hometown of Chicago) before he joined an investment banking firm and then became a congressman from Illinois. Others included Larry Summers, yet another former Treasury secretary, former head of the World Bank, a former Harvard professor (he had been president of the school but had been forced to resign after questioning the math aptitude of women), and a managing director of the hedge fund D.E. Shaw; and Timothy Geithner, the president of the New York Federal Reserve, who in that position was the banking system's chief regulator after the Federal Reserve chairman himself, Ben Bernanke.

Bernanke, for his part, was largely a copy of his former boss and predecessor, Alan Greenspan. During his long career in government and as an economist, Greenspan fancied himself a free-market guru and devotee of Ayn Rand, who favored putting the United States back on the gold standard, which meant the nation's supply of money would be based on the amount of gold stashed away in Fort Knox. He was first appointed by President Reagan in the mid-1980s but survived through the Democratic administration of Bill Clinton primarily because he had long ago given up his free-market credentials, seemingly cheering on the Clinton tax increases during the early part of the administration, as well as the massive changes to the financial system Clinton advocated later on at Rubin's behest.

They were changes made under the guise of deregulation and largely supported by Republicans who considered themselves supporters of the free market, the grandest goal of all being the elimination of the Glass-Steagall

Act, which forbade banks to mix trading activities with safeguarding of customer deposits. While the free-market nature of these efforts is still in debate, what isn't in debate is the result: Massive banking empires were created, allowing financiers to merge risk-taking trading businesses with commercial banks that held federally insured bank deposits.

The result? Companies like the gargantuan Citigroup, run by Sandy Weill, that were—as America was about to find out—so huge and carried so much bad debt on their books that their collapse would threaten to destroy the entire financial system. More than any single bureaucrat during the past three decades, Greenspan was truly Wall Street's best friend. When the banks lost money, he made sure they never felt too much pain, lowering interest rates and pumping money into them whenever the markets snapped. It was a pattern he'd repeatedly used over the years, from the 1994 junk-bond crisis to his response in 1998 to the collapse of the hedge fund Long-Term Capital Management and later to the dot-com crash of 2000 and 2001.

Now Wall Street was looking for a new friend, and it had its sights set on Obama, a newly elected U.S. senator from Illinois who long before he began a charm offensive with members of the Wall Street elite had started his political career in Chicago as a young "community organizer," mobilizing people in poor neighborhoods to protest big companies who were moving their manufacturing jobs overseas (the protests were largely unsuccessful) and creating a jobs program for teenagers living in Chicago's depressed South Side (which was moderately successful).

As a local politician, he had earned some name recognition, and he gained even more as a U.S. Senate candidate from Illinois, when (on his way to a landslide victory) he gave a rousing speech at the 2004 Democratic National Convention.

In that speech, he couldn't help but express his fondness for Big Government. He waxed eloquent about how the government-run Federal Housing Administration program did so much good because it allowed his grandfather to buy a home after he returned from World War II. Of course, he failed to mention the role of other government agencies, Fannie Mae and Freddie Mac, in creating the housing bubble that, within four short years, would become a housing crash. He talked about how government had helped a child from Chicago's South Side learn how to read. He added that the American people "don't expect government to solve all their problems. But they sense, deep in their bones, that with just a slight change in priorities, we can make sure that every child in America has a decent shot at life, and that the doors of opportunity remain open to all."

Even so, from what they knew of him, the bankers felt that in this ambitious, charismatic young man they might have found their guy. The chatter among top Democratic fund-raisers on Wall Street was that Obama understood their importance and would do little to dismantle their power and influence over the nation's economy. Despite his lack of experience in the big leagues, his time as a community organizer had taught the young Barack Obama about power—namely, how one's relationships with influential people can make a difference. As reported by the *National Review*'s Byron York, one of Obama's defining experiences as a community organizer came after suffering a setback in his effort to get asbestos removed from a housing project. York quotes an old friend of Obama's summing up the future president's reaction: "He said, 'I need to go there [Harvard Law School] to find out more about power. How do powerful people think? What kind of networks do they have? How do they connect to each other?' "

Another story, this time in *New York* magazine, quoted a law school friend of Obama's, Julius Genachowski, as saying, "Other states vote; New York [i.e., Wall Street] invests." It was a lesson the young candidate would take to heart. The same story contains an anecdote that illustrates just how much Obama had learned about how to sway Wall Streeters: In trying to persuade investment banker Robert Wolf to support him over Hillary Clinton, Obama arranged for a two-hour private dinner with Wolf on the night that George W. Bush was announcing his plan for the surge in Iraq.

But before the Wall Street elite would endorse Obama, they needed to see what sort of mettle he had. The man largely responsible for convincing the bankers to meet with Obama was Mark Gallogly, a veteran investment banker. Gallogly is one of those Wall Street executives who rarely appear in the *Wall Street Journal*, nor even the Wall Street gossip rags, but are powerful in their own right. Gallogly grew up in a heavily Irish-Italian section of Providence, Rhode Island, and had been a lifelong Democrat. He had had a thirty-year career on Wall Street, the last sixteen as one of the top executives at the private-equity firm Blackstone, before starting his own private-equity firm that specialized in media deals.

If the public face of Blackstone was the firm's eccentric founding partner Steve Schwarzman (maybe best known for throwing a lavish, celebrity-filled birthday party for himself just weeks before Blackstone became the first private-equity firm to go public, pegging Schwarzman's net worth at close to $6 billion), Gallogly was known as the silent partner who made the trains run on time.

In so doing, he came to know just about everybody on Wall Street, and it didn't hurt matters that during his years at Blackstone he had also become increasingly active in Democratic Party politics.

A new generation of Wall Street leaders had begun filling the executive suites. They were men more like Jamie Dimon, a committed supporter of Democratic causes, than the old-line Republicans who used to control Wall Street. They all considered themselves to be capitalists, but they also believed they were progressives and were willing to use their money and clout to spread a left-of-center political agenda.

Gallogly was cut from the same cloth, and he was all too eager to introduce the junior senator from Illinois to the most powerful men in the world. He did so simply by telling them, "There's someone I'd like you to meet."

With his fine features, neatly combed silver hair, and piercing blue eyes, Gallogly looked like a politician himself. But he was content to make his money as a banker while staying in the political background and quietly campaigning for others who looked poised to advance the Democrats' agenda (and not incidentally, his interests and those of Wall Street). And in Obama he saw the complete package.

As far as Gallogly was concerned, the man running for president wasn't the Barack Obama that many on the right were now warning about as his campaign began to gain momentum in 2007. He wasn't the guy who had sat idly by in the pews of Trinity United Church of Christ on the South Side of Chicago listening to the fiery Reverend Jeremiah Wright delivering anti-American and anticapitalist rants. Or the Barack Obama who associated with the socialist terrorist William Ayers (Ayers was a member of the Weather Underground, a terrorist group that bombed government buildings in the 1960s) on Chicago education reform.

Gallogly had first met Obama in 2004 at a dinner with other senators after Obama was elected to the Senate, and the two had hit it off immediately. Gallogly found Obama to be an incredibly moderate person in terms of temperament and policy. He wasn't anticapitalist, Gallogly believed; he just wanted to spread the wealth. He wasn't anti-American; he just wanted an open dialogue so the country could get beyond the struggles of the past.

More than that, he appeared truly smart.

"This is one of the most competent, intelligent people I have ever met in public life," Gallogly would later rave to his Wall Street friends. In conversations with them, Gallogly dismissed talk of Obama's being a socialist as "absurd" and gave little thought to Obama's connections with Reverend Wright. "That never really worried me," he told people.

Maybe even more, in Obama, Gallogly probably saw someone who he thought would be good for both the country and *himself*. But like any good Wall Street veteran, Gallogly always did his homework before making a trade. Since at least 2006, Obama had been speaking sporadically with Wall Street executives, people like hedge fund manager Orin Kramer and Robert Wolf, a senior executive at UBS. Both were major Democratic fund-raisers, but what gave Obama his first dose of Wall Street cred was the endorsement of George Soros. The billionaire hedge fund manager,

champion of far-left causes through political action committee MoveOn
.org, had met Obama the way many of the Wall Street rich and powerful
make acquaintances—through a neighbor who lived next door to his posh
weekend home in the Long Island village of South Hampton.

That particular neighbor, Jacques Leviant, a successful investor in his
own right, was asked to approach Soros by an old girlfriend, the Chicago
socialite Sugar Rautbord, who was smitten with Obama's brand of politics,
as were a number of other wealthy Chicago socialites, such as Penny Pritzker, heiress to the Hyatt fortune, whom Obama had wooed with promises
to change the world.

Leviant himself was moderately conservative, though he has given to
both Democrats and Republican candidates over the years. That said, he
brokered the introduction to Soros, and pretty soon Soros, the financial
industry's king of all liberals, was swooning over Obama as well.

Even so, in deciding whether to raise money for Obama's campaign,
Gallogly did his own research. He talked to business leaders in Chicago,
including Andy McKenna, who sits on the board of McDonald's and is a
longtime Republican who sat on the boards of both the Chicago White
Sox and the Chicago Cubs baseball teams. You couldn't have found a more
establishment person than McKenna, and Gallogly discovered he wasn't
the only one impressed with Obama. McKenna "raved" to him about how
"sensible" the junior senator seemed to both him and to other members of
the Chicago business community, how he wasn't that liberal despite his
reputation for associating with left-wing loons like Reverend Wright and
Bill Ayers, but most of all how he wasn't antibusiness. Obama seemed to
understand one of the core values, maybe *the* core value, of capitalism: It's
best to put people to work—the country as a whole will prosper and grow
when as many of its citizens as possible are working, earning, and creating
wealth.

At least that's what McKenna said, and what Gallogly came to believe,
after dozens of private meetings with Obama. The man who found common ground with revolutionaries and socialists convinced them both he
was at heart a capitalist.

With that Mark Gallogly soon became a force, albeit a largely invisible one, behind Wall Street's effort to elect Barack Obama. How truly close were the men? That's difficult to determine. Gallogly meets frequently with Obama and the two discuss public policy, but like any good Wall Street trader, he keeps most of the details of his meetings private. But despite the secrecy surrounding them, there's no doubt those meetings occur. Gallogly serves as a member of the President's Economic Recovery Advisory Board and, according to the *Washington Post*, has attended at least five meetings with the president; of course, it's impossible to tell if other meetings have occurred and been left unreported. It's a telling sign, by the way, that the Economic Recovery Advisory Board, designed, according to its Web site, "to [reflect] a diverse set of perspectives from across the country and various sectors of the economy," is dominated by former or active members of the Wall Street establishment and/or members of the boards of directors of prominent Wall Street firms. What's more difficult for Gallogly to keep private is how much money he raised for Obama while Obama was running for office. By the time the 2008 presidential election was over, Gallogly would have raised somewhere between $200,000 and $500,000 for Obama, according to election records.

These are big numbers that Gallogly won't refute. He also won't refute his enormous wealth, amassed during his long years on Wall Street. So why would someone like Gallogly, who had become rich thanks to the (alleged) free market, be a Democrat, and support high taxes and increased governmental meddling in business? If you ask him, he'd give you the same answer that his colleagues and fellow Democrats Jamie Dimon and Larry Fink might give you. "I want to give something back," he'd say, or, "Money isn't everything."

But like these so-called enlightened capitalists, Gallogly understands just how good Big Government policies have been for Wall Street, and for him personally. More than that he understands that Wall Street is hardly the bastion of the "free market" it's made out to be.

What Gallogly and every Wall Street CEO knows is that the housing bubble, which showered countless billions of dollars on Wall Street, was sparked primarily by the policies of Big Government—beginning in large part with President Clinton's Department of Housing and Urban Development, which was charged with increasing homeownership from its then-current level of around 60 percent of the population to 70 percent. It accomplished this largely by prodding the government mortgage companies, Fannie Mae and Freddie Mac, as well as private banks, to make risky "subprime" loans to those who would otherwise not be eligible for a mortgage. These loans, named for their relatively high risk of default because they were made to riskier borrowers, were packaged by Wall Street firms into mortgage bonds that became the biggest moneymaking business on the Street, a process known as "securitization."

While the story may be familiar to many readers, it's perhaps worthwhile to pause and review how this system worked.

Beginning in the Clinton administration and continuing throughout the Bush years, the mortgage companies Fannie Mae and Freddie Mac started buying up mortgages from the banks, mortgages that those banks were making to riskier and riskier borrowers. Why were they making these crazy loans? Since Fannie and Freddie would buy pretty much any mortgage any bank made, and thus take all the risk off the banks' books, there was no reason for the banks not to try to lend to anyone who asked them for cash. At the height of the insanity, loans were being given to practically anyone despite obvious red flags: lies on an application, a history of bad credit ratings, even lack of a job. There's also evidence that loan officers would simply rewrite applications to change or eliminate negative information that would prevent the loan from being accepted because the banks knew they could dump the mortgage on Fannie and Freddie the minute the papers were signed.

Fannie and Freddie would then make these loans, or guarantee them, so they could be processed into bonds—combining the streams of income from many of these mortgages into a single security known as a mortgage bond, which they would sell to investors, earning enormous profits in the process for the chosen Wall Street firms that conducted the bond sales to finance Fannie's and Freddie's operations. The firms kept many of these bonds on their own books as well, because they earned such tremendous returns.

The beauty of the whole process, the thing that made investors snap these loans up whenever they could get their hands on them, was that because the mortgages that went into these bonds were made to risky borrowers, they carried high rates of interest, meaning the bonds in turn would generate high yields, or returns, for their owners. Normally in the world of finance, high returns imply high levels of risk as well, but the compliant ratings agencies happily gave these bonds their coveted triple-A rating, the same rating given to the safest bonds in existence, U.S. Treasury bonds. Because these bonds were composed of so many mortgages, which were unlikely to go into default at once, investors were led to believe they were safe.

But as any farmer can tell you, if you take a lot of pieces of horseshit and put them together, what you get is nothing more than a big pile of horseshit. And the bonds, no matter how many mortgages were in each of them, were still composed of thousands and thousands of shitty loans made to people who should never have been given mortgages in the first place.

What's more, the financial firms, looking to increase profits even more, got more and more creative with their financial engineering, developing new bonds composed not of mortgages themselves but of other mortgage bonds; at the peak, just before the collapse began in 2007, the firms were even selling bonds that were composed of other mortgage bonds that were in turn composed of the mortgages themselves. So one mortgage made to one risky borrower could end up as part of a whole stew of crazy financial instruments (all unbeknownst to the original borrower, of course).

While the mortgage bond opened the housing market to the masses, it ironically made housing less affordable; prices shot up because just about anyone could get a loan that would be packaged by Wall Street into a seemingly risk-free security. The rest of the story is known to anyone who's not been living in a cave for the past several years: The housing bubble created by this furious borrowing and lending eventually burst as people realized the inflated prices of so much American real estate bore little or no relation to its actual value. As a result, many of the insane subprime mortgages went belly up as well, and with that, in a chain reaction, so did the value of the bonds based on those mortgages, the value of the bonds based on those other bonds, and so on.

This, of course, is the *Reader's Digest* version of how the crisis worked. Anyone interested in exploring the sheer lunacy of the process in more detail might enjoy reading any of the many books on the crisis, which make for fascinating and depressing reading.

But my goal is not to do what these other books have already done, so let's return to Johnny's Half Shell.

As Gallogly and all investment bankers—including those at the secret meeting—know, pushing banks to make terrible loans is just one way Wall Street has made a fortune off Washington. While a fiscally conservative McCain administration would presumably be looking to lower spending, which would mean less borrowing and less money for Wall Street, Obama would not. To take just one example, which was no doubt in the minds of those in the room, if Obama became president, he would likely support a "green agenda" that would mean potentially tens of billions of dollars in federal money and incentives going into new businesses like solar and wind power, not to mention renewable energy and ethanol (as General Electric and its Republican-turned-Obama-supporting CEO, Jeffrey Immelt, would soon discover). While Big Business feasted off this largesse, the bankers would get a piece of the new action as well, namely the fees for bringing those companies public and the high stock prices for their direct investments in the nascent industries. But the green agenda was just part of it.

This is, of course, exactly the opposite of the assumption made by most Americans, thanks in large part to the left-leaning media, that because investment bankers are rich, they must favor Republicans because, by definition, Republicans favor lower taxes on the wealthy and on big business. And while, of course, no one *likes* high taxes, what's more important than the tax rate is how much income you make in the first place: paying 30 percent of your money in taxes if you make a million dollars is better than paying a 20 percent tax rate on an income of only half a million.

In fact, a year after the secret meeting, in June 2008, as the markets were getting skittish and candidate Obama's economic team was fanning out trying to cool the fires, Greg Fleming said to me as the inevitability of a Democratic president and his high-tax agenda became clear, "We're all going to have to accept taxes are going up but we can live with it."

Fleming was not alone. He and his rich Wall Street brethren could live with those higher taxes under an Obama administration because they'd still make as much or more money under Obama than they would have under McCain or another Republican.

After all, it was under a Democratic administration (with the help of prominent Republicans like free-marketer Senator Phil Gramm) that the Glass-Steagall Act, a Depression-era law that prevented certain kinds of banks from combining, was repealed, allowing the big firms to swiftly grow in size.

While many of these characteristics (love of Big Government, "green agenda," etc.) are hardly unique to Barack Obama among Democrats, he alone seemed to have the complete combination of characteristics the bankers were looking to purchase. And make no mistake about it, "purchase" is the right word to use: These men, used to evaluating the characteristics of multibillion-dollar deals, approach politics as they do any other trade, and Obama, with his perceived probusiness outlook on life and charisma, not to mention his seeming moderateness and his close ties to Wall Streeters such as Gallogly and those who for years had been perfecting the Wall Street–Big Government link, seemed like a sure bet.

Knowing all this, it's no wonder Gallogly was able to convince his high-powered colleagues to meet this fresh-faced candidate from Illinois as they sipped some wine at a Washington hot spot.

To be sure, all the attendees were looking for a president who represented something new, even if they each came with their own agenda. In the case of Larry Fink, the CEO of what would become the largest money-management firm in the world, BlackRock, it was a quest for something other than the sleaze of the Clintons and for someone who could play favorably internationally, where the Republican brand was toxic (Fink did much of his business overseas as a money manager for large foreign pension funds).

In the case of Dick Fuld, CEO of Lehman Brothers, it was a search for someone who appeared to believe in the free markets but also understood the need for government to fund projects and initiatives, especially those close to Fuld's heart, such as the federal housing agencies Fannie Mae and Freddie Mac, whose mission it was to expand homeownership to the masses and, incidentally, keep Lehman's mortgage bond business alive. But as it turned out, that mission may have been the primary cause of the housing bubble and subsequent collapse. Fuld didn't seem to mind: When these agencies weren't guaranteeing loans to people who couldn't repay them, they were issuing massive amounts of debt to finance these activities, and Lehman Brothers earned huge fees assisting in this effort before it imploded later in 2008 as the third casualty of the financial crisis after Bear Stearns and mortgage lenders Fannie and Freddie.

And Warren Spector, Bear Stearns's president, was simply searching for someone whom he could believe in. These were tough times for Spector. Despite a net worth that exceeded $300 million, he was in the crosshairs at Bear Stearns, where he had made his mark as one of the top traders of mortgage bonds, the complicated securities that would lead to Bear's massive losses and ultimate demise a year later.

At issue for Spector was how he had managed—or failed to manage—the two large Bear Stearns hedge funds packed with mortgage debt, the

High-Grade Structured Credit Fund and High-Grade Structured Credit Enhanced Leverage Fund. They weren't exactly household names, not even on Wall Street, but that would change as the funds became the first casualties of the declining market. For that reason, Spector's job was now clearly in jeopardy, and that was a humiliating blow to someone who just months earlier had been seen as the likely successor to Bear's CEO, James "Jimmy" Cayne. (And indeed, just a couple of months after this June meeting, Spector would be fired from Bear Stearns.)

With his Wall Street career in decline, Spector now turned to politics. On paper he supported Hillary Clinton, even inviting her for a private meeting with senior executives at Bear Stearns. But based on everything he knew about Obama, he thought the young senator was someone he should be listening to. And like Gallogly, Spector had been impressed immediately after his first meeting with Obama which had occured back in 2004 at a private lunch in Bear's gleaming Midtown Manhattan headquarters. In fact, he had been so impressed that years later, when Gallogly arranged the Washington dinner, he flew down from New York on a private jet to make sure he could attend.

Paul Volcker, the former Federal Reserve chairman, thought he should be listening to Obama as well, but for different reasons. He was looking for someone—anyone—who he thought had a clue about the excesses of Wall Street. Despite his long years in the financial markets, and most famously his years as Fed chairman, when he had shown the political will to raise interest rates and put a halt to the massive inflation of the 1970s, Volcker hated what most of the men in the room stood for: making money—sacks of it—simply by trading all sorts of financial products, but most notably the toxic bonds that were at the heart of the then-burgeoning crisis. Volcker had believed that the financial innovations of the past two decades had been setting the stage for a massive implosion—the beginnings of which were already happening. He hated that the men in that room who took all this risk were basically protected by the Federal Reserve and the federal government, and Volcker had watched in dismay as his successors at the Fed, Alan Greenspan and Ben Bernanke, did all they could to preserve that status quo. Knowing that the bankers at the Fed and the politicians on Capitol Hill would backstop them in the event of trouble, Wall Street's risk taking rose to enormous heights.

Volcker and Gallogly knew each other from Democratic Party circles, and when Gallogly called and asked if he would like to attend the private sit-down, Volcker asked for some literature—articles, maybe a book or two—on the young junior senator from Illinois. There was, of course, a myth already being created about Obama—the notion that he was post-partisan, something that Obama himself had promoted in his two autobiographies, putting himself forward as a man who could see virtue in all sides of the argument and then, after reasoned consideration, come to an independent conclusion about the right way to go.

Despite the fact that it was largely contradicted by his far-left voting record as a state senator and now a U.S. congressman and by his associations with people like Ayers and Wright, the media accepted Obama as a moderate without much debate. Likewise, the more Volcker read about Obama, the more he accepted him as an agent for banking reform, even as Obama wooed the very same bankers who would oppose it. A few days after Gallogly sent Volcker the material, Volcker said he liked what he had read, and Volcker was in.

But while each of the men in the room was looking for something new, they also wanted something old. While Volcker may have somehow come to believe Obama had the personal history to possibly upend the status quo—namely his background in "progressive" politics as a community organizer—everyone else in the room showed up because Gallogly's pitch was pretty simple: In the end, Barack Obama really was someone Wall Streeters felt they could work with, despite all the noise they might have heard about Obama's far-left views and his associations with some of Chicago's more unsavory characters, like criminally convicted businessman, real estate developer, and Democratic Party fund-raiser Tony Rezko.

In 1995, Rezko became literally one of the first three people to ever make a campaign contribution to Obama, and he would help to raise millions over the years for him, particularly when Obama was in the Illinois state senate, where he could influence legislation involving real estate. Their association didn't end there; Obama and Rezko became close friends, so much so that Rezko hired Obama to do some legal work for him in the 1990s.

Obama's association with Rezko was in many ways emblematic of his dealings with business in general (and more specifically with Wall Street). As with his relationships with Jeremiah Wright and William Ayers, who helped Obama solidify his left-wing political credentials in Chicago, Obama's relationship with Rezko gave him access to amazing amounts of campaign cash over the years, though it would also raise questions about his judgment. During the Democratic primaries, Hillary Clinton mocked Obama's reference to Rezko, calling the land developer a "slum lord." In 2008 Rezko would end up being convicted on sixteen charges: six counts of wire fraud, six of mail fraud, two of corrupt solicitation, and two of money laundering for offering campaign contributions in exchange for state contracts.

Being someone who spent years as an Illinois state senator before representing the state in the U.S. Senate, Obama had been surrounded by the notoriously corrupt world of Illinois politics: Disgraced and soon-to-be-impeached governor Rod Blagojevich was caught on tape attempting to sell his appointment to fill Obama's now-vacant Senate seat. But Obama also made very productive use of his time in Chicago, forging deep connections not just with real estate developers and powerful albeit controversial local political players like Wright and Ayers but also with key business leaders, which would put him in good stead later in his career. What's more, he built relationships with others who would themselves create a web of Wall Street ties—like Valerie Jarrett, a real estate lawyer who ran a firm that specialized in profiting off its strong relationships with Chicago-based developers, and of course a certain ambitious young man named Rahm Emanuel.

Like Gallogly, Warren Spector had long been involved in Democratic Party politics, though he knew very little about Obama's ties to the likes of

Wright, Ayers, or Rezko, he would later say. And like some of Obama's other supporters, Spector said he really didn't care. The more he got to know Obama, the more he judged him as his own man, someone who was smart, educated about Wall Street in a way that went beyond simply asking for campaign contributions. He seemed to really appreciate what bankers did—the financial innovations, as in mortgage bonds, that people like Spector produced had a direct social benefit by expanding loans and housing to more and more people.

As the executives milled around the room with wineglasses in their hands, Obama immediately spotted Spector and walked over to him. "Glad you could make it, Warren," Obama said. "Good to see you, too," Spector responded. Spector might have been impressed with Obama, but he wasn't quite sold on Obama's being the next president because he was still leaning toward supporting his rival, Hillary Clinton.

That was about to change. After a couple of glasses of wine, the group sat down and each man formally introduced himself to the candidate. Most, like Dick Fuld and Larry Fink, did so matter-of-factly, and Obama gave them both friendly hellos. Those who had not already met Obama expected a night of policy analysis from the wonkish candidate, not exactly the most exciting way to end a hard day at the office.

But Spector immediately livened up what had begun as a dull affair. Inside Bear Stearns, Warren Spector was not known for his sense of humor, and the strain of the firm's recent problems was clearly weighing on him. The failing Bear Stearns hedge funds had been big financial news. Some pundits were saying they were harbingers of a broader decline of Wall Street because many of the biggest firms, most notably Bear itself, had invested in the same toxic housing bond investments that were found in Bear's hedge funds.

As a result, Bear's stock was getting crushed, and with that the rumors had begun swirling that Spector's boss, Jimmy Cayne, a right-wing conservative (the political opposite of Spector), was getting ready to fire him over the problems that had begun with the losses of the Bear hedge funds, which were clearly under his watch. Spector's problems with Cayne had been brewing for years. Just three years earlier, Cayne had publicly chastised Spector for his public support of Democratic presidential candidate John Kerry. (Cayne, despite his personal political views, thinks it's bad business to overtly support any political party—unless, of course, there's business to be gotten.) Since then the two had barely spoken and with the hedge funds disaster, their relationship turned even more toxic.

Yet tonight Spector was unusually glib, as if he knew the end of his career at Bear was approaching and with it a great weight was coming off his chest. He would soon be a free man, free to start his own hedge fund; free to start his own film production company (called Tashtego Films); and free possibly to be part of history—the election of President Barack Obama, the nation's first black president and, most important (although by no means unprecedented), a progressive who could work with Wall Street.

When it was Spector's turn to talk, he announced himself to the group as "Warren Spector, the current scourge of Wall Street." Everyone laughed, including Obama, who had undoubtedly read in the financial papers about the problems at Bear Stearns.

Spector certainly broke the ice that night, and then, as the conversation began, Obama did much of the talking. Gallogly immediately knew he was hitting a home run as candidate Obama expounded on his vision about the future of America, one unburdened by the politics of the past and one in which the financial sector and capitalism flourished, according to people who were there and who were immediately impressed by Obama's rhetoric.

- - - - - - - - - - -

But in reality, the pose Obama assumed at this meeting downplayed his alter ego, what some would say is the *real* Barack Obama, the ultraliberal politician and community activist who lobbied on behalf of the far-left housing advocacy group known as the Association of Community Organizations for Reform Now, better known simply as ACORN.

ACORN billed itself as the largest community action group in the country, with 350,000 active members who lead marches, protests, and voter registration drives in advancing its far-left agenda. And it's no stranger to the community activist turned president; Obama worked closely with ACORN during his days as a community organizer, and his campaign paid an ACORN affiliate more than $800,000 for its get-out-the-vote efforts.

It was ironic that Obama would be glad-handing some of the same bankers who had been targets of many of ACORN's protests, including claims that the big banks were at the center of a plot to redline inner-city neighborhoods and that they refused to lend to minority communities out of sheer racism.

Less ironic but more scary is ACORN's own record of abuse. The organization would make the news for numerous alleged criminal activities, including encouraging prostitutes to evade the law and, much more sinister, possible voting fraud. (Examples that would be amusing if they weren't so scary and scurrilous include a voter application form for "Mickey Mouse" submitted by ACORN in Orlando, Florida, and registration forms sent in by ACORN in Las Vegas that included the names of the entire starting lineup of the Dallas Cowboys.)

But none of that mattered to the high-powered executives in the room. Obama was demonstrating the skill that, even more than his vaunted oratorical ability, has served him most usefully throughout his political career: a chameleon-like quality that allows him to be all things to all people (not unlike the previous Democratic president, Bill Clinton).

Earlier in 2007, the closely watched rankings of the *National Journal* ranked Obama *the* most liberal U.S. senator in the entire Congress, based on his votes to expand government health-care benefits, as well as other spending initiatives. In fact, he was ranked as more liberal than Hillary Clinton, who was ranked sixteenth despite her long-standing desire to create government-run health care. But unlike Hillary, Obama had a reasoned, calm demeanor that appealed to the bankers, who still remembered the bruising national drama of the Clinton years.

Obama had voted against George W. Bush's successful "surge" of troops in Iraq, which would finally turn the corner on bringing peace to that troubled land and limiting Al Qaeda's operations, and he had repeatedly voted yes on questions of massive government entitlements—yet at this meeting he wasn't asked a single question about either of these issues, according to people who were there.

Obama once considered Reverend Wright his spiritual mentor, despite Wright's espousal of so-called Liberation theology in his church in Chicago, the Trinity United Church of Christ. Liberation theology interprets the Bible through the prism of Marxism, yet no one asked how it could possibly be squared with the candidate's newfound faith in capitalism. Nor did anyone ask how a candidate vying for the presidency of the United States could admire a man who said such things as "God damn America" or "[T]he Jewish vote, . . . that's controlling [Obama]" or, concerning the September 11, 2001, terrorist attacks, "America's chickens are coming home to roost." (Obama was eventually forced to disavow Wright and these statements, but only after intense media pressure.)

Instead of the ultraliberal activist, the man at the meeting was Obama the moderate, the one who impressed Gallogly, Andrew McKenna (the chairman of McDonald's), and now just about everyone at Johnny's Half Shell as a centrist politician. And unlike most politicians he was also quite entertaining.

In addition to discussing his "post-partisan" philosophy, Obama cracked a few jokes. To the stodgy bankers in the room he was simply cool. As Greg Fleming would later recall, Obama never once spoke about massive new programs like government-sponsored health care, higher taxes, or even income redistribution, all of which would become hallmarks of his administration's agenda just a couple of years later. Instead Obama spoke about "helping the less fortunate" (which when adroitly phrased sounds like simple social concern, a basic sense of morals and ethics, not a call for an outright welfare state), about "getting health-care costs under control," and about "the need for a strong financial sector," according to people in the room.

They also listened to the captivating junior senator from Illinois explain why he should be president and proclaim his respect for the principles this country was built on, including the virtue of hard work and, despite his leftist background, the business community. If Obama displayed any hint of his radical past, no one seemed to notice, nor did anyone care. He had won them over, impressed them as a man of the future, open to ideas and to wise advice.

That night and over the next two years, Big Business and Wall Street, the alleged epicenter of capitalism and bastion of free markets, would fall head over heels for maybe the most liberal presidential candidate since FDR. Wall Street bankers and firms would help Obama raise over $100 million for his campaign (see the front of this book for a partial list of the amounts raised just by some of the firms and people mentioned here—the numbers are eye popping). Their man would use the huge monetary edge Wall Street provided to decisively outadvertise and outspend his opponent, naval war hero and senator John McCain, and become the forty-fourth president of the United States.

In a supreme irony, perhaps *the* critical turning point of the campaign occurred in the fall of 2008 at the height of the financial crisis, when the very banks that were funding Obama were in danger of going under; it was at that time that Obama's calm and steadfast demeanor set him apart from his competitor in the eyes of many voters.

In fact, betting on Barack Obama may have been the best investment Wall Street made in 2008, or indeed ever. For much of the campaign, McCain and his running mate, Sarah Palin, were either ahead or running neck and neck with Obama and Joe Biden, yet the Wall Street money kept pouring in to Obama.

Undeterred by the financial crisis and the subsequent bailouts, Wall Street sent checks totaling nearly $15 million to Obama, compared with around $9 million to McCain—this during a year in which many of the firms barely broke even despite billions of dollars in government bailouts.

Goldman Sachs would eventually rank as Obama's second-largest contributor. And it wasn't alone. Citigroup lost close to $19 billion in 2008, yet donations from its bankers and traders put the firm sixth among Obama's top contributors. Jamie Dimon was on the Federal Reserve Board, and according to his press office, he refrained from direct contribution, but one of his seconds-in-command, JPMorgan Chase chief financial officer Mike Cavanagh, didn't. He held one large fund-raiser outside JPMorgan headquarters for then-candidate Obama that helped raise nearly $100,000 for the campaign. Meanwhile over at Morgan Stanley, John Mack switched his support to Obama at the prodding of one of his top executives, a man named Tom Nides, who had held various jobs inside the Democratic Party over the years between stints on Wall Street. Nides became one of Obama's biggest supporters on the Street, holding a number of fund-raisers actually inside Morgan Stanley headquarters.

Nides would eventually be offered various jobs in the Obama administration but chose to stay at Morgan as one of its highest-ranking executives. He also chose to run Wall Street's primary lobbying organization, and with that, Morgan Stanley became one of Obama's favorite bankers, handling various deals for the administration, including the sale of its ownership positions following the government bailouts and takeovers of banking giant Citigroup and General Motors.

But Nides and Morgan Stanley were hardly the only beneficiaries of Obama's new economic agenda. In truth, the entire Street benefited because, in the end, it was Wall Street's money that helped a former community organizer, the disciple of a preacher who once proclaimed, "God damn America," defeat his moderate Republican opponent (who had spent seven long years as a prisoner of war) and become president of the United States.

2

THE LEFT SIDE OF WALL STREET

B arack Obama assembled an amazingly effective coalition to win his historic presidential election in 2008: Moderate suburbanites, young people, and minorities combined to give him a 53 percent share of the vote over John McCain, who had won the GOP nomination. But a key piece of the Obama coalition that received far less notice from the mainstream media and had a far greater impact on the election result was Wall Street—or to be more precise, the heads of the major Wall Street firms. These were people like Lloyd Blankfein and Gary Cohn, who run Goldman Sachs; Larry Fink, head of the world's largest money manager, BlackRock; and Wall Street's current rock star, Jamie Dimon—who united to provide one of the most liberal politicians in generations unprecedented access to the Wall Street piggy bank, even as the financial collapse in late 2008 put their very survival in jeopardy.

It was that access to Wall Street's cash that gave Obama's campaign early traction; according to the Center for Responsible Politics, Goldman Sachs, Citigroup, JPMorgan Chase, UBS, and Morgan Stanley all ranked among the top twenty U.S. corporations that bundled donations to the candidate. To be sure, Obama famously raised the majority of his campaign cash from "individuals," that is, average people who were so inspired by his personal story and his plans for America that they gave whatever they could to the campaign. The Obama campaign bragged that it had more than 250,000 individual donors, a presidential campaign record, with many of these coming from people decidedly different from typical Wall Streeters, who generally bundle scores of $2,300 checks (the maximum amount a single donor can contribute to a candidate) during fund-raisers.

But Wall Street's support for Obama was important—vitally important—not just for his successful presidential run but for his campaign against Hillary Clinton for the nomination. That's because Wall Streeters like Gallogly and the crew at Johnny's Half Shell provided the seed capital for the Obama campaign. As attorney and political strategist Jack Burkman explains, if it weren't for that early and continued Wall Street support, who would have paid for those massive rallies where Obama raised $200 each from ten thousand or more adoring fans?

"People tend to associate Republicans with Wall Street, but the truth is, it's the Democrats that are in bed with the Street," says Burkman, who advises mainly Republican candidates. "And that's certainly true with Obama. He's been in bed [with them] from the beginning. And that was crucial to his victory. Obama raised a lot of money from individuals, but it was the Street's initial support that was crucial to his success. Without Wall Street's initial support, he doesn't have credibility. That's why Hillary was so freaked out when Obama started to woo Wall Street. It gave him the money to hold those megarallies that galvanized his support. It got the ball rolling and allowed Obama to access more people and raise more money. None of that would have happened without Wall Street's support. No doubt about it. Without Wall Street, Obama would not be in power today."

And as reported by *New York* magazine's John Heilemann, Obama rewarded these generous contributions to his campaign by letting some of these bigwigs, including Dimon and UBS's Robert Wolf, into his inner circle. It's worth noting that UBS is under investigation for tax fraud and is one of the biggest purveyors of subprime loans and debt.

The sheer scale of Wall Street's profits, beginning with the Bush bailouts and continuing with policies advocated by the Obama administration, is mind-boggling: Take just one firm alone, Goldman Sachs. Just over a year after the entire financial system nearly collapsed, Goldman reported profits in excess of *$13.4 billion* for 2009. Nor is Goldman alone in reaping the benefits of having put Obama into office. The other major firms reported gigantic profits as well. In the first quarter of 2010, Goldman, JPMorgan Chase, and Bank of America *all* reported that their trading activities didn't lose money on one single trading day—an extraordinary achievement made possible only by the generous support of the American government and taxpayers.

Once again, the irony of Wall Street's love affair with Obama is that the conventional wisdom (as put forth in the mainstream media) about the Street's relationship with the president is so different. If you read the *New York Times*, you would think that Obama was leading the anti–Wall Street charge that has now targeted Goldman Sachs, which is fighting securities fraud charges brought by the SEC (whose chairman, Mary Schapiro, was appointed by Obama). Or that Obama's landmark victory was a rejection both of the mindless greed of bankers that led to the market crash and of eight years of Republican rule— a rejection, that is, of everything from the war in Iraq to the business-friendly environment of the Bush administration, which in the media's portrayal allowed Wall Street to run wild, sowing the seeds of a banking system collapse that could be stopped only by the unprecedented expenditure of hundreds of billions of dollars in bailout money.

During the 2008 presidential campaign, as I pointed out, Wall Street, like the majority of voters, fell in love with Barack Obama and overwhelmingly supported him over John McCain, a politically moderate Republican (with a very immoderate temper) who vowed he would cut taxes rather than raise them, as Obama promised. But paying a few more bucks in taxes never really bothered the men who run the big Wall Street firms. What they look for in a president, or for that matter any elected official, is someone they can work with; someone with an appreciation of what they do and who can help them in times of need. The bankers at the big firms may grouse that Obama has used banker bashing as a political weapon as the 2010 midterm elections approach and Wall Street's unpopularity with the public grows, but according to a senior executive at Goldman Sachs (the target of much of the abuse) and others, he's doing it not out of conviction but out of convenience, because he needs to show a legislative victory in the financial reform bill, and attacking Wall Street is the best way to drum up popular support for the initiative, which he has now signed into law. As a senior executive at Goldman recently told me, "Obama couldn't give a shit about all this anti–Wall Street stuff. He needs to bash us to get his bullshit financial reform through Congress." (The notion of financial reform being "bullshit" is something we'll discuss later in this book, but suffice to say, Wall Street is already finding ways to dance around the legislation.)

If you think the facts behind the financial collapse are complicated, the story of why the financial services firms went out of their way to support Obama is really quite simple. Simply put, in Obama they saw an ally, someone who would support them while in McCain they saw someone who at best was noncommittal to their agenda. The former POW and famously cantankerous senator never had much of a relationship with Wall Street for two reasons: First, he was a senator from Arizona, not exactly a financial services mecca, and for the most part, he couldn't stand being in the same room with guys who compared trading bonds for a living with warfare. As a man who had survived the brutality of war in the most literal sense, he found their talk unbearable.

And it was an attitude that permeated his staff. "These guys couldn't give a shit about what we think," an exasperated Steve Schwarzman snapped at an aide when he came back from a strategy session at McCain campaign headquarters in Washington. As opposed to his former partner Gallogly, Schwarzman was a staunch Republican. But the founder of the private-equity giant Blackstone with a net worth well into the billions of dollars wasn't used to being told his views didn't have much merit, even if that was the message he received from McCain's staffer one afternoon. The actual message delivered to Schwarzman from the McCain aide was actually more polite, primarily because it was delivered by the aide and not by McCain himself. But the meaning was the same. It was as if the old man, who despite his temper can be disarmingly charming, had told Schwarzman to "shut the fuck up," as he had told so many people during his long political career.

Even so, Schwarzman was one of the few Wall Street executives who continued supporting McCain, and not just because he was a registered Republican. He had actually listened to some of Obama's plans while other CEOs were busy swooning over the rock star who would be president.

"They didn't add up," he remarked at the time. Listen closely, Schwarzman told his friends, most of whom didn't believe him, and beneath the soothing rhetoric is a radical agenda of spending, spending, and more spending. Schwarzman couldn't understand why his friends on the Street— and he knew just about everyone of note at every major bank—didn't understand what they were supporting; they worked on Wall Street, after all, so why couldn't they add?

It dawned on him after attending a few meetings with both John McCain and his staff. "This guy just doesn't give a shit about what we think," he thought, and Obama did. With that Schwarzman also concluded that his own vote and the money he would like to raise for McCain would be overwhelmed by the Wall Street juggernaut lining up behind the community activist turned Wall Street's best friend.

McCain, it should be noted, did have some other Wall Street supporters, most notably Merrill Lynch CEO John Thain, but the rest of the Street, it appears, abandoned him. Why? In various interviews, some of the Wall Street CEOs and their senior staff told me they didn't want another four years of what they saw as the failed policies of the Bush administration. Others say they couldn't bring themselves to vote for a ticket that included Sarah Palin, who they believed was insufficiently educated in foreign affairs or, for that matter, anything else. To the Wall Street elite, as to most of the East Coast intelligentsia, the notion of what they saw as this rube from Alaska being the proverbial heartbeat away from the presidency was unthinkable.

John McCain, meanwhile, never came across as a guy who would go to bat for Wall Street; he didn't have a close personal relationship with any of the big CEOs, as Obama had with Gallogly, with Bob Wolf of UBS, later with Jamie Dimon of JPMorgan Chase, or with Blankfein's number two, Gary Cohn, who was an early supporter. In fact, based on his conversations with Treasury secretary Hank Paulson, a former CEO of Goldman (and Blankfein's ex-boss), it seemed that McCain was so angered by the burgeoning financial crisis and what it had done to his campaign (turned an even race into one that favored Obama) that he seemed like a guy who, if he had his way, would let them all, Goldman included, simply fail.

Another possible reason for the bankers' support of Obama over McCain was McCain's natural distrust of their motives.

"Why the fuck would you do that?" snapped McCain into his cell phone, his face turning red and his finger jabbing in the air as if he were pointing right at his target. He wasn't, of course. The target, Treasury secretary Paulson, was at the White House, where he had just unveiled the latest bailout plan for Wall Street: a multihundred-billion-dollar program to keep Wall Street alive.

The financial crisis had severely wounded the McCain campaign, which made the old fighter pilot even more ornery toward Wall Street types like the Goldman banker turned Treasury secretary. And now McCain felt that the crisis and the government's solution—to just give the banks money to prop them up—would put his campaign on life support.

McCain was huddled with campaign chief Rick Davis and advisers Greg Wendt and Douglas Holtz-Eakin in a conference room in his campaign headquarters in Crystal City, Virginia, overlooking Reagan National Airport.

It was a few weeks after Lehman's failure, and the financial system was still in shambles, with banks losing money, losing clients, and falling into insolvency. Paulson said the new batch of money—and he recognized it was indeed a lot of money—was needed to save the banking system and the economy. Without massive direct infusions of capital the big banks—nearly every firm, including his old firm—were doomed. And if that happened, no one would lend, no one would borrow. The banking system would shut down. The economy, already in a fragile state, would collapse. Think bread lines and the Great Depression.

McCain wasn't buying the entire sob story. What little he knew of Wall Street he didn't like. He considered most of the people who ran the banks spoiled brats and ruthless opportunists. Why wouldn't they just take the money, wait out the panic, and then begin using the taxpayer funds to pay themselves big bucks, with bonus season quickly approaching?

McCain's advisers weren't witness to the whole conversation, just Mc-Cain's blunt responses, bitten lips, and angry gesticulations as he listened to Paulson explain the plan. "Huh? What the fuck?" McCain said at one point. "How the fuck can you trust them?" he screamed at another.

He was, of course, right not to trust Wall Street, which, just weeks after getting its collective ass saved, handed out billions in bonuses to traders and bankers (Goldman doled out $4 billion in bonuses in the bailout year). That was of little consequence to McCain, who reluctantly went on to publicly endorse the Paulson bailouts and lose the election, in large measure because he lost Wall Street support—the millions of dollars in campaign contributions that other Republicans often count on to combat attack ads like those that Barack Obama unleashed in all those battleground states that McCain lost.

"Thank God he's not our president," one senior Wall Street executive told me, referring to McCain, the day after Barack Obama made history and became the nation's first African American president. "Obama is at least smart; he'll know what to do about the economy. McCain would be a disaster."

At this point, explaining some of Obama's blind spots—his liberal voting record, his associations with Ayers and Wright, and his plan to balance the budget while expanding the war on terror to include Afghanistan, creating a new health-care entitlement, and proposing nearly $1 trillion in stimulus spending—could do little to convince any of Obama's many Wall Street supporters that they had made the mistake of a lifetime. Not only were they thrilled to support a winner and someone who so eloquently articulated their own desires to change the world (as long as they made their millions in the process), but they simply hated McCain because they knew he hated them.

And as the election season wore on, they came to love Obama. In addition to meeting with the bankers at Johnny's Half Shell, Obama continued to meet with the big Wall Street executives throughout 2007 and 2008 at fund-raisers and private events, where he came across as nothing short of a moderate. If John McCain was sneering and screaming at Paulson about the mess his friends on Wall Street had put his campaign and the country in, Obama calmly asked for advice in fixing the system. Yes, that's right, advice. He was asking the very men who had created the problem to come up with ways to fix it. He wanted a partnership to spur the economy that would help him do all the great things he wanted to do, from fixing the health-care problem to creating a "green" economy to help save the environment.

"And who could be against that?" Jamie Dimon quipped one afternoon, as he thought back on the reasons he found Obama so refreshing. Dimon, the son of a stockbroker, who had been working on Wall Street ever since he graduated from Harvard Business School, saw so much he admired in Obama that while he didn't officially support Obama (press aides say that because he was on the Federal Reserve Board he couldn't overtly support anyone) he let it be known that he wanted his top executives to do what they could to get this breath of fresh air elected. And they did, and they weren't alone.

They had good reason, because Obama seemed so smart and polished and, most of all, moderate to the Wall Street titans, people like Larry Fink, John Mack of Morgan Stanley, Greg Fleming, and many others. As much as Dimon loved Obama, he couldn't hold a candle to the love shown by Lloyd Blankfein and Goldman Sachs.

In September 2008, when the financial collapse was at its peak and Wall Street's world was collapsing, Goldman contributed $596,000 to the Democrats, including then candidate Obama, nearly eight times what it gave the Republicans that month. JPMorgan Chase gave nearly $230,000 to the Democrats, nearly two and a half times what it gave the Republicans.

Obama rewarded the bankers' expectations and eagerly filled key jobs in the administration with their surrogates, who quickly enacted policies that added to their bottom lines during the next two years and further supported the notion that the big banks must be kept alive at all costs.

Yet with the surge in profits during 2009 and into 2010 came something that not even President Obama saw coming: a surge in outrage. Obama had planned a massive stimulus package to stop the rising unemployment he was saddled with. The plan was simple: Give states money to fund infrastructure projects, and people would be put back to work. That was the theory Obama sold to Congress, which in turn sold it to an increasingly desperate public. The reality was far different. The states hoarded the cash and kept their bloated bureaucracies in place. To be sure, some of those "shovel-ready" jobs were in fact created, but not enough, not even close to spur the economy into hiring, and unemployment skyrocketed. In some industries, like construction, joblessness rose to above 20 percent.

Wall Street's support for Obama certainly isn't completely devoid of ideology, but its driving force is without a doubt the opportunity to make money from his Big Government agenda. The Wall Street executives who lined up behind Obama will say they are all committed liberal Democrats who were looking for someone new—a postpartisan president, so to speak, who could shape the country in ways others couldn't or wouldn't. "Hope and Change," Obama's campaign slogan to millions of new voters, minorities, and young people resonated in Wall Street boardrooms as well, a special irony given that so many of his far-left supporters would have felt sick knowing that the message they were embracing so eagerly was also embraced by the same men they felt embodied the laissez-faire, free-market capitalism that they so detested.

Despite the seeming differences between these two groups, on some level most of today's Wall Street brass have more in common with Obama's young, idealistic supporters than meets the eye. The new breed of Wall Street executive is far more progressive, far more *liberal*, and thus believes to a far greater degree in his or her broader responsibilities to the country, to mankind, than his or her predecessors, who many assumed were myopically focused on their individual net worth and their firms' bottom lines.

Maybe that's why it seems Dimon has gotten along so well with Obama for the past year. Both are cut from the same cloth. Obama is the essence of a limousine liberal who distrusts the masses clinging to "their guns and their religion." Dimon, despite his skills as a chief executive, isn't far behind. For a CEO who runs a company that does investment banking and safeguards customer deposits in branch offices across the country, Dimon isn't bashful about spouting the liberal talking points.

He has railed against measures to scale back illegal immigration, likening people who worry about border lawlessness to xenophobes who would have kept his grandparents from immigrating to the United States from Greece; he has called for increased spending on inner-city schools, some of the most free-spending, profligate bureaucracies in the country; he has advocated for increased spending on the country's infrastructure, despite the fact that the cities and states that do much of the road and bridge work can't afford to go into any more debt to pay for these projects. At work, he tells his staff that "giving back" to society is a necessary ingredient to being a Wall Street executive.

It's why shortly after taking over at JPMorgan Chase, Dimon began requiring executives to contribute substantially more in health-care premiums to subsidize their lower-wage colleagues. Similarly, Dimon has instituted what Noam Scheiber of the *New Republic* has described as "nanny-state paternalism" at the company. At a recent health-care conference, Dimon said, "[I]f a JPMorgan Chase employee has diabetes and we don't see claims for insulin and for eye exams, they get a phone call."

All this is why his staff says when he retires he'll most likely become a college professor, a line they used whenever rumors have swirled that Dimon's close relationship with Obama would lead him to a job in the White House, possibly succeeding Tim Geithner as Treasury secretary.

Dimon isn't alone among the Wall Street life embracing progressivism. John Mack openly supports health-care reform (he and his wife have created a charity dedicated to promoting health-care reform and alternative medicine), and in 2007 he made waves by announcing that he had switched parties to endorse the Democrats, namely then-candidate Hillary Clinton for the 2008 election because of her record supporting that cause. He also serves as chairman of the board of one of New York's biggest hospitals (NewYork-Presbyterian).

Hank Paulson was an avowed environmentalist as CEO of Goldman Sachs before he led one of the greatest ever governmental interventions into the free markets as Treasury secretary. In that position he was one of the key architects of the now-infamous Wall Street bailout, which *New York Times* columnist Gretchen Morgenson estimated in one column well exceeds the already enormous $89 billion the Obama administration says it cost taxpayers.

In other words, these guys may drive around in limousines, but they proudly wear their liberalism on their sleeves. What may make them different from many of their liberal peers is that they rarely shy away from an opportunity to turn a profit, especially when turning that profit allows them to satisfy their social consciences at the same time.

With Barack Obama, Wall Street wasn't just betting on his new "hope and change" agenda, which, when boiled down, came right out of FDR's playbook from the 1930s: Big Government programs, taxes on small businesses, new entitlements, and more. They were betting that while Obama would lead America in his own liberal image, he would have no stomach for changing Wall Street's role in government; namely, its ability to make money through its partnership with Big Government.

It's a mutually beneficial relationship—and it always has been. As I've explained, the big Wall Street firms have earned huge fees underwriting America's debt binge by scooping up the Treasury's bonds and distributing those bonds across the globe. That government policy, begun under the Clinton administration, couldn't have been accomplished without Wall Street.

The mechanism that allowed the banks to lend so freely and give mortgages to millions of Americans who otherwise would not have qualified for a loan was in fact something called the mortgage bond, created, ironically, by BlackRock founder and CEO Larry Fink back in the early 1980s, when he was a Wall Street bond trader. The mortgage bond allowed banks to remove these risky loans from their balance sheets and put them into the hands of investors, and Fink went on to make a fortune from its broad acceptance in the banking business.

These bonds may have been the root cause of the 2008 financial crisis, but for years they were some of the most lucrative inventions Wall Street had ever come up with. They added trillions of dollars in profits to the bottom lines of the banks as home ownership soared.

And government, in turn, was happy. The stated social goal starting with the Clinton administration was to expand housing "penetration" (i.e., the percentage of the population that owned their own homes) from 60 percent to 70 percent, a dramatic increase that could be achieved only with the willing cooperation of the big banks in buying those mortgages from Fannie Mae, Freddie Mac, and elsewhere and putting them into bonds to sell to investors. So Wall Street made piles of money and Big Government saw its mission accomplished, all at the same time.

In 2006 Wall Street made so much money from these housing bonds that the average salary for the CEOs of the top seven firms was $50 million. Even though these same bonds turned sour just a couple of years later when their depressed values forced the banks that held them into near or total failure, the partnership between Wall Street and Big Government survived as the Bush administration set the stage for a bailout of Wall Street as the president's final act in office.

Just a couple of months after the bailouts, the Obama administration's policies—some of them held over from Bush's bailout and some of them new to the game—began to kick in, and Wall Street, fresh off nearly driving the country (and arguably the global economy) to ruin, began one of the greatest periods of profitability in years. No firm illustrated this better than Goldman Sachs. In the second quarter of 2009, while many Americans were pondering the possibility of the next Great Depression, Goldman rolled the dice and generated a then-record $8.3 billion in trading profits, enough to push the overall firm to a $3.1 billion quarterly profit. Goldman was not alone. After months of write-downs, in the first quarter of 2009 Goldman, Bank of America, Citigroup, and Morgan Stanley generated a combined $7.4 billion in profits. The next quarter was even better. Feasting off low interest rates from the Federal Reserve and generous government subsidies, those firms made nearly $11 billion in combined profit.

But these profits weren't derived from activities that actually helped the broader economy, such as investing seed capital in start-up companies or lending to small businesses, the original intention of the bailouts. Rather, the windfall came from essentially the *same* risk-taking activities that had led to the financial crisis—borrowing cheaply thanks to the low interest rates supplied by the Federal Reserve; using that borrowed cash to buy bonds, essentially financing Barack Obama's spending spree through the purchase of some Treasury bonds but mostly government-supported mortgage-backed securities (the government was now actively buying these beaten-down bonds as another way to help the banks holding them repair their balance sheets); and, of course, pocketing the immense profits.

In one sense the protections given to banks and the profits they produced can be seen as a form of hush money. Small-business owners and average citizens are now shocked and worried by the massive amounts of debt issued by the new administration for various programs, including the $800 billion stimulus package that fell far short of the administration's expectations. But there's been barely a peep from the financial experts on Wall Street, who downplayed the impact all this borrowing might have on the economy and the markets. Why would they do that? Wall Street has earned countless billions in fees from this activity. Not even a report in March 2010 from Moody's Investors Service, one of the big credit-rating agencies, that the United States might lose its triple-A rating could wake them from their stupor. And their silence doesn't end there. The big firms barely said a word about health-care reform, even as its passage in the spring of 2010 created a massive new entitlement on top of the already massive Obama spending plans and plans to raise taxes. After all, mandatory health care may hit small businesses hard in terms of higher taxes, but Wall Street's clients, the big pharmaceutical and insurance companies, will flourish because, under the law, those who remain uninsured will be guilty of a crime and as they receive insurance coverage they will undoubtedly use more medicine. And of course, when the government borrows money to finance this expensive new plan—well, you know who's raking in the fees on all that debt (here's a hint: it's not the National Small Business Association).

If this isn't enough to demonstrate the liberal mind-set of those on Wall Street, let me ask you a question: When was the last time a major Wall Street firm openly advocated tax cuts as a way to spur the economy? Tax cutting was something that even Obama's own economic adviser, Larry Summers, had once called for—that is, before he joined the spending-happy Obama administration. Summers is a particularly interesting example of the principle of "bought and paid for." He was one of the architects of Wall Street's alliance with Washington. He was at the forefront of both the Wall Street bailouts and deregulation during the Clinton years—as deputy Treasury secretary under Clinton he helped repeal the Glass-Steagall Act, allowing the big banks to combine their risk-taking trading activities with the safeguarding of everyday customer deposits. The repeal of Glass-Steagall led directly to the creation of the megabanking giant Citigroup, which required one of the biggest bailouts during the financial collapse. Summers would later be well rewarded for his connections to Wall Street. He earned about $8 million at hedge fund D.E. Shaw and in speaking fees from financial companies between stints as the president of Harvard. In his new role as one of Obama's economic advisers, Summers, along with numerous other members of the administration, remains close to many of the top executives of the big firms.

Summers has been a White House sounding board for Wall Street during the past two years, but he isn't alone. Wall Street's friends are placed throughout the Obama cabinet, thus ensuring that Wall Street has had a huge say in the reshaping of the financial business in the aftermath of the 2008 collapse, including the current financial reform legislation. And despite Obama's calling the bankers "fat cats," CEOs like Dimon and Blankfein had made numerous trips to the White House attempting to ensure that the president doesn't do anything that really costs them money. It's rather like letting the wolves guard the henhouse, only in this case the wolves gained access by making generous campaign contributions.

It's only fitting that the firm that went the most head over heels for Obama—Goldman Sachs—has emerged from the carnage as the most profitable of the big investment banks. After all, Goldman was feasting off Big Government and making huge profits. And Goldman has been the target of public outrage for handing out some $20 billion in bonuses nearly a year after the financial collapse, while nearly a quarter of all construction workers remain unemployed.

"It's pretty amazing," explained a twentysomething Goldman Sachs trader to me in 2009. "We're making money in so many different ways it's frightening."

He was bragging about the enormous pool of wealth he and Goldman found themselves sitting in just months after the financial collapse had nearly destroyed his Wall Street career and forced him to use his Ivy League education and top-flight MBA to do something other than speculate on bond prices. But the federal government, first under George W. Bush and then under Barack Obama, had once again made the world safe—and highly lucrative—for speculators.

Beyond even just the direct and indirect bailouts, what the young trader was now bragging about was how policy makers had created a no-lose market for him and his trading buddies.

"We're making money with our eyes closed," he laughed.

As he explained it, the gravy train began with what we've already covered, namely the Federal Reserve's policy of taking interest rates down to zero. This then lowered the cost that this trader and his many counterparts paid to borrow funds and invest them in whatever they wanted.

The government handouts included the new "too big to fail" policy, which the Obama administration made clear it wouldn't change from the Bush years. Under this policy, companies and investors with capital could lend to Goldman and the rest of the Wall Street banks without worrying that a bad bet here and there from the traders would put the firms out of business and cost them their investment. Why? Because any bank receiving this special designation would be bailed out by the U.S. taxpayer, and that protection was better than anything any insurance company could give them. As a consequence, Goldman's borrowing costs fell even further.

On top of all this there were the various guarantees the banks received—

that the government wouldn't let them default on their own long-term debt and that the banks could borrow from the government. And as an added layer of protection, investment banks like Goldman and Morgan Stanley were now treated like ordinary commercial banks (though I've never known anyone to open a checking account at Goldman or the House of Morgan).

Yet by becoming commercial banks in name only, Goldman and Morgan had access to government funds through the Fed's discount window, something that had only been available to banks with traditional deposits.

Meanwhile, the American public was told that these measures were designed to save the banking system. After all, without big banks, where could small businesses—widely regarded as the engines of any economic recovery—get loans to expand and hire again? The problem was that small businesses couldn't get loans. The dirty secret was that Goldman and Morgan Stanley never made loans to small business and never will, and as for the big banks, like Citigroup and JPMorgan Chase? They were copying the business models of Goldman and Morgan Stanley, so instead of making money by lending to businesses, they were now trading bonds, which, with all these programs and gimmicks, were on a government-subsidized rally, as the young Goldman trader explained to me. "It's almost criminal," he snickered.

Like most young men who go to Wall Street, this trader was drawn to Goldman Sachs for the opportunity to make millions, and after nearly losing it all, it didn't matter that he was getting rich off the American taxpayer or that Obama promised to squeeze entrepreneurs and small businesses with higher taxes. The young millionaire even explained that, thanks to a fat 2009 bonus, which was derived from all of these government gifts, he planned to retire early.

But Wall Street had help in another place too. The Financial Accounting Standards Board—the chief regulator of the accounting industry—basically stemmed the flow of losses at the big banks in April 2009 by relaxing rules that forced the firms to price (or "mark") their assets at actual market value (as opposed to a "model" value, which allows firms to mark assets at whatever they feel they are worth). Before this change went into effect, this "mark-to-market" accounting had helped expose to the world the enormous degree to which Wall Street had become a gambling den rolling the dice in some of the most speculative securities ever created. This accounting rule had forced the firms to take losses on those securities by marking them to the actual, often near-zero values, even if they had no intention of selling those bonds any time soon. It was this type of accounting treatment that nearly forced them out of business in the fall of 2008, and now that hurdle was being removed. It's good to have friends in the right places.

Now the mark-to-market rule was gone, thanks to political pressure to relieve the banks of a massive burden during their time of alleged need. What's more, the Federal Reserve (with the support of Obama's Treasury secretary, Tim Geithner) spent most of 2009 purchasing on the open market $1.3 trillion of debt, much of it consisting of similar securities to the banks' depressed mortgage bonds while Geithner planned to have the Treasury subsidize hedge funds' purchases of mortgage bonds. All of this made the type of investing the Goldman trader was boasting about a no-lose proposition.

"Any way you look at it," this trader boasted, "we're going to have an amazing year."

The trader's comments were, of course, an honest and stark contrast to the absolute horseshit spin (forgive the blunt language, but there's no other way to describe it) coming out of his firm, and out of all the major firms. As the banks' PR flacks told it, all that money was being made the old-fashioned way—just by using brainpower and skill to game the markets.

Given all the money being made at Goldman, Lloyd Blankfein must have known he had the most to lose from profiting so soon after the bailouts. Goldman's bonus numbers in the spring of 2009 were on a record pace, and suddenly the big firm came up with a new PR campaign. While other Wall Street firms tried to downplay their near-death experience in 2008 or simply thank the American taxpayer for the bailouts, Blankfein chose to take it on directly and ordered his PR staff to rewrite history. As the flacks at Goldman put it, the firm had never really needed the bailout money that it had been given in 2008, nor did it need all the handouts it was receiving as the new administration took over. In other words, the Bush White House had forced it to be bailed out back in 2008, shoving $10 billion in capital down its throat on top of other measures, just as the Obama White House was forcing it to make so much money now.

When word of Goldman's new PR strategy, articulated by its sharp-tongued spokesman (and highly paid partner), Lucas van Praag, began to spread, even rivals at Morgan Stanley were shocked. "Why are they drawing so much attention to themselves?" one press official asked me.

At JPMorgan, Dimon's PR staff were more subtle than Goldman's (they shied away from arguing with reporters about whether the bank had needed to be bailed out), but they were nearly as duplicitous about JPMorgan's postbailout progress. The bank, they said, was simply "earning" its way out of the banking crisis.

If that was the case, if the Street really didn't need all these special programs, then why did it continue to use them? And why did they never cease to butter up the new president who was handing out free money? In fact, just the opposite appeared true. Dimon, who was now a regular visitor to the White House, spoke glowingly about how he first met Obama years earlier while he was the head of Bank One in Chicago (which he later merged with JPMorgan to become CEO) and Obama was an Illinois state senator. Sources inside JPMorgan say that during the presidential election, while Dimon's PR staff said he had to remain technically neutral, Dimon appeared to encourage his staff to funnel money to the Obama campaign and began briefing Obama on the banking crisis. If Obama seemed to be the better versed of the two presidential candidates on the intricacies of the banking system during those days, it was because he had Jamie Dimon, by most accounts the best manager on Wall Street, lending him a helping hand.

And that help continued. Dimon took his family to the presidential inauguration, and during Obama's first year in office, Dimon was seen around the White House so many times directly with the president that he became known in Washington as the "shadow Treasury secretary," the man Obama trusted most when it came to the economy.

Meanwhile, the real Treasury secretary, Tim Geithner, was busy meeting with Lloyd Blankfein. The Goldman CEO didn't have the warm and fuzzy relationship with the president that Dimon had (no one, it should be pointed out, feels particularly warm around Blankfein), but he and Goldman had supported the president enough during the campaign that, like Dimon, Blankfein also had an open invitation to the White House. Records show that Blankfein met with Geithner a whopping twenty-two times in 2009, more than any other CEO.

What were they discussing? Spokesmen for Dimon and Blankfein characterize the meetings as casual visits to discuss banking policy and how it would affect Wall Street, which might well be true. But what they're leaving out are the details of those meetings. Those details, I am told, often centered around TARP (the Troubled Asset Relief Program)—the bailout program that injected hundreds of billions of dollars of capital into the banks following the collapse of Lehman Brothers in September 2008. Now that the firms were making money again, they were no longer worried about surviving; their big concern was how much they would thrive. And they couldn't thrive unless they could pay their traders bonuses that matched their performance, even if that performance was subsidized by the American taxpayer.

But under TARP, these bonuses were capped—as long as the firms owed that money to the government, the government's "pay czar," a man named Ken Feinberg, limited the amount of money each firm could pay its top-earning traders. Feinberg was already sending a chill through Wall Street. Citigroup was forced to sell Phibro, its profitable commodities-trading unit, because Feinberg would not allow it to pay Andrew Hall, the head of the unit, the $100 million he was owed under his contract.

With all this in mind, Blankfein and Dimon spent more time in Washington than ever before. In addition to meeting with the president and Geithner (some of those "meetings" occurred over the phone), they met with members of Congress, including Democrat Chris Dodd, who ran the banking committee of the U.S. Senate, and Barney Frank, his counterpart in the House of Representatives. Blankfein and Dimon's pitch was pretty direct: Now that their firms were healthy again, they asked to be allowed to pay back the TARP money so they could pay their people what they (thought they) deserved.

But for some government officials, it wasn't as easy as just paying back the government's money with interest. The investment banks were still saddled with toxic debt that was being propped up by the feds. That TARP capital would be needed if the system went south again. Blankfein and Dimon had won over Geithner, their longtime friend; he gave them the sign-off, as did Ben Bernanke at the Fed. But Sheila Bair, the FDIC chief, was hesitant. She was, after all, the bureaucrat who would have to bail out the banks if the system seized up again, and she barely had enough money to handle the dozens of small community banks that were failing, it seemed, by the day.

But Dimon and Blankfein continued to press: The system was better, they assured the administration, and their firms were better—they spun a tale of a Wall Street that had learned its lessons from the past. They claimed they no longer used massive leverage and wild trading strategies to make money.

More than that, in order to survive in the long term they needed to retain talent, people like that young Goldman trader I spoke with, who could make serious money trading at a hedge fund if Goldman was no longer able to pay him the big bucks.

Dimon, notorious for his quick temper and lack of patience, was about to explode as the paper pushers in Washington kept dragging their feet through the late winter and early spring of 2009 on the firm's repaying its TARP money. During a town hall meeting with his employees, he explained his frustration when he was sitting before one of the numerous congressional committees investigating the banking crisis. "While I was sitting there, I was thinking I should raise my hand and say, 'I will wire you back the (TARP) money if you let me leave right now,'" Dimon quipped to massive laughter and applause.

By the spring of 2009, the administration, for all its misgivings and concerns about the safety of the banking system, finally succumbed to the relentless pressure. JPMorgan Chase, Goldman, and Morgan Stanley would be allowed to repay their TARP money by the summer; Citigroup and

Bank of America, given their mammoth size and equally mammoth problems, would do so later in the year.

And so, of course, the bonuses began to flow again.

There is a theory, promoted for years by the banks and accepted as gospel by their defenders in government, that helping Wall Street profit is good for the country: As the banking system improves and strengthens, small businesses will have access to credit, while entrepreneurs will be able to find more capital to expand. This is, of course, the argument Bob Rubin, both inside the White House and later as a Wall Street executive, has made for years, first to Bill Clinton and now to Barack Obama. But small-business lending has fallen significantly despite the improving profits of the banks.

Look no further than Citigroup. In the first quarter of 2009, the company made $1.5 billion in profit. The next quarter, it earned $4.2 billion. But the bank's consumer lending fell. In the first quarter of 2009, Citigroup had a little more than $301 billion in outstanding consumer loans. But in the next quarter, that number fell to $292 billion. By the end of the year, it fell to $270 billion, a 10 percent decline. While the bankers were getting rich trading with the government, the average Joe was having trouble getting a loan. Same story for Bank of America. It earned $4.2 billion in the first quarter of 2009 and another $3.2 billion in the next quarter. Like other firms, these profits were driven not by taking risks on businesses and people but simply by trading some stocks but mostly bonds. In the first quarter of 2009, the bank generated $7.5 billion in trading profits. In the second quarter, the bank's traders made even more money: $7.7 billion. But in those same two quarters, outstanding consumer loans fell to $543 billion from $564 billion, a decline of more than 3 percent. By the end of the year, Bank of America's outstanding consumer loans fell to $531 billion, a decline of more than 5 percent. In fact, it seems that the big banks have plowed most of their profits into massive new bonus pools to reward their employees as the benefits of Big Government continue to flow to Wall Street through Obama's second year in office.

It is Wall Street, after all, that gets to profitably underwrite the trillions of dollars in state, local, and federal debt that will be sold in the coming years to support Obama's Big Government agenda—government-run health care, the $800 billion economic stimulus program, expensive climate control legislation, and any of the countless other programs that the new administration plans to unleash that will grow the national debt to historic proportions.

With that in mind, now is the time to take a closer look at just how the Wall Street firms benefit from the expansion of government and what the consequences can be for the rest of us.

For decades Wall Street has been doing wonders to keep Big Government at as big a level as it can, almost always at the expense of the average American taxpayer. When Rudy Giuliani was mayor of New York City, his staff members reached out to their friends on Wall Street and cooked up an idea to plug the city's massive budget deficit: They would create a dummy corporation that would sell bonds for the purchase of the city's water system. Water taxes would pay off the debt over time, the city was assured, and the proceeds of the bond sale would flow right into the mayor's hemorrhaging budget.

Everyone seemed to benefit, except the taxpayer. The Giuliani administration wouldn't have to make politically painful budget cuts, and the firms underwriting the city's bonds would make a fortune—their bonus checks coming right out of the pockets of taxpayers. In Giuliani's defense, he inherited a massive and unwieldy bureaucracy from his predecessor, David Dinkins, and by the end of his eight years in office had cut the size of New York City's government more than any of his predecessors or, for that matter, the man who succeeded him, billionaire businessman Michael Bloomberg.

But the fact remains that a big reason New York City and, for that matter, New York State, have some of the highest taxes in the country, crippling business development and forcing the middle class to move elsewhere, is because all that tax money is needed to pay off loads of debt piled up as politicians balance the books with Wall Street chicanery. By the time Giuliani left office, the city was shelling out a little more than $2.5 billion a year in debt-service payments; today the city is paying closer to $5 billion annually—that's more than $7,000 for every citizen in the city, according to the *New York Daily News*.

Wall Street firms are supposed to have their own research arms to analyze the safety and the security of these bonds. But like the rating agencies that are paid by the city to rate its bonds and have given the big spenders a free pass, the big firms have barely raised an eyebrow about New York's massive indebtedness (approaching a combined $200 billion), and when they do, it is usually in hushed tones.

Meanwhile, New York City chugs along, with mayor after mayor praying that those Wall Street bonuses keep on flowing so their tax revenues keep growing. But other municipalities, where budgets aren't supported by people making millions a year in salary, face a very different reality.

Just ask the citizens of Orange County, California.

Orange County, a sunny suburban oasis south of Los Angeles, is known for its political conservatism (an airport named for conservative icon John Wayne is located there) and its beautiful beaches. It is the last place you would have thought would engage in shady and dangerous fiscal practices. But back in the early 1990s, facing a burgeoning budget deficit and a public that didn't want to pay for it (and didn't want to cut spending, either), the county's treasurer, Robert Citron, turned to Wall Street for help.

He found a partner at Merrill Lynch in Michael Stamenson, a top salesman of bonds and other financial products, mostly to state and local governments. If you were a young broker who wanted to be a player at Merrill Lynch back in the 1990s, Michael Stamenson had simple advice for you: Possess the "tenacity of a rattlesnake, the heart of a black widow spider, and the hide of an alligator."

This philosophy had paid off for Stamenson, who, while at Merrill, had amassed a small fortune—one much larger than that of any of the government bureaucrats who were his clients. That fortune bought him three homes in which he threw lavish parties, featuring valet parking; a seven-figure income; a beautiful young second wife; and, most of all, the admiration of his colleagues. "I would say that Stamenson is exceptional as far as understanding the investment philosophies and goals of the clients he works with," former Merrill CEO David Komansky once told the *New York Times*.

It's fair to say that Stamenson was at ground zero of Wall Street's love affair with Big Government. He built his business by catering to local municipalities, which had huge investment pools that needed to be put to work—meaning they needed to be invested in securities that would produce higher-than-average returns so those returns could be directed back into the budgets of states, counties, and cities (if there's one thing I've learned in decades of reporting on politics, it's that no government bureaucrat *ever* wanted a smaller budget).

In the early 1990s, Stamenson's expertise was in high demand. The economic downturn that had begun with the implosion of the junk bond market in late 1989 hit the real estate market hard and fast, and tax revenues began to plummet. State and local budgets in California and New York were hit particularly hard. Both were among the highest-taxed states in the country, with all that money going to support massive spending plans: lavish deals with unions, generous welfare benefits, and more. Politicians in both states refused to cut services—fearing a backlash from unions and other interest groups—and they could raise taxes only so much.

So they turned to Wall Street, and in large part to Stamenson, for help.

Robert Citron seemed like a typical client of Stamenson's in that he was Orange County's longtime treasurer (for twenty-four years) and he knew his way around Wall Street—he had been dealing with the big firms for years to underwrite his county's debt and, more important, to help him manage the county's various investment pools. The way the county's budgeting worked, tax money from local governments and school districts in the county were funneled into the countywide pools, and Citron was in charge of investing the money.

Citron appeared to be a modest man. A Democrat in a largely affluent Republican county, he ate regularly at the local Santa Ana Elks Club, a dingy local hangout that offered unlimited soup and salad for $4.50. He bought his clothes at local outlets and favored bright polyester pants and pastel blazers. He liked turquoise jewelry and often spoke of his fondness for USC, his alma mater.

But those quirks aside, it was his supposed financial acumen and, as it turns out, zeal for successful risk taking that had made him a local legend. Under his watch, Orange County's investment pools produced the type of returns that would make any fancy hedge fund manager green with envy. As a result, tax increases remained a distant reality despite massive government spending on everything from roads to new schools. During much of Citron's tenure as treasurer, spending grew a whopping *10 percent* annually.

That's why the massive returns from his hedge fund (for that's what the investment pool he ran really was) were so important; despite Orange County's reputation for staunch conservatism, Big Government was flourishing in the warm California sun, and it was being paid for by Citron's investment strategy, which was no different from that of a typical hedge fund investing in exotic securities that could blow up at any moment.

Helping Orange County pay for this largesse was Wall Street—or, to be more precise, a consortium of Wall Street lenders that included Credit Suisse but was led by Merrill Lynch, thanks to Stamenson's relationship with Citron.

Needing to drum up revenues to finance the county's big spending, like the finance ministers would do in Greece years later (thus leading to their national economic collapse in 2010), Citron frequently bet on derivatives known as swaps, or instruments whose value would fluctuate widely depending on the direction of interest rates. In one case, he purchased $100 million worth of securities whose value would increase if interest rates fell but would plunge if interest rates rose.

The strategy worked for years, and Citron was a local-government superstar, the Oracle of Anaheim, so to speak. But in 1994, the Federal Reserve began raising interest rates and Citron stopped looking so omniscient as losses in his investment pools began to mount. Under the deal he had cut with Merrill, the county had to post "collateral," or make payments to the Wall Street firms on the other side of its swaps, as its losses mounted. Citron couldn't just walk away from these deals; to do that would be a financial death sentence, a black mark as far as Wall Street was concerned, making it difficult to sell bonds and finance the county's operations in the future.

But by the middle of the year he didn't have much choice; rates kept rising, and the investment pool was now in serious condition, and so was the county's budget, which was losing hundreds of millions of dollars to satisfy the collateral demands of the Wall Street dealers who had once been Bob Citron's best friends but were now the single largest reason the county was in dire straits. The losses were soon insurmountable, and on December 6, 1994, Orange County, one of the nation's richest counties as measured by its per capita income, declared bankruptcy.

The bankruptcy filing led the way for huge budget cutbacks, particularly for the 187 school districts that had money invested in Citron's fund. Of course, Orange County's pain was Wall Street's gain. According to the *New York Times*, between 1993 and 1994 Orange County bought nearly $6.3 billion in derivatives from Merrill Lynch, transactions that generated nearly $100 million in commissions for the firm.

The bankruptcy set off a series of lawsuits. Citron would plead guilty to six felony counts. The *Los Angeles Times* described his misdeeds: "misappropriating public funds, falsifying documents and misleading nearly 200 government agencies that trusted him to invest their money." Because of his guilty plea (a surprise, as he at first stated he would fight the charges in court), Citron spent just a year in jail.

Merrill got off relatively cheaply.

"They're getting off completely. It's a joke," said an official at the Securities and Exchange Commission, embarrassed and outraged by the settlement the SEC had reached with Merrill over its dealings with the county.

When he said those words to me, four years had passed since Orange County's bankruptcy; it was now 1998, and Wall Street was leading the nation in an economic renaissance, or so the Clinton administration liked to say. New cutting-edge companies that were supposed to make money off the Internet were coming to market every day; stocks were on a roll, and not just those in the stodgy S&P 500 index of the "old" economy.

These were the stocks of the dot-com rage, and they were making Middle Americans rich, people who for the first time began buying individual technology stocks based on research reports by Merrill Lynch's Henry Blodget or Jack Grubman of Citigroup, many of them touted on the business news channel CNBC.

As for Merrill's dealings with Orange County? Investigators working on the case, according to an SEC official, wanted Merrill to suffer in a big way, possibly with a fraud charge and a large fine. But Merrill hired a team of sophisticated and—more important—politically connected attorneys who argued that it was Citron who had been hooked on risk and that it was *his* decision to roll the dice. Merrill merely supplied the heroin, which he could have gotten from any other firm.

It's hard to imagine a drug dealer getting off with a slap on the wrist with that defense, but much to the chagrin of the investigators on the case, that's exactly what happened. Senior SEC officials succumbed to Merrill's pressure, and a settlement was crafted that left much of the SEC staff, and those reporters still covering the case, including me, stunned.

Merrill had already settled with local prosecutors, thus escaping criminal charges that would have shuttered the firm more than a decade before its 2008 collapse, by paying a large but manageable $470 million to settle civil and criminal litigation into its role in the bankruptcy. The Securities and Exchange Commission demanded just $2 million to end its investigation. There were no individual charges (Stamenson got to keep his job at Merrill). And in neither case did Merrill have to admit to wrongdoing, even though its actions had helped convert Orange County's municipal finance department into a casino and led to the largest municipal bankruptcy in U.S. history.

As Greece does today, Bob Citron and Orange County nearly twenty years ago exemplified what can go wrong when Wall Street high finance is used to mask the reality of runaway government. Part of Merrill's defense that appeared to resonate with its primary regulators at the SEC was that it merely served as a middleman for Citron and had no responsibility to stop him from carrying out his scheme, while Citron himself attempted, in turn, to tap into the growing anger over Wall Street's indifference to the scandal. He claimed to be an "unsophisticated investor" who was largely duped by the smart Wall Street crowd.

Stamenson, of course, disputed that account, describing Citron as a "highly sophisticated investor." While Citron had only visited Wall Street four times in his life, he had known all the big dealers well, including the salesmen who peddled bonds.

Orange County and its taxpayers, meanwhile, were the ones who suffered the most; had their government not gambled away their money, they might not have had the decades of lavish spending that they did, but they wouldn't have the dire collapse, either. Sound familiar?

One thing neither side can dispute is how the Orange County bankruptcy displays in vivid detail the symbiotic relationship between Wall Street and Big Government, and all its disastrous effects. Stamenson had donated $4,000 to Citron's successful reelection campaign, which helped ensure that the investment strategy would continue. He also would actually write Citron's talking points for him when the treasurer made presentations about his management of the pools to Orange County's board of supervisors.

But despite the enormous cost to taxpayers, Orange County marked the beginning, not the end, of risk taking in the municipal market. The reason? Well despite the magnitude of the implosion—at their height the pools were valued as high as $8 billion—both government and Wall Street got off pretty easily.

As a result, the market for financial products used by Robert Citron to keep his Big Government alive (for a time) continued to flourish, and Wall Street, like a dope pusher living on Park Avenue, couldn't have been happier.

3

DEEP, DEEP ROOTS

"Where's Sandy, where's Sandy?" Reverend Jesse Jackson nervously asked. He was huddled with some key advisers in a rather unusual setting for the controversial civil rights activist: a reception held inside the headquarters of Travelers Group, the massive brokerage and trading empire run by financier Sandy Weill.

The year was 1997 and the reception was being held to commemorate Jackson's new civil rights organization, the Wall Street Project. But there was much more at stake—for both Jackson and Weill—than the seemingly simple goal of Jackson's group to create more diversity in the financial services industry.

Weill wasn't content with merely running a firm like Travelers, which combined selling insurance to consumers with peddling stocks and bonds to small investors through a brokerage unit, and of course doing its own trading and deal making.

He had his eye set on creating the world's ultimate "financial supermarket" by purchasing a large commercial bank and merging it with Travelers. Weill's vision was to combine commercial banking, including customer deposits, with the risk-taking trading activities found at Wall Street firms like Goldman Sachs and Morgan Stanley. The profits would be huge, he predicted, because clients would shop at one place for all their banking and investment needs.

But he faced formidable obstacles in creating his dream, which a few years later would turn into the nightmare named Citigroup. Under the Glass-Steagall Act, a deal of this nature would create something that was in violation of the law. To forge ahead with his plan, Weill would have to spend a few million dollars on lobbyists to get the law repealed once and for all.

An even bigger challenge would be more political than financial: the government's housing advocates, people like Congresswoman Maxine Waters and others, who would view the potential merger as an opportunity to demand major concessions from the company in exchange for their vote of approval. They would protest, hold hearings showing alleged racial disparity in lending practices, and force Congress to think twice before allowing the merger—unless Weill's banking empire stepped up its lending to poor communities.

But Sandy Weill had an answer to that as well: Jesse Jackson. The famed civil rights activist wasn't above demanding that banks give more loans to the poor, even if the poor couldn't repay them. Indeed, he had been using his stature inside Big Government, his access to key lawmakers, and now his friend President Bill Clinton to achieve his political and financial goals for years. Lately, he had developed a simple but lucrative new business model wherein he would threaten protests of the lack of diversity of various corporations, including, now, the big Wall Street firms. He labeled this latest campaign the Wall Street Project, whose purpose was to bring greater diversity to the nearly all-white and all-male power structure at the typical Wall Street firm. Jackson told me those firms that donated money to his new Wall Street Project were simply demonstrating their commitment to diversity. The firms that gave called the money the price of doing business and, in a rare moment of candor, a form of extortion.

Jackson's Wall Street Project had very little practical effect on the diversity of Wall Street—women and minorities remain largely absent from the senior ranks of the big firms. But the focus on Wall Street helped his organization reap many benefits. For the five or six years the Wall Street Project existed, the money from the banks to his various groups soared. "Blood money," is how one senior Wall Street executive described the donations. It's easy to understand why Jesse Jackson had his eyes set squarely on Wall Street's blood money, with its vast riches from the 1990s stock market boom, its nearly all-white-male executive ranks, and its movement toward political correctness. The big Wall Street firms and banks that were feasting off the Internet bubble—selling stocks of dot-com companies (many of them eventually worthless) to small investors—as well as the Big Government—earning fees through selling its bonds to finance the nanny state, through municipal financing projects, and through the lucrative debt that an expansive housing policy creates—had found that those profits came at a price: the embrace of contemporary liberalism.

Jimmy Cayne, the CEO of Bear Stearns, used to joke about how he could avoid an extended conversation with Jackson during the glory years of the Wall Street Project. "Rev. Jackson, I'm such a fan of yours," Cayne said he'd told Jackson. "But the only money I can give you is from the Bear Stearns Charitable Foundation." The foundation had it own executive director and management, so, as Cayne explained, the firm wasn't the target of a shakedown; its foundation was.

Jimmy Cayne may have dodged the bullet of having to deal directly with Jesse Jackson (Bear Stearns actually financed a minority-owned brokerage that donated significant sums of money to the Wall Street Project and benefited from Jackson's push to force corporations to hire minority-owned brokerages as underwriters), but nearly every major firm had tagged diversity as a primary goal. Firms like Merrill, for instance, even encouraged gender- and race-based groups and clubs inside the firm, even if the senior ranks of the firms remained all white and largely male.

All of this created a tremendous business opportunity for Jackson. He would scare the daylights out of Wall Street by showing how it violated not just its own diversity goals but also civil rights laws, unless, of course, the big firms made him rich (he was already a millionaire) by donating to his organization and by making sure that minority-owned firms that were part of the Wall Street Project gained access to the Big Government largesse that usually flowed only to the big firms, namely lucrative municipal bond contracts and other forms of corporate welfare.

Weill's idea was simple yet ingenious: Instead of fighting Jackson, he would partner with him. He would lend Jackson his name, his offices in Midtown and around the city, and one of Travelers Group's lawyers, Harold Levy (who went on to become New York City schools chancellor), to raise money for Jackson's Wall Street Project, which was supposed to promote diversity on Wall Street but did little more than promote Jesse Jackson. Weill would enlist his friends in the effort, including New York Stock Exchange CEO and chairman Richard Grasso, who gave Jackson and his civil rights group access to the famed floor of the NYSE to hold fundraisers and access to his Rolodex of millionaires.

And according to people who worked with Weill at the time, he would and did buy off Jackson with events like this one, held inside Travelers' luxurious headquarters in Midtown Manhattan.

It was a pretty odd scene. Corporate executives are usually the ones seeking out and kissing up to Jackson, fearing that they might be the next target of one of his patented shakedowns. But here was Jesse Jackson, an imposing figure in his own right, nervously waiting for the arrival of a short, overweight, and balding investment-banking chieftain.

When Weill arrived at the event, he was surrounded by aides and a bodyguard. He shook some hands before making his way to Jackson, who promptly hugged him and thanked him for all his help. Weill thanked Jackson as well, and with good reason: Within the next year, Weill would purchase banking giant Citicorp and merge it with Travelers to create Citigroup, and he would enlist Jackson to keep his mouth shut about the firm's poor record in lending to minority communities and its near lily white management team and, equally important, to persuade friends in Washington to support the death of Glass-Steagall.

Big Government's alliance with Wall Street, of course, has historical roots, including many that I have uncovered during my long career as a reporter. These roots long predate Jesse Jackson's Wall Street Project and the historic Orange County, California, bankruptcy filing. In fact, Orange County was just one instance of how Wall Street and Big Government have worked arm and arm, often to the detriment of the average taxpayer, not just on the local level but on the state and national levels as well.

Rating agencies like Moody's Investors Service, Fitch, and Standard & Poor's slapped all those fictitious triple-A ratings on the mortgage debt, enabling the Wall Street firms to sell the bonds that allowed banks to meet the requirements of the Community Reinvestment Act, which hands out loans as part of the social policy goals of Big Government. While they were doing that, the raters became the useful idiots of the tax-and-spenders at the state and local level. Despite broad public support for lower taxes and smaller, more efficient government, the rating agencies all but threaten states to keep taxes high or face downgrades in their debt ratings.

And of course, on the national level, the alliance between Big Government and Wall Street has been responsible for bailout after bailout.

It's important to remember that the embrace of Wall Street and its largesse is a bipartisan sin. The George W. Bush administration cut taxes but not the size of the U.S. government, and Wall Street prospered through the issuance of government debt and through the continued use of the mortgage-backed security to further the housing policies that began in the Clinton years and continued under Bush.

But George W. Bush never proclaimed himself to be the president of change, to be the leader who would set the greed merchants on Wall Street straight even while he all but promised to make them rich. That distinction belongs to Barack Obama alone.

Obama made good use of his time in Chicago, cultivating financial as well as political connections. And few were more important than Jamie Dimon.

When he took the top job at Bank One, Dimon moved his family to the Second City and enticed his Citigroup cronies to join his new firm, which he vowed would one day match the size and strength of Citigroup, and he immersed himself in the midwestern political culture. While in Chicago, he forged his close ties to Rahm Emanuel, to the ruling Daley family (he went on to hire one of the Daleys as a top executive), and, according to Dimon himself, to a young state senator named Barack Obama.

It's no coincidence, either, that shortly after their first meeting, Dimon made donations to a number of Chicago-based charities that no doubt were and remain close to the then-future president's heart. Dimon serves on the board of the University of Chicago, to which he donated $1 million, and he also gave money to the Museum of Contemporary Art Chicago, Big Brothers Big Sisters of Chicago, the Chicago Community Foundation, and the Chicago Public Education Fund.

And Obama's close friend and future chief of staff Rahm Emanuel was linked closely to Wall Street as well, having worked for Goldman Sachs and receiving a salary of $3,000 per month in the early 1990s to "introduce us to people," as one Goldman partner said at the time. And that's exactly what he did, and more.

The overall market for the derivatives traded by the big investment houses and used by big corporations and Big Government to massage earnings and debt levels exploded (well into the tens of trillions of dollars) between 1998 and 2008—that is, until the financial system collapsed as these financial products that had been invented to reduce risk pushed the financial system to the breaking point.

Much has been said and written about this period of excess, which allowed America to go on a spending spree. The conventional wisdom in the media is that everything that caused the crisis was the result of deregulation, the free-market sin of allowing unscrupulous bankers to lend to risky "subprime" borrowers, letting the Wall Street traders run wild without adult supervision, and maybe most of all the explosion of various new forms of debt and "derivatives" of that debt that made Wall Street so rich while the wages of average American stagnated. In 1989 the total amount of the derivatives market stood at $2.4 trillion. Twenty years later the markets had undergone a radical transformation with more than $450 trillion worth of complex derivatives contracts being held by various financial players.

The proponents of these newfangled financial products said they had a proven societal benefit. The risk reduction that derivatives created allowed those risky subprime borrowers to buy homes through the magic of

Wall Street financial engineering, such as the mortgage bond and its various iterations, like the collateralized debt obligation.

The great financial collapse of 2008 occurred after a period of reduced regulation of mortgage lenders, Wall Street, and its traders, but Wall Street's historic implosion was equally the result of large government bailouts, which had the cumulative effect of allowing the big Wall Street firms to skirt the full consequences of their risk-taking actions. In other words, government didn't just let Wall Street run wild; it virtually condoned Wall Street's wildness by bailing it out whenever it ran into trouble. For example, in 1998, the Federal Reserve slashed interest rates, creating free money for the brokers whose risk taking had led to large losses. Ten years later, the federal government, as we all know, would play a direct role via bailouts in ensuring that the Street survived the downside of gambling.

What's more, the men at the center of this massive government subsidy for Wall Street gambling would benefit mightily from this protection and continue to do so even today, as they shuttle back and forth between Wall Street and key jobs in the federal government. They include Emanuel, now the president's chief of staff (and according to some, the second-most-powerful man in America, behind the president himself) but formerly a lobbyist for Goldman Sachs; Larry Summers, formerly deputy Treasury secretary, Treasury secretary, and adviser to the giant hedge fund D.E. Shaw and now a chief economic aide to the president; and a man who more than anyone else epitomizes all that is wrong with the alliance of Big Government and Wall Street: Robert Rubin.

Known by his friends simply as Bob, Robert Edward Rubin is a short but intense man who speaks in a commanding yet understated tone. Those who know him describe him as part intellectual, part risk-taking gambler. According to the *New York Times*, when he worked at Goldman in the 1980s, he would pester coworkers with questions during holidays and even called a colleague to ask a mundane question during the second half of the Super Bowl. He seemed too intellectual to be sitting at the trading desk, making bets like a professional Vegas gambler.

But Rubin saw trading as the key to success on Wall Street as the Street's traditional lines of business, such as advising companies on stock deals or mergers and acquisitions, began to show lower and lower profit margins because of increasing competition. Trading, however, couldn't be commoditized, especially at a firm like Goldman, which recruited the best and the brightest from top-ranked schools. The Goldman trader (so those at the firm believed) was far superior to the competition because he was simply smarter and would be willing to trade against even his own clients for the greater good of the firm (something that, as we'll see, would land the firm in hot water in 2010).

The art of risk taking was Rubin's forte, and he instilled it in a generation of future Goldman leaders, people like bond trader Jon Corzine (who would go on to run the firm before embarking on a political career as a liberal U.S. senator and governor of New Jersey) and a commodities salesman named Lloyd Blankfein, who, like Rubin, openly embraced risk.

Bob Rubin was a trader through and through, and in his mind, men like him were essential to the survival of modern Wall Street. It came as no surprise to any of his colleagues at Goldman that amid the clutter of his office, one thing stood out: a photo of former Goldman chief Gus Levy, the legendary trader who began the firm's push into the wild side of the Wall Street business model many years earlier.

Rubin graduated from the London School of Economics and received a law degree from Yale. But he made his fortune during his nearly three decades at Goldman Sachs, mostly in the trading pits, as an "arbitrageur"— a fancy Wall Street term for someone who takes big bets in the markets by trading debt and other esoteric securities.

During this time, he was active both in Democratic Party politics and among the Wall Street elite, where he helped set the financial business's lobbying agenda. Under Rubin, Goldman would hire numerous young and talented politicos, mainly Democrats, including a young Rahm Emanuel as a "consultant," to help the firm win lucrative investment-banking contracts from municipalities and businesses. When he retired from Goldman as its chairman, he took a job as the chief economic adviser to President Bill

Clinton, and shortly after that he made his greatest "contributions" to public service as Clinton's Treasury secretary.

Rubin has earned kudos for prodding the Clinton administration to cut the nation's deficit through a massive tax increase, initially slowing economic growth and igniting a massive rally in the bond markets—which just happened to benefit Rubin's old firm, Goldman Sachs, along with the rest of Wall Street. Economists are divided, mainly along ideological lines, over whether the Clinton tax increases did indeed help spur the massive economic recovery that began in 1995 or whether it was the result of political gridlock in Washington, where the Republican-run Congress blocked many of Clinton's spending initiatives and forced him to govern from the center, enacting policies that the far Left hated, such as cuts in capital gains taxes and welfare reform.

Either way, one thing is certain: Bob Rubin was Wall Street's inside guy within the Clinton administration, where he appointed top officials who believed, as he did, that Big Government and Big Finance could work and prosper together. The massive amounts of debt sold by the federal government to finance that Big Government needed to be auctioned first to the Wall Street firms, which took healthy fees before they sold it to their customers. Likewise, municipal governments needed Wall Street to underwrite their debt, and as in the case of Orange County, pump up returns with fancy, and risky, bets on the markets.

Meanwhile, Rubin's massive risk taking on Goldman's trading desk was being replicated across Wall Street and could only be accomplished through government policies in one form or another. Sometimes it would take more than just Federal Reserve interest-rate cuts to save Wall Street, as Rubin himself began to argue in early 1995, just as Bill Clinton appointed him Treasury secretary.

"The objective of promoting United States exports, jobs, security of our borders, in our judgment, is being accomplished," Rubin said in 1995. He was describing what was at the time the largest intervention by the U.S. government in the free markets in memory. In January of that year, the bond markets had seized up with the sudden devaluation of the Mexican peso. America's southern neighbor, a major trading partner, was on the verge of default, and Wall Street panicked.

The big firms had suffered a tough year in 1994, particularly in the bond markets, as the Fed raised interest rates and the banks saw the value of their bond holdings begin to sink. Amid these losses, Wall Street viewed its investments in Mexico as a savior of sorts. (The Street ignored, of course, the fact that economic booms are normally followed by steep busts, especially in economies that, like Mexico's, are just beginning to embrace free-market economic principles.)

So now Wall Street was realizing it had bet wrong, as it was holding billions of dollars' worth of Mexican bonds, currency swaps, and other securities tied to the peso. In other words, if Mexico went down, Wall Street would certainly suffer massive losses and, God forbid, smaller year-end bonuses.

Robert Rubin, President Clinton's Treasury secretary and onetime Goldman Sachs boss, was about to orchestrate his first bailout.

Of course, in terms of size and scope the response to the Mexican "peso crisis" would barely resemble the massive banking bailouts that would come some fifteen years later, when President Bush and his successor, Barack Obama, pumped trillions into the banking system. But the peso crisis *was* a dry run for the bailouts that would be coming in 1998 (following the collapse of the hedge fund Long-Term Capital Management) and in 2008. Many feel, as do I, that the peso bailout was a critical signal to Wall Street that it could take as much risk as it wanted because the government was always there, ready and waiting to help the bankers out when their risk taking went bad, as it always eventually does.

Rubin's plan was to buy pesos on the open market and then issue $50 billion in guarantees on Mexican debt. The move was unprecedented because it was done by the administration—the Treasury Department, to be exact—without congressional approval.

And that's where Rubin faced the heaviest criticism. Taking some of the most intense flak was Rubin's deputy, Larry Summers. Some members of the Senate Finance Committee viewed Summers with as much suspicion as Rubin because he was the point man on the bailout. Some called for his resignation. Senator Alfonse D'Amato of New York would later accuse Summers of outright lying about the true state of Mexico's financial health prior to the crisis, citing Treasury documents that showed that officials had become increasingly alarmed by Mexico's trade deficit well before the crisis itself.

"The looting of America, on behalf of the new world order, has begun," wrote the economic populist Pat Buchanan. "Never again should a President be allowed to disregard the will of Congress to raid the U.S. Treasury to bail out Wall Street banks or a foreign regime." Buchanan went on to accuse Rubin of supporting the Mexican bailout to enrich his old investment-banking firm, Goldman Sachs. It's unclear if helping Goldman was indeed Rubin's motive (he denied any such thing), but there is no doubt the bailout aided the firm by stabilizing the already skittish markets and preventing further losses for Goldman and its fellow firms.

In selling his bailout plan to the American people, Rubin argued that a Mexican default would be catastrophic for the world economy, that it presented "systemic risk." A Mexican collapse, he argued, would trigger a massive wave of defaults around all the world's emerging markets, creating a tidal wave of fiscal pain that would eventually envelop the United States. Playing off anti-immigrant sentiment in the border states, Rubin, who when he was in the United States spent most of his time shuttling between Washington and New York, argued that a collapse of the Mexican economy would spark a rush of illegal immigration to California and Texas.

If the fear of millions of Mexicans running into our backyard wasn't enough, the administration also tried to sell the bailout as a jobs-saving necessity, claiming that the U.S. economy had seven hundred thousand jobs that were dependent on a thriving Mexican economy. And so the first great government-run bailout was enacted.

The bailout didn't exactly turn around the Mexican economy as Rubin and company had predicted, mainly because Mexico was saddled with a huge debt burden to repay the U.S. government. So why didn't it just walk away and default on all those bonds? Rubin, like any good bond trader, would have made it clear to Mexico that if it did that, Mexico would be virtually barred from the borrowing markets, a disaster for any government. A Mexican default, in Rubin's view, would have threatened the stability of not just the South American economies but, more important, his beloved friends on Wall Street and his old firm, Goldman Sachs.

There would be consequences for Mexico's mistakes, but not for the Wall Street firms that held Mexican paper. Because of Rubin's actions, the big firms avoided massive losses and were able to generate big bonuses. And with that, Wall Street and Big Government came to understand the meaning of teamwork. The big firms would underwrite the massive amounts of debt being sold to keep the welfare state afloat, and the welfare state would bail out the big firms from some of their most disastrous forays into risk.

Following the Mexican bailout, the notion of "moral hazard" (the financial theory that the ability to take risk without consequences leads to even greater and more reckless risk taking) was solidified in every Wall Street CEO's and trader's mind. Rubin and his team would say that such bailouts are a necessary evil to prevent such massive losses that the entire financial system would undergo a gut-wrenching "systemic" collapse. Maybe so, but the lack of consequences taught the Wall Street risk takers a valuable lesson, even if they had slept through this part of college economics class: When they lost money and it came time to pay the bill, the government and the American taxpayer would provide backup—again and again.

None of that seemed to matter to Rubin or even to most members of Congress, who, despite some initial dissent, slowly but surely came to believe that the plan was a success. Nearly two years after the bailout was passed in a lavish ceremony in the Roosevelt Room, White House officials were nearly giddy with the news that Mexico had repaid its $13 billion bailout to America—three years ahead of schedule.

A reporter peppered President Clinton with questions about a recent decline in the value of the peso—an indication that despite all the money spent, the country's economy was still ailing, even if the government had paid back the loan. Clinton, grinning from ear to ear, passed the question to Rubin, explaining, "You've made so much more money than I have, and so should be the one to answer the question."

The usually reserved Rubin, who has been known to be low-key about his vast fortune, couldn't contain his excitement at the president's calling attention to his money-making prowess. "There is a point to that!" he said. Later in the ceremony Summers would joke that he would love just a slice of the estimated $580 million in profits the U.S. government claimed to have made on the deal, even as the Mexican economy imploded, thanks to the stiff terms Rubin negotiated.

"Larry, anything you can negotiate I'm happy to split with you," Mr. Rubin shot back.

Whether the Treasury actually turned a profit really doesn't matter (that $580 million in "profit," after all, is barely a drop in the bucket of the U.S. government's titanic spending); it was the moral hazard that was created, the belief in the minds of Wall Streeters that their friends in DC were ready to ride to the rescue.

Rubin, of course, didn't need the money he was joking about with Summers, and in a few years he would become even more wealthy thanks to his ability to help arrange benefits for the securities industry.

In 1998, Rubin was still at the Treasury Department, but he was setting the stage for his return to Wall Street. It was around this time that the massive Citigroup merger was announced. It was a landmark deal: Citigroup was the combination of a commercial bank, Citicorp (one of the world's largest banks), with Traveler's Group, the massive brokerage, investment-banking, and insurance empire run by Sandy Weill.

There was just one problem with the deal: It was technically illegal under the Glass-Steagall Act, which, as discussed at the beginning of this chapter, Weill had been campaigning for years to abolish.

So as soon as the merger was announced, Weill and his team of lobbyists went to work in Washington. Rubin was one of their main contacts to do the job. One of the odd things about enlisting Rubin in this effort was that when he had been at Goldman he had argued against Glass-Steagall's repeal. The reason: Creating a megabank like Citigroup would have put a partnership like Goldman at a megadisadvantage. But times were changing. Goldman was now in the process of going public—raising money and capital to grow and compete in the securities industry, where size mattered. And maybe more than that, Rubin didn't want to remain in government forever. He wanted a job on Wall Street. In other words, Citigroup, with its "financial supermarket" business model—whereby it not only opened bank accounts to average people, made loans and mortgages, sold CDs and mutual funds, et cetera, but also sold insurance, traded bonds with the likes of Goldman and Morgan Stanley, underwrote public offerings, sold debt to large institutional clients, and did all the other activities that ordinary investment banks did—seemed like a perfect fit for Rubin in his postgovernment life.

But first he would have to undertake his second bailout of Wall Street.

———————

"Yes, Gary, what is it?" asked Robert Rubin one Saturday afternoon in mid-September 1998. Rubin had been relaxing at his home in New York City when he received a call from Gary Gensler, a former partner of his at Goldman, who was once again working for him at Treasury as assistant secretary for financial markets.

Gensler is one of those people in government whose power far outweighs his name recognition. There are many bureaucrats running around Washington, but there are very few who can say that they play a major role in controlling an industry that pumps out trillions of dollars in revenues each year. In other words, Gensler was the point man in the vast federal apparatus that monitors Wall Street when times are good and bails out the big firms when they aren't so good.

And the news from Gensler wasn't good. The hedge fund Long-Term Capital Management (known as LTCM), run by trading whiz John Meriwether, had made massive profits in recent years from trading esoteric bonds based on computer models designed by Nobel Prize–winning economists. LTCM had made fortunes from exotic bets on little-known corners of the financial world, like Danish mortgage bonds, of all things. But now it was imploding, literally ready to collapse, because it had bet enormously wrong on the direction of everything from the bonds issued by the U.S., European, and Japanese governments to the share price of the Royal Dutch Shell petroleum company.

Instead of letting LTCM fail—a move that true free-market devotees would advocate as a way to punish excessive risk taking and teach the gamblers not to gamble—Rubin's idea was to bail it out. Once again, as with the Mexican peso, Rubin worried about systemic risk. Rubin was concerned about this possibility because the big Wall Street firms, which dealt with LTCM, piggybacked (i.e., copied) many of its trades and would lose massive amounts of money too.

The panic selling an LTCM collapse, Rubin thought, would lead to massive losses in the market at all the major firms, including his old firm, Goldman Sachs. At least two firms, Lehman Brothers and Merrill Lynch, might take such heavy losses they might not survive. Goldman would have to postpone, maybe indefinitely, its IPO.

As Rubin put it in his biography, *In an Uncertain World,* "In normal circumstances, the government shouldn't worry about the tribulations of any particular firm or corporation. But if the situation threatens the financial system, some kind of government action might be the best among bad choices."

The solution that the Treasury and the Fed came up with demonstrated the true strength of the ties between the big Wall Street firms (or at least most of them) and their benefactors in Washington. The firms were summoned to the offices of the New York Federal Reserve Bank, the most important of the Fed's regional banks because it provides oversight of the banking system and conducts "open-market operations" that control the nation's money supply. The solution was pretty simple: The Fed was ready to pump money into the banking system in an effort to help eliminate the losses on the bad trades the banks had copied from LTCM. Each of the big banks (with the exception of Bear Stearns, whose CEO refused to join the effort) would each pony up around $300 million (Lehman Brothers could just afford $100 million) and buy the fund's assets for $3.6 billion.

Taken another way, they each spent hundreds of millions to save countless billions, because after a few hectic weeks and some modest losses at Merrill Lynch, Lehman, Goldman, and the rest, Wall Street recovered. It wasn't just the dot-com bubble, then in full swing, that generated such massive profits for the Wall Street firms that took all those fleeting Internet companies public. The bond markets exploded as well, thanks to the Fed's dumping all that money into the system with low interest rates. In the months after the LTCM collapse, Wall Street was standing tall. Combined with the revenues from underwriting dot-com IPOs, the soaring trading revenues breathed new life into Lehman Brothers and Merrill Lynch; Morgan Stanley had one of its longest periods of prosperity in years, as did Goldman Sachs, Rubin's old firm, which finally completed its long-awaited IPO.

With Wall Street on a roll, Main Street prospered as well. It didn't matter that many of the dot-com stocks underwritten by the Wall Street firms would turn out to be busts. It didn't matter that President Clinton's chief regulator, Arthur Levitt, chairman of the SEC and the man charged with making sure mom and pop investors get a fair shake, seemed blind to this massive fleecing of the investment public. It also didn't matter that the bond traders who were minting money once again by buying, selling, and packaging esoteric debt had been given the signal from government that they could take as much risk as they wanted without suffering the consequences.

Everyone was happy, at least for the moment.

It is impossible, of course, to know whether letting market forces take their course and allowing LTCM to fail would have created the type of financial tsunami that Rubin feared—the same tidal wave that nearly destroyed the system ten years later when Lehman Brothers was allowed to fail. Wall Street was smaller then, and the risk in the system from derivatives and the funky mortgage bonds that would doom the banks in 2008 was far, far less.

But one thing is certain: By bailing out Wall Street, Rubin and his cohorts at the Federal Reserve essentially doubled down on moral hazard. It's why, for example, insurance companies insist on deductibles or copayments; if they didn't, customers would have no reason to, say, worry about getting into a car accident (aside from the possibility of personal injury) because they wouldn't bear any cost for doing so. In the context of Wall Street, bailouts create a moral hazard by planting the idea in the minds of firms that if one of their competitors is bailed out, they will be too if they run into trouble. As a result, these firms have no qualms about engaging in reckless and excessive risk taking.

And yet first with the Mexican peso crisis and later with the LTCM bailout, the federal government was introducing moral hazard into Wall Street in a big way. Unsurprisingly, the risk taking on Wall Street would rise over the next decade to unprecedented levels. Until, of course, the system came crashing down.

The dot-com bubble would end in 2000, and by the time President George W. Bush took office in 2001, a mild recession had set in, soon compounded by the September 11 terrorist attacks, which caused a major sell-off in the market. A new government was in power, but "Rubinomics" was administered from Washington once again. Following the attacks, the Fed began slashing interest rates to historic lows, igniting the bond markets once again and setting the stage for the biggest housing bubble of all time as banks, flush with cash, lent money to anyone with a heartbeat.

Robert Rubin was at one of those banks.

"I had a number of offers," Rubin would later brag, "but Citigroup was the best." Rubin, of course, was talking about his new gig at Citigroup, where he carried the amorphous title of "chairman of the executive committee." Before he left the Treasury Department in July 1999, Rubin did several things. First, he began looking for a job on Wall Street. He held extensive talks with Hank Greenberg, the fair-minded but volatile CEO of insurance giant American International Group (AIG). They couldn't reach a deal, Greenberg later said, because "I didn't want to pay him $8 million a year to fly around the world."

Citigroup and its CEO, Sandy Weill, ultimately would pay him this much and more, offering Rubin a job at Citigroup to advise on its businesses, do deals, consult with bureaucrats in Washington, and generally think big thoughts. He did all this for an estimated $15 million per year, not counting stock options. Rubin also received a seat on the board of directors and a promise that he would have no responsibilities as a supervisor. This meant nobody really reported to him, and if anything went wrong, he could blame someone else.

"I did that once," he later said, referring to his job running Goldman Sachs, "and I didn't want to do that again." No, Rubin had bigger goals. He told the *New York Times* that what he really wanted was some type of job at a large financial institution that would give him time to "fish, read books, and play tennis, but life is a trade-off." With such a plum assignment, it was little wonder his colleagues at Citigroup could hardly contain their envy. "Bob has the best job in the company; no line responsibilities. But he will be a full partner" was how co-CEO John Reed described Rubin's position. And why would Rubin need to work all those long hours? He was, after all, on Clinton's speed dial. With Big Government connections like that, Citi was sure to have a massive year, even if Rubin spent much of his time playing tennis.

Of course, a lot would go wrong at Citigroup over the next decade, and to be fair, Rubin wasn't without accomplishments at the firm. But by far his most notable—and probably most historic—"achievement" in his time there was doing what he'd meant to do for years—repeal the Glass-Steagall Act.

By late fall 1999, just before Rubin was to begin his job at the firm, Citigroup was still technically an illegal enterprise. The Glass-Steagall Act wasn't dead quite yet. And that's when Rubin went to work, participating in the massive Wall Street lobbying effort to kill the law once and for all and thus allow the big firms to grow even bigger.

Rubin's old firm, Goldman Sachs, shuddered at the thought of competing with the massive Citigroup empire—which could entice clients with bank loans in order to get other types of deals. A decade earlier, as chairman of Goldman, Rubin would have been lobbying against its repeal. But times were changing.

Glass-Steagall was finally repealed in late 1999, and Rubin ended up on the cover of *Time* magazine as one of the wise men of the great economic boom of the late 1990s. Despite his fame, it's difficult to tell exactly how much influence Rubin had over his old boss, President Bill Clinton, in killing the law.

But two things are certain: The end of Glass-Steagall made Bob Rubin richer than ever before, and it paved the way for the eventual collapse of the economic system nine years later. The megabanks like Citigroup, Bank of America, and JPMorgan Chase weren't the only culprits in the massive risk taking that occurred in the decade preceding the 2008 financial collapse, but their existence propelled the others to take more risk. Bear Stearns, Lehman Brothers, Morgan Stanley, and even the great Goldman Sachs, the one firm that seemed to reduce risk taking to an art, ramped up their borrowing so they could compete with the big banks.

Profits soared, at least for a while, and Wall Street fulfilled its end of the bargain it had struck with Washington, namely aiding and abetting the policy goal of treating the earned benefit of homeownership as something nearly approaching a right of citizenship. Under President Clinton, the big mortgage lenders, Fannie Mae and Freddie Mac (which in essence function as part of the government), were pushed to guarantee loans to people in lower and lower income categories. Meanwhile, Clinton's housing secretaries, Henry Cisneros and Andrew Cuomo (who as I write this book is running for governor of New York, after serving as the state's attorney general since 2006), did all they could to use policies such as the Community Reinvestment Act to make sure banks gave mortgages to the disadvantaged, regardless of the borrowers' ability to repay.

So Wall Street did its part as well: With Washington giving its blessing to a policy of "housing for all," the Street came up with new ways to implement that policy. Banks, of course, couldn't do it alone. They had just so much capital from which they could make loans. Luckily, they had a fallback plan: the plain-vanilla mortgage-backed security, developed by Larry Fink and others on Wall Street in the late 1970s and early 1980s, morphed into several new generations of bonds, including the "collateralized debt obligation," or CDO. A CDO is a gigantic stew of mortgages packed into bonds that are in turn packed into a bigger bond.

The CDO was supposed to lessen risk while at the same time allow banks to sell mortgages to riskier borrowers. The more mortgage bonds were packed into a CDO, the more diversified the risk would be, thus the less likely the entire bond would fall into default. That was the theory, at least. Because after all, what would possibly cause mortgages to simultaneously go into default in Denver, Miami, and Las Vegas? The buyers of these CDOs were safe because even if a few of the mortgages that lay behind these financial concoctions went belly up, the majority would still be earning their nice, fat payments, and the CDO would continue to generate cash for its owners. (This was because technically the firms made sure the CDOs were "overcollateralized," i.e., had some extra cash packed into them to account for a few defaults.)

Investors flocked to these instruments because they produced such large returns. Liberals who advocated housing as a right, as opposed to something that must be earned, saw the CDO as a savior because it allowed banks to keep making risky mortgage loans. Everyone seemed fat and happy. The housing bureaucrats in the Clinton administration achieved their goal of raising the number of people in homes from 60 percent of the population to 70 percent. Wall Street's profits soared, and Bob Rubin eventually started earning as much as $15 million per year at Citigroup, one of the biggest players in the CDO markets, even though he would later concede he hadn't the foggiest idea how one of these supreme examples of financial magic worked.

The partnership between government and Wall Street was working, until it wasn't.

"SO, DO YOU WANT
TO COME TO THE ADMINISTRATION?"

"Hello, this is Warren Spector and I'm calling to see if you have voted yet."

It was the twentieth call Spector had made that hour, and yet none of the people on the other end recognized his name or the role he played as the number two executive at Bear Stearns during the burgeoning financial crisis, which ironically was now propelling *his* candidate, Senator Barack Obama, closer and closer to the presidency.

It was the week before the 2008 presidential election, and Spector was canvassing for voters in Palm Beach, a key battleground district in the all-important war to win Florida, a state that had trended Republican in recent years but was clearly now up for grabs. Spector was seated in a large room with other volunteers, mostly college kids, a key force behind Obama's surging campaign. Like the people on the other end of the telephone, no one in the room seemed to have a clue that just a year earlier, their fellow volunteer, Warren Spector, now sitting with them in this drab room, had been among the most powerful people on Wall Street.

Those days seemed so far away. Not long after Wall Street's meeting with Obama at Johnny's Half Shell in Washington DC, Spector had gotten the ax. The Bear Stearns hedge funds he was supposed to be overseeing had failed, giving his boss and longtime nemesis, Jimmy Cayne, the reason he was waiting for to fire his number two. Cayne, of course, would have done it sooner if he had thought the board and investors would have allowed it.

Still, not all of the animosity between Cayne and Spector had to do with business. Spector was acknowledged by all, including Cayne, as an expert in the bond market, particularly the highly lucrative mortgage-bond market, and with him running that part of the business, Bear had become one of the most profitable firms on the Street. That business was now the root cause of the firm's demise.

Instead, the rift can be traced, at least in part, to politics. Spector wanted Cayne's job, and Cayne was doing everything he could to block him, including at one point a few years earlier telling Bear's thirteen thousand employees in a memo that his number two had basically violated company policy when he overtly supported Democratic presidential candidate John Kerry.

"Free speech should not be confused with directly or indirectly using the company to endorse personal political views or agendas," wrote Cayne, whose staunchly conservative views are well known on Wall Street.

Once the hedge funds—some of the riskiest investments in the market, packed full of toxic CDOs and even CDOs squared (CDOs of CDOs, believe it or not)—blew up, Cayne had his excuse to fire Spector, which he did, announcing that a new team would be put in charge to get the firm on the right track. Whatever Spector's faults, Bear could have used him and his expertise in the bond market in the months ahead: A contagion spread throughout Wall Street, and the result of thirty years of risk taking in esoteric securities aided and abetted by both large and small government bailouts began to set in. The big firms were gambling just as the Bear Stearns hedge fund managers had, and they had all loaded up their books with billions of dollars in toxic mortgage debt.

Bear Stearns itself was hit particularly hard, in no small part, Cayne and others believed, thanks to Spector. After all, Spector had been in charge not just of the hedge funds but of the entire bond division. Spector would point out that he wasn't the only executive in charge of monitoring the firm's enormous risk taking (legendary trader Alan "Ace" Greenberg often ran the risk committee meetings). Either way, Bear was the first domino to fall during the great financial crisis that began to unfold in March 2008. But it wasn't the only one. The giant mortgage lenders Fannie Mae and Freddie Mac—which the government used as vehicles to carry out its policy of homeownership as a civil right—would go next, as would hundreds of billions of dollars of taxpayers' funds that would be appropriated to bail them out. The bailouts of Fannie and Freddie, by the way, would only work for a while—as I write this book the *New York Times* was reporting that the cost of bailing out Fannie and Freddie could exceed the cost of all the rest of the bailouts combined. With the bill standing at $145.9 billion in June 2010, the Congressional Budget Office is predicting that the final tab could reach a mind-boggling *$389 billion*—more than a third of a trillion dollars to bail out just these two troubled firms. Later in the fall of 2009, Lehman Brothers would collapse too, though unlike Bear and Fannie and Freddie it would not receive a bailout. Instead it would be forced to declare bankruptcy, a rare show of government restraint when Wall Street had bet wrong.

But as Spector sat in Obama's Palm Beach campaign headquarters, the outgoing Bush administration had come to the conclusion that letting Lehman fail had been a mistake. Following its collapse, a financial panic had set in, threatening to plunge the nation into economic chaos. At least that's what the public was told, and while Federal Reserve chairman Ben Bernanke and Treasury secretary Hank Paulson were predicting unimaginable disaster without unprecedented government support, they were still grappling with how best to save the remaining big investment firms and banks—Citigroup, Bank of America, Merrill Lynch, JPMorgan Chase, Morgan Stanley, and even the great Goldman Sachs.

Over the next six months, they would all receive hundreds of billions in direct and indirect aid from the government to stay afloat as policy makers embarked on a messy, and ultimately successful, rescue effort. Of course, success in this case entailed keeping in business a failed behemoth like Citigroup, which ignored repeated demands from investors to downsize its bloated operations until it was far too late.

But this afternoon, as he dialed one call after another, Spector seemed like he had not a care in the world. And why should he? He had been forced out of Bear in August 2007, nearly a year before the firm's crash and forced sale to JPMorgan Chase for a measly $10 a share. Many of the executives had lost their life savings, which had been tied up in company stock, but not Spector. As soon as he was fired, while Bear's stock price remained at a healthy $100 a share, Spector sold everything and almost instantaneously became $300 million richer.

Spector was known inside Bear for his lack of emotion. Some, like Cayne, considered him moody and arrogant, a by-product of a privileged life (an upper-middle-class upbringing, a fancy MBA, and so on). Cayne was so disdainful of Spector's attitude he used to refer to Spector as "Lord Fauntleroy." Others who took a more nuanced view of Spector pegged his attitude as an indifference to his job; even while he was gambling billions of dollars of company money in esoteric bond markets, Spector acted as if he had better things to do, like read the *Sunday Times* book review.

But Spector was now legitimately excited to be working for the man he believed was going to be president, even if his post-Bear lifestyle was being mocked by Cayne, now Bear's disgraced ex-CEO (in addition to allowing the firm's risk taking to expand to dangerous levels under his watch as CEO, Cayne had been playing bridge while the firm was imploding in March 2008, when he still held the title of company chairman). Cayne, who had always incessantly questioned Spector's manliness, was now having a field day as he received a report from a former Bear Stearns executive who said he had spotted Spector at a local country club in "tight, tight shorts with a poodle under his arm."

Others who know Spector say he was just trying to fit in with the campaign staff, many of them college students who didn't even own a business suit. Originally a Hillary Clinton supporter, Spector had slowly but surely become a convert along with the rest of his good friends on Wall Street who had attended that initial secret meeting in Washington a year earlier. During the nomination process, Obama had initially seemed like a long shot. But even as the Wall Street elite bet wrong on their investments in toxic mortgage debt, they soon bet right on Obama, who would go on to beat Clinton thanks to his strong Wall Street support.

They also bet, as we saw earlier, that they were getting the Obama who had displayed himself so elegantly that night in Washington and dismissed his reputation as a Marxist with ties to terrorists. "Obama's a moderate," another early Obama supporter, Larry Fink, would assure his friends and colleagues as they dined at his favorite Upper East Side restaurant, Sistina, and discussed his impressions of the man who would be president.

Fink wasn't alone. Tom Nides, the Morgan Stanley executive and über-lobbyist who had convinced his friend and boss former Republican John Mack to vote for Hillary, now sealed the deal for him to vote for Obama. Jamie Dimon had steered JPMorgan Chase more or less unscathed through the financial crisis, even if the government had forced the bank to take $25 billion in capital as a precautionary measure, but as Election Day approached, the press officials at JPMorgan were giddy over their boss's support for Obama and the pending wave of Democrats to take office that year. And with good reason: JPMorgan supported Democratic candidates and committees at a much higher rate than it did Republicans while Dimon's personal donations show a significant preference for Democrats. Between 1989 and 2009, he and his wife donated more than $500,000 to Democrats and their committees, twelve times more than he gave to Republicans, according to a study conducted by the Center for Responsive Politics, which tracks political contributions.

While most of Spector's Wall Street colleagues showed their support by giving money, Spector gave his time and energy as well. At first, Spector, who splits his days between his luxurious homes in New York and Martha's Vineyard and a palatial estate in Palm Springs, Florida, got involved in the campaign because he was bored. In the midst of the ongoing turmoil he certainly wasn't going back to Wall Street; in fact, given his enormous wealth, he didn't have to.

But it wasn't long before working for Obama became something more fulfilling. Being part of an effort to bring "change" to the country was filling a void in Spector's life. While many men, like Dimon and Nides, loved Obama because they believed he was a moderate—someone Wall Street could do business with and, of course, make money from—Spector, now out of the securities business and someone who had always been involved in Democratic Party politics, was personally satisfied for the first time in years. He was part of something that was "good" and would "make a difference"— clichés, to be sure, but Spector didn't mind. After decades of making money on Wall Street, Spector found purpose in helping elect not only the first African American president of the United States, but also a man with the wisdom to change the direction of the country, to make it more appealing abroad and better for the masses here at home.

Spector and Obama first met in the spring of 2004. It was a lunch meeting arranged through a mutual friend and held at Bear Stearns's private dining room in New York City. At the time, Obama wasn't that far removed from his days as a community organizer who would look at Wall Street as the enemy of the poor and middle class. He was a local state senator vying for a seat in the U.S. Senate. Spector didn't really know who he was, and he didn't really have time to waste on political neophytes, but he took the meeting anyway because his friend assured him that he would just "fall in love with this guy."

Before the entrees arrived, he was blown away.

"Brilliant" was how he would later describe Obama to his wife, the actress Margaret Whitton. Over lunch, the two discussed politics and the state of the economy, although oddly (not in retrospect, of course), the conversation stayed on the big-picture issues and never got into specifics. Rather, Obama left Spector with the impression that he was a "guy of clear intelligence . . . a winner," without ever really explaining the details of his worldview.

Obama's conversation with Spector would, of course, be repeated dozens of times with Wall Street executives, including Spector's next encounter with him in Washington DC as the candidate eyed the ultimate prize in politics, the presidency. He would make sure to speak in broad, albeit grand, generalities about matters of great importance: how as a nation we needed to better support the underprivileged; how we needed to get health-care costs under control; and how we needed to reestablish the American brand in Europe and around the world, where hatred of the Bush administration's foreign policy had translated into hatred of America.

The great irony, of course, is that Wall Street is a place where some of the world's best salesmen make millions by telling people what they want to hear. And that's exactly what Barack Obama was doing to Spector and the rest of Wall Street with grand results: turning the tables and making the sale.

And it was working, thanks to people like Warren Spector.

When he had first met Obama in 2004, Spector had had no idea that this guy would become the president. But he had liked his chances to become the U.S. senator for Illinois, so he had introduced him to people who could help him win that election, which he had.

Now, just four years later, Spector was helping the young senator win his most important campaign. And the ultrarich mogul was getting a kick out of being part of the primarily student- and retiree-led campaign for "hope and change," to boot.

"I would never be allowed to do this at Bear," Spector would later remark to friends about the time he spent on Obama's campaign. "I'm so glad I got the opportunity." When they weren't working the phones, Spector and the other volunteers would venture out to minority neighborhoods, knocking on doors, handing out flyers, and reminding people to vote on Election Day for the man who would make history as the first African American president.

It was grueling work, at least for most of the volunteers, who slept on cots or on the floor of the campaign office. Spector would often work twelve hours a day as well, but his idea of slumming it was retreating to a nearby luxury hotel to recharge at night. But in the end he felt it was well worth it.

Warren Spector had survived Jimmy Cayne, who continued to ridicule him behind his back, and he had survived Bear Stearns with his vast fortune intact, while Bear itself collapsed. And if you talk to friends of

Spector, they'll tell you he felt he was doing something great—helping bring change to the nation in the form of Barack Obama.

On Election Day 2008, the remaining heads of the big Wall Street firms were, of course, still fighting for survival. The total collapse of the financial system that had followed Lehman's bankruptcy filing continued to send shock waves through the banking network. One bailout followed another. There was TARP, which eventually consisted of government-mandated direct infusions of cash into each and every firm. That was preceded by the government's takeover of giant insurer AIG, which had run out of money to cover its insurance contracts on imploding mortgage bonds held by firms like Goldman Sachs. If AIG couldn't make good on those contracts, Goldman would have to write down and take massive losses on those bonds and would probably go out of business as well. But once the government stepped in, Goldman was saved, at least for now.

And at least the bank heads and their compatriots were on the verge of helping to bring "hope and change" to the White House. With the economy and the financial system in tatters, all the polling showed that Obama and his vice presidential pick, Joe Biden, would easily beat the McCain-Palin ticket, and much of Wall Street, particularly those in the executive suites, was rejoicing. Bush fatigue had set in on Wall Street despite the fact that most firms had split the ticket in the 2004 elections, giving equal amounts to the Democrats and Republicans in both Congress and the presidential election. Now these same executives were high-fiving over their decision to flood the Democrats with money as the leadership of all three branches of government skewed decidedly to the left.

To hear the CEOs themselves tell it, eight years of George W. Bush had left America a broken land. Deficits were out of control (even though Wall Street had made countless millions selling the debt that supported those deficits). The economy was sinking. President Bush, they all complained, destroyed the country's reputation overseas, where they had extensive operations; his aggressive foreign policy (including the wars in Iraq and Afghanistan) made it difficult to travel overseas and meet clients, and alienated those clients as well. About the only thing they couldn't blame on Bush was the financial crisis—even the most left-wing executives on Wall Street had to grudgingly admit that was at least in part their doing. And as for John McCain? They believed the maverick who had never really cottoned to Wall Street would make a bad situation even worse.

As they saw it, Bush, like McCain, was never *really* one of them. He wasn't anti–Wall Street; far from it. His Treasury secretary, Hank Paulson, had worked at Goldman. Less boldfaced names populated other areas of the administration; the president's chief of staff, Josh Bolten, was a former Goldman partner. But the guys in suits felt that the president himself was too Texas, too "cowboy," to really understand the needs of Wall Street. To the typical Wall Street executive, Bush came off as the type of guy who would rather chat with a small businessman running a modest manufacturing plant than play golf at John Mack's fancy club in Rye, New York, where most of the Wall Street power elite belong. And they were right.

But Obama appeared so comfortable in their presence; to the bankers and executives who listened to Obama in private chats during the campaign (and that included all of the major CEOs), this was a guy who could have easily worked at a big Wall Street law firm if he hadn't gone into community organizing first.

Once the euphoria of Election Day itself had passed for Obama's supporters in banking, all the signals seemed to indicate that the ease and friendliness Obama had displayed to Wall Street during his campaign was about to translate into Wall Street's having even more influence in the new administration than it had had with the old one.

Tim Geithner, the president of the New York Fed, was a career bureaucrat (part of the coterie of regulators who never saw the crisis coming) and a devotee of Bob Rubin, who was still at Citigroup and seemed destined for some top job in the new administration. But in public Rubin's reputation had been crashing as the market did, as the megabank needed one bailout after another to survive, and it became clear that while Rubin claimed no responsibilities at Citi in return for his multimillion-dollar salary, he nonetheless was one of the key architects of the bank's failed business model. Traders who worked there at the time say that he prodded the firm to take more and more of the types of risks that eventually led to its near insolvency. Rubin also stubbornly supported Citigroup's labyrinthine structure, which mixed customer deposits (checking and savings accounts that are insured by taxpayers through the FDIC) with the risk taking on the trading desks; thus ensuring that as the bond traders doomed the bank, it was the taxpayers who would be on the hook to make the depositors whole.

Yet even as he was about to resign from Citigroup, Rubin had been making inroads with Obama, giving him private briefings about Wall Street and the economy. Rubin may be the best-known Clintonite on Wall Street, but what is less known is that his son Jamie Rubin, who had also served in the Clinton administration and who was now working in private equity, had, like Gallogly, been one of Obama's earliest supporters from the financial sector. Jamie Rubin, along with Gallogly and people like UBS's Bob Wolf and veteran hedge fund manager Orin Kramer, were known on the Street as Barack's Bundlers for their ability to raise money for the candidate when he was contesting Clinton for the nomination, even when he was considered a long shot to win.

Bob Rubin, for all his toxicity as one of the architects of the financial crisis, was embraced by the new president. Indeed, Obama seemed to be more impressed with Rubin than Citigroup's stockholders were; the company's owners were now in open revolt against Rubin, questioning his massive salary and lousy results. Yet Geithner and another Rubinite, Larry Summers, fresh from making a quick $8 million for two years' work at the hedge fund D.E. Shaw and speech making, were the odds-on favorites to become Obama's Treasury secretary.

The links between the new White House and Lower Manhattan wouldn't end with Geithner, Rubin, and Summers, however.

"It's Rahm," Tom Nides told John Mack not long after Obama's election as president was made official on November 4, 2008. He was, of course, talking about Rahm Emanuel, one of the most powerful and aggressive

Democrats in Congress, who had just been chosen to be the most powerful man in the new administration (after the president, of course): the chief of staff.

Nides, as it turns out, was one of the first people to know with any degree of certainty not just that Emanuel was Obama's choice for chief of staff (it had been rumored for some time before the election) but also that he would accept the offer. And there was good reason for Nides's insider information: He and Emanuel had been close friends for years, working their way up through the Democratic Party together back in the mid-1980s. While Emanuel chose to make a career primarily in politics and Nides primarily on Wall Street, both understood just how much they needed each other.

At least superficially, they are an odd couple. Emanuel is short, lean, and intense. He loves to scream and curse, not just at aides but also at reporters and even members of Congress: at anyone who stands in his way. One famous anecdote recounts how, after Bill Clinton's election, Emanuel repeatedly plunged a steak knife into the table, screaming the names of the people whom he saw as the president's enemies and shouting, "Dead! . . . Dead! . . . Dead!" after each one.

Nides is taller, softer around the middle, and affable—traits that made him so successful as a Washington DC flack and lobbyist and as an executive at Morgan Stanley, where his chief duties included lobbying and PR management ("flackery").

In reality, they have much more in common. Both have straddled the Wall Street–Washington nexus for the past twenty-five years, and done so successfully, something that might come as a surprise in Emanuel's case. Indeed, much has been made of Emanuel's long political career—as a party operative; a Clinton administration hatchet man (where his tough style earned him the nickname "Rahmbo"); later as Chicago's representative in Congress, where as chairman of the Democratic Congressional Campaign Committee (DCCC) he emerged as a leading force in helping the Democrats take control of the House; and finally as Obama's chief of staff.

Much less has been made of Emanuel's impressive, and extensive, ties to Wall Street. They began with a stint in the early 1990s as an outside "political consultant" for Goldman Sachs, where he used his deep connections in the Chicago political community to help the firm secure municipal bond and other government contracts—nearly twenty years before he would become the second-most-powerful person in the country, he was already working to deepen the bonds between Wall Street and Washington.

During those years as a consultant for Goldman, he started to develop a network of friends on Wall Street, including a young senior executive named Jamie Dimon and, of course, his friend Tom Nides, who a few years later started working at Morgan Stanley. When Emanuel's deep ties to Goldman were first reported, he was in the Clinton White House. He quickly and vociferously attempted to quell speculation that former Goldman chairman and Clinton economic adviser Bob Rubin had gotten him the job. "Rubin had nothing to do with it," he told me at the time.

Maybe so, but the Clinton White House was a Wall Street–friendly place, deregulating the markets; bailing out their friends at the banks when they felt it to be necessary, as they did during the Mexican peso crisis and the LTCM collapse; and passing laws that allowed them to grow and take enormous risk (e.g., by ending Glass-Steagall). With that, it was only fitting that Emanuel's next gig after the Clinton administration would be on Wall Street: In 1999, in the midst of the dot-com bubble, he worked for a quick couple of years at the investment bank Wasserstein Perella, where he earned an equally quick $16 million before entering politics once again as a member of the House.

People on Wall Street like to joke that Emanuel doesn't have much of that $16 million left because of his free-spending wife. But if so, he made up for the lack of personal cash in political pull. Once back in the House, Emanuel used his Wall Street connections again, this time to raise millions of dollars as head of the DCCC, where he and his fellow Wall Street travelers, like Tom Nides, helped deliver the most liberal congressional leadership in the modern era when Nevada senator Harry Reid became majority leader of the Senate and San Francisco congresswoman Nancy Pelosi became the first female Speaker of the House (and one of the most liberal ever).

Now ensconced at Obama's side in the White House, Emanuel was ready to deliver for his buddies on Wall Street. After the election Tom Nides's boss, John Mack, effectively retired from the day-to-day management of Morgan Stanley, stepping down as CEO (though he remained chairman), while Emanuel's good friend Nides was stepping up: He became Morgan's chief operating officer—one of just a handful of top executives reporting directly to the new CEO, James Gorman. In addition, Nides was appointed the new chairman of Wall Street's chief lobbying group, the Securities Industry and Financial Markets Association, also known as SIFMA. It was here that Nides began to plot Wall Street's comeback after the disastrous 2008, something he was relying on his friend in the White House to assist him with.

The billions in taxpayer-financed bailouts and the recession caused by the financial crisis weren't things that endeared Wall Street to Main Street. The country was angry, even if Obama didn't appear to be (his nickname inside the campaign was "No Drama Obama"). During the campaign and after the election, Obama had had numerous meetings with his Wall Street kitchen cabinet about the banking crisis that lingered through the end of the year.

Lurking in the background, of course, was Bob Rubin, always willing to lend his sage advice and perspective as a survivor of past crises, even if that same advice may have contributed to the current one.

Obama, by all accounts, listened intently. There would be new rules, no doubt, he said, and now that the Democrats were in charge of just about everything (having built bigger majorities in the House and Senate), Wall Street was bracing for some class warfare coming from the liberal politicians.

Tom Nides was one of those unofficial advisers as well, even if he was a former Hillary supporter. According to people who know him, after the 2008 election, Nides wasn't really worried about attacks coming from the Democrats—after all, the House leadership included Wall Street's favorite liberal, Representative Barney Frank, who had been helping the Street lighten regulation and finagle Congress for years. And then there was the Street's favorite Senator, Chuck Schumer of New York, who never passed up the chance to tax, spend, and regulate, unless it involved Wall Street: As the ranking member of the banking committee, awash in Wall Street campaign cash, Nides was betting that Schumer would never kill the golden goose.

Instead, Nides believed if Wall Street truly faced a threat, it was from the Republican Party, particularly the Republican members of the House. As he saw it, *they* were the renegades who had voted against the initial plan to bail out the banks, the Troubled Asset Relief Program, which caused the markets to tank more than six hundred points that afternoon, and *they* were the ones now being influenced more and more by the Tea Party—a nascent political movement that viewed Big Wall Street as the evil equivalent of Big Government.

Obama lived up to Wall Street's expectations and began assembling a senior staff that had little of the "hope" and even less of the "change" he had promised in his campaign. In fact, he began to assemble a group of regulatory bureaucrats who looked like they had been plucked right out of the good ol' Clinton days, which made Wall Street, and Nides, now its chief lobbyist, absolutely giddy.

Rubin was gone, a casualty of the financial crisis, but after Obama announced Rubinite Tim Geithner's selection as Treasury secretary, the market rose to close over four hundred points higher from its low—this on the news that the country's finances would be run by a man who not only had missed the entire financial crisis, allowed Fannie and Freddie to implode, and permitted AIG to go on an unparalleled risk-taking spree, but who had been a key voice in favor of bailing out the financial system in 2008. Wall Street had other reasons to rejoice. Larry Summers, fresh from getting booted out as president of Harvard University after implying that women were bad at science and math, and even fresher from leaving the hedge fund where he had made millions doing almost nothing, would become the new president's chief economic adviser. Banks and traders from other big firms found high-ranking jobs as well: Gary Gensler, Rubin's old pal from Goldman Sachs and later at Treasury, snuck back in to government as head of the Commodity Futures Trading Commission, which regulates one of the core businesses that helped get Wall Street in trouble, the use (and abuse) of derivatives.

The only sour note amid the general euphoria sweeping the Street over team Obama was that somehow the Crazy Old Man, Paul Volcker, had made his way into the administration as a senior economic adviser. The former Fed chairman was as anti–Wall Street as ever, and top executives were warned that he wanted to once and for all rein in the excesses that had produced the 2008 financial collapse. They were also told not to fear: The president planned to keep Volcker around like a crazy uncle, for window dressing, and nothing more.

With Geithner, Summers, and lesser-known names like former Citigroup banker Michael Froman (a law school buddy of the president), and Phil Murphy, former Goldman Asia region chief and finance chair of the National Democratic Committee, in place (Froman as a deputy assistant to the president and Murphy as ambassador to Germany), Nides and Wall Street *knew* they had an administration they could work with. "Could you imagine who John McCain might have picked for the Treasury?" was a standard joke among the Wall Street hierarchy as they thought back to the presidential campaign and wondered what a McCain presidency might have looked like if, say, the financial crisis had come to a head after the election rather than before. In fact, Nides and the rest of Wall Street had barely gotten to know McCain during the campaign, except through the filter of Hank Paulson, who had briefed the Arizona senator on the financial collapse. And that was hardly a briefing: What was reported back to the heads of the big firms was that while Paulson was busy saving their collective asses, McCain was busy chewing out Paulson's ass. Hank Paulson, then the Treasury secretary and the former CEO of Goldman Sachs, is an imposing man, about six feet three inches tall, hunched over even as he normally stands, with steely blue eyes and a voice that's more like a rasp. He played football at Dartmouth, and while he could be exceedingly polite and accommodating to clients (he was a longtime investment banker) he's also known for his mean streak when challenged, as McCain had done to him in the fall of 2008 on a nearly daily basis.

Inside the Goldman boardroom or even at Treasury, such a confrontation would constitute fighting words for Paulson, who is known for frequent outbursts and cutting off people who he believes are wasting his time. According to Wall Street executives who spoke to Paulson, the former Treasury secretary believed firmly that McCain was wasting his time, as was his running mate, Sarah Palin, who called him from time to time as well.

But Paulson's temper was no match for McCain, who truly appeared disdainful of the former investment banker now leading the bailout of his old firm and the rest of the Street. It's what seemed to separate Obama from McCain; at least, that's what Paulson's remarks about his meetings with McCain and Obama conveyed to Wall Street. Obama treated Paulson and the rest of the Wall Street elite with respect during his meetings and telephone calls around the time of the crisis, as if they were partners and would rise out of the crisis together.

McCain, on the other hand, barely spoke to the Wall Street elite, unless, of course, he was pissed about the bailouts and what they did to his campaign. It was clear, at least to most of Wall Street's ruling figures, that McCain seemed to think Wall Street wasn't a partner but the enemy, the reason why the country was sinking into a near depression, and the reason why after running neck-and-neck with Obama for so long, his own campaign was now losing ground and would ultimately fail.

So Paulson, as he told his friends on the Street, just took the abuse. He didn't like being screamed at by McCain, but he wasn't about to pick a fight with a senator who had survived a couple of jet crashes, years as a North Vietnamese prisoner of war, and thirty years of politics. Especially not when, as he and the rest of the Street hoped, after November, McCain would go back to being the crazy senator he'd always been and Wall Street would breathe a collective sigh of relief that grew louder with each and every appointment by the new president-elect.

In the late fall of 2008, the heads of the big firms, of course, had seen better days. They were beaten and bruised, though bailed out. John Mack seemed barely alive, in a state of exhaustion after working nonstop for weeks and having barely saved Morgan Stanley, something that would not have happened were it not for a combination of government bailout money and the sale of a chunk of the company to a Japanese bank. Ditto for Goldman; it was a bitter pill for Blankfein to swallow, but with the bailout money from the feds and a cash infusion of around $5 billion from Warren Buffett, as well as the side benefits of the AIG bailout, which will be explained in more detail later, Goldman escaped almost certain death, as had Citigroup, Bank of America, and JPMorgan Chase. Jamie Dimon's prowess at risk management had kept JPMorgan from immediate implosion, though he, like the rest of them, recognized that without the federal government standing in the way, his firm could have gone down the tubes as well.

But at least they now had Obama, they all reminded themselves during their fancy lunches at San Pietro and expensive dinners at the Four Seasons in the days and weeks after the election, a man not much different from themselves, a man whom they could do business with.

Nides himself was giddy with excitement. Morgan Stanley was known for its blue-blood Republican ties, but he had convinced Mack, a former Bush fund-raiser, to jump to the other side. After a year of fund-raisers for Obama, Morgan Stanley was now clearly part of Obama country, and Nides one of the president's closest allies. And the payback would be grand.

"So, do you want to come to the administration?" Those were the words Nides heard from his close friend Rahm Emanuel not long after Obama's victory, according to bankers briefed on the matter. For his hard work during the campaign, for his political skill in laying out to Mack and the top brass at Morgan that 2008 would be a Democratic year, Nides was being offered a reward: a substantial job in the new administration, perhaps a key post at the World Bank or maybe as number two to Tim Geithner at Treasury. Whatever it was, the job would be a prestigious one.

Nides thought hard. Usually such jobs in government lead to even bigger jobs on Wall Street later, and with the Republican Party in disarray, political talking heads were already speculating about a second Obama term, which meant that Nides's connections—not just Rahm Emanuel but also those he would make at government on the new job—would be there waiting for him when whatever "private sector opportunity," as such positions (which often involve lobbying one's former colleagues in government) are euphemistically labeled, came his way.

But in the end, Nides declined—at least for the moment. He was making too much money, or to be more precise, was ready to make too much money, at Morgan Stanley now that his pals were running the country. Plus, he hoped the bailouts would have the same effect they had had in the past and Wall Street would soon begin to recover. Just look at the profits it had amassed in 1999, after the 1998 implosion of LTCM. That year, Wall Street had had one of the greatest runs in its long history, and despite the current dismal state of affairs, many on Wall Street believed prosperity was right around the corner once again if Obama, of course, remained a friend and ally as he had promised during the campaign.

Emanuel, meanwhile, assured Nides he had an open invitation to change his mind and join up with the winning team—to "give back," as the Wall Streeters who hop between government and finance call their frequent government forays. That made Nides relax a little because having friends in Washington was more important than ever for the remaining Wall Street firms and banks.

These banks owed their very continued existence to Big Government, and as Nides knew full well, they would owe their profitability and big bonuses to Big Government's continued largesse as well. Wall Street, if it was to not just survive but thrive once again, would need the key ingredients of the Bush bailouts, the levers provided by Big Government, to remain firmly in place: the guarantee of the banks' survival known as "too big to fail" and the superlow interest rates granted by the Fed that allowed them to borrow cheaply and earn money simply by investing in something that returned just a little more, not to mention direct capital infusions (a fancy way to avoid using the hated term "bailouts"). All this, controversial as it was, ultimately allowed the banks responsible for one of the worst economic crises in history to make a ton of money while the rest of the country suffered.

But Nides, like his more powerful Wall Street brethren Lloyd Blankfein, Jamie Dimon, John Thain, Ken Lewis, Vikram Pandit, and the heads of the other banks, didn't represent the rest of the country; they represented themselves, and they had made an investment in the new administration of "hope and change" to not change things too much.

Basking in the glow of being Obama's guy, Nides gave his first speech as the new head of the Wall Street lobbying group SIFMA, in which he laid out his game plan for how Wall Street and Washington would navigate an uncertain future. The event was held at the Marriott Marquis hotel, just a block from Morgan Stanley's headquarters in Times Square and conveniently located just a short distance from the Midtown Manhattan headquarters of the other big banks, which, with the exception of Goldman, no longer considered the Lower Manhattan financial district home.

It was a star-studded affair. Among those in attendance was Jamie Dimon, who was basking in his stature as the new king of Wall Street, having navigated J.P. Morgan through the financial crisis better than the rest. There was, of course, a good reason why throughout the campaign, his PR team kept telling reporters that Dimon was avoiding direct involvement in presidential politics because he was on the board of the New York Federal Reserve. After all, Wall Street execs who serve on the board of the New York Fed have a role in the policy making that directly affects their own profits and losses. If that sounds like a conflict of interest, well, it is. What's more, the board helps elect the New York Fed president; most recently, in 2003, the board had chosen Tim Geithner, who was now going to be Obama's Treasury secretary.

In other words, without Jamie Dimon's raising a dime for Obama (though others inside JPMorgan Chase had raised many, many dimes) the king of Wall Street was already close to one of the men who held Wall Street's purse strings—and now that same man was working for the president. In fact, it wasn't just Dimon but Wall Street as a whole was thrilled with Geithner's appointment; upon the news of his selection, the Dow jumped 6.5 percent.

The reason: Traders viewed Geithner as a familiar, steady hand. "At least he didn't appoint Bill Ayers," one trader told me after the announcement. Another reason for the apparently euphoric reaction was that Geithner (who, public myth believed, used to work on Wall Street) was ready to do whatever it took to make the banks profitable again. In reality, he, like the vast majority of Obama's senior staff, has no real business experience. Geithner is actually a career bureaucrat, albeit one with a soft spot for the banks, as he's spent pretty much his whole career in Lower Manhattan. *New York* magazine's John Heilemann even quoted one hedge fund manager as saying, "No one here would ever hire Tim to run a business, because he doesn't understand how to run a business. He's a good guy, a smart guy, with a good heart. But he's, you know, a regulator."

The Street's somewhat condescending attitude toward Geithner would be reflected in the rapid 382-point drop in the market after Geithner released his half-finished crisis-response plan in early 2009. It came just weeks, of course, after the news that Geithner would be Obama's Treasury secretary had sent stocks soaring. The problem now was that Wall Street had expected so much from Geithner and he seemed to be delivering so little, at least initially. When Wall Street fully digested the economic plans of Geithner and Obama, stocks would post one of their strongest rallies in decades, rising from six thousand on the Dow Jones Industrial Average to more than ten thousand, even as unemployment remained at great recession levels. Traders began to bet that even if Middle America remained depressed, Wall Street and the banks would prosper, and thus so should the markets.

As Heilemann observes, "The irony here was rich, of course, since Geithner's stabilization scheme would turn out to be strikingly favorable to Wall Street, as all would eventually see. From the outset, his aim was never to punish the banks. Quite the contrary, it was to save them—by pouring money into them, restoring confidence in them, treating them with kid gloves. . . . 'His office was there and he was deeply enmeshed in that culture and he had those relationships,' says one of his best friends."

Nides, of course, had his own pull inside the Obama administration in the form of his buddy Rahmbo, which is why he felt confident enough during his speech to the group to promise hope and opportunity, just as his new president might have done, to an industry that was beaten, bruised, and hated by the general public.

"We are navigating these waters with prudent but deliberate resolve," Nides said during the speech, with Dimon and the rest of Wall Street listening intently. "We will work with policy makers to fashion meaningful but sensible reforms."

Listening to Nides that night, people in the audience seemed to forget, at least for the moment, that the financial collapse had ever happened.

Others weren't so sanguine.

5

"WE KNOW EACH OTHER FROM CHICAGO"

While Tom Nides, Jamie Dimon, and others were celebrating the news of Obama's victory, Joe Perella was digesting that news at his usual corner table in his favorite restaurant, San Pietro, in Midtown Manhattan, where the Wall Street elite gather each afternoon to dine. Perella is no ordinary Wall Street executive—he's a legend in the arena of investment banking after a forty-year career in which he worked at the top of two large investment banks (First Boston and Morgan Stanley) and launched two "boutique" investment houses, the first one with Bruce Wasserstein (the same bank that Rahm Emanuel would later work for) and a second with a former partner from Morgan Stanley.

Unlike his friends seated at the other tables, Perella wasn't giddy with excitement over the Obama presidency and the prospect of tapping into the wealth that Big Government can shower on Big Business. Rather, he was worried about the future, not just for Wall Street but also for the country. Perella is a tall, intense man who loves to eat expensive Italian food and gossip. Despite being among the most connected, respected, and charismatic executives on the Street (his affability is one of the main reasons he has such deep relationships with just about every major CEO in corporate America), he's known for an occasional outburst of emotion.

Now was one of those times. "I can't believe these guys voted for Obama!" he snapped as he sat in San Pietro watching his friends wolf down expensive pastas with what seemed like not a care in the world, just a couple of months after financial Armageddon. Many of Wall Street's top brass were now bragging about how well they knew the new president, not just how much they liked and admired him. "We knew each other from Chicago," Jamie Dimon boasted one afternoon. The way Dimon explained it, the two had become acquainted when Dimon was CEO of Bank One, the large Chicago-based bank, and Obama was just a state senator on the rise.

Dimon always took great pride in his ability to understand the political side of his job as a Wall Street executive; back when he was Sandy Weill's right hand at Citigroup, he had made sure that his firm hired political advisers across the country, helping the firm meet politicians in charge of municipal bond business. It should thus come as no surprise that under Dimon, Citigroup had become one of Wall Street's top underwriters of municipal debt, particularly in the Chicago area that gave both Obama and Emanuel their start in politics. That's because one of those political advisers Dimon hired while he was at Citigroup was the law firm of Daley & George, run by Michael Daley, the brother of Chicago mayor Richard Daley. Now at JPMorgan, Dimon was turning to another Daley brother, Bill, who, like his siblings, is a mover and shaker in Democratic Party circles. He's built local ties to people like Emanuel and Obama's chief political adviser, David Axelrod, and, of course, the president himself. On the national level Daley served as secretary of commerce for Clinton and chairman of Al Gore's failed presidential campaign in 2000. Dimon hired Daley (whose ties to the Obama administration were so close that he was approached about becoming ambassador to China) after deciding that the firm's government outreach efforts were insufficient (he graded his own contributions in this area as *D* level).

Daley, now Dimon's vice chairman at the bank, was, according to people there, largely responsible for handling political matters, including the biggest political matter now at hand, how to influence the White House, where a Chicago native had just won the presidency. And with Daley on the case, the Dimon-Obama relationship was flourishing even more.

Like the rest of the Chicago business elite, and indeed the Wall Street elite, Dimon has said he was impressed with Obama's obvious intellectual gifts and smitten by his charm, so smitten, in fact, that he would later admit he had no idea that in a South Side Chicago church Barack Obama had come to love and admire the radical minister Jeremiah Wright. Perella, on the other hand, had begun researching Wright after hearing on NPR that the minister who had once preached "God damn America" and spewed anti-Semitic bile was also Obama's "spiritual mentor."

Even as far as radical pastors go, Wright pushed the boundaries. He once called Italian Americans "garlic nosed"; blamed "them Jews" for Obama's leaving his church during the campaign, and honored Nation of Islam leader Louis Farrakhan as a leader who "truly epitomized greatness" while preaching a Marxist religious doctrine known as Liberation theology.

This is the guy all these jerks voted for? Perella thought, as he heard John Mack's and Larry Fink's continued assessments—both before and after the election—of Obama as "moderate."

Initially, Perella had just kept shaking his head in disbelief. But now he couldn't take it any longer. One weekend shortly after the election, Perella was hanging out at a friend's estate in East Hampton, New York, and the conversation turned to Obama and how lucky the country was to have someone of his skill and intelligence in the White House, particularly after eight years of the "failed" Bush presidency. Perella soon discovered that he and his wife were the only people there who had voted for John McCain—and he couldn't take it anymore. As he listened to the dialogue, he realized this group of very rich, very smart New Yorkers, who received most of their information from the left-leaning *New York Times*, had no idea that Obama was not just a little left of center but was ranked as the *most liberal* U.S. senator by the prestigious *National Journal*. They had no idea that during his years as a state senator (a relatively low-level office that nonetheless he had held longer than any other elected position to date) he wasn't exactly a profile in courage, that rather than take an actual stand by voting "yes" or "no" on important legislation, he frequently merely voted "present" as a way to avoid taking either side. They had never listened closely to all those speeches where he waxed poetic about hope and change while more than hinting at his expansive (and expensive) spending plans like socialized medicine that would certainly lead to massive tax increases. And more than anything else they had no idea about his connections to the radical Reverend Jeremiah Wright, despite the fact that when videos of the reverend's rantings were made public, Obama and his wife, Michelle, feigned disbelief that their "spiritual mentor," the man who had baptized their children and served as the family pastor for nearly two decades, actually harbored such thoughts.

"Everyone here lives in New York State [one of the highest taxed states in the country], so what makes you think this guy won't raise your taxes to sixty percent?" Perella snapped. "In this economic environment, that's crazy."

For a second the room went quiet, and then someone leaned over and repeated what Mack and Fink told Perella earlier: "Oh don't worry, Obama's really a moderate."

Moderate on Wall Street, yes, but Main Street was quickly coming to another conclusion about its new president. Soon after taking office, Obama was met with the beginnings of a backlash from average Americans against the elites who had gleefully led government's expansion to unprecedented size, and maybe most of all against the Wall Street elite who had brought the country to financial ruin. They demanded accountability and expected Obama to deliver on his promises of hope and change.

So President Obama promised not to let the great financial collapse of 2008 pass without teaching Americans an important lesson: that everything we had been taught about the economy since the Reagan presidency, specifically that economies work best when they are unfettered by government, was wrong. Wall Street's recklessness was exhibit A as Obama put capitalism on trial and, like Moses bringing his people to the promised land, President Obama said he would lead the American people to a new understanding of the limits of unfettered, unbridled capitalism.

It was, of course, more myth than truth. Wall Street's greed had been subsidized by government for decades, thus allowing the casino that Wall Street became to grow and grow.

Even so, as he officially took office, and well into his first year as president, Obama swore to hold the Wall Street elite responsible for the financial collapse, and now for the smoldering economic collapse that took unemployment to nearly 10 percent. As unemployment grew seemingly by the day, the president and his advisers promised there would be no more reckless gambling—the stern hands of Big Government would make sure of that. There would be solid, responsible financial reform and, more than that, a reform of the economic mind-set; Wall Street businessmen would be held accountable as they never had been before, and they would be taught that there was a greater good than just making money. They would pay higher taxes (in fact, anybody making $250,000 a year would do so) and they would have to further subsidize his plans to level the playing field, namely his new government-subsidized health-care plan and the new stimulus package of $800 billion in spending projects (or, in his words, "shovel-ready jobs") that would put Main Street back to work immediately.

What our new president didn't say was that while these taxes would be distributed evenly among businessmen regardless of where they worked, the real benefits of "Obamanomics" would be distributed unevenly. The higher taxes to pay for his vast expansion of government would hit hardest the owners of so-called small businesses, the vast array of companies that fall clearly outside the Fortune 500 listing of the biggest employers in America. These companies may be called "small," but when they're taken together they represent a majority of jobs in America.

The common media stereotype of a small businessman is someone like Joseph Wurzelbacher, better known as "Joe the Plumber," who was starting a plumbing business and during the presidential campaign chastised Obama for promising to raise his taxes (one of the promises Obama would eventually keep) and trying to redistribute wealth. But more typical small businesses are the ones that are considered the engine of the economy mainly because they are the ones that do most of the hiring when the economy recovers—not the giant firms that make headlines. These small businesses, according to stock market analyst Peter Sidoti, employ anywhere from two hundred to two thousand people per company. They have a stock market value of as little as $2 billion (which makes them "small" by comparison with larger firms but still important), and if Sidoti's research was accurate, they were about to engage in a massive elimination of jobs, not jobs on Wall Street but those of ordinary, hardworking Americans.

Sidoti, it should be noted, has been a research analyst for thirty-five years, but of a caliber different from the more well-known Jack Grubman and Henry Blodget, the glitzy, publicity-hungry duo who will live in infamy for being thrown out of the financial business in 2003 after securities regulators found they placed positive recommendations on stocks of companies that their private e-mails showed they really didn't believe in. Instead, regulators believed their recommendations were designed to win investment-banking deals; these same companies were kicking back huge fees to their firms (Citigroup and Merrill Lynch) for this business.

In contrast, Sidoti looks like an accountant. He keeps a low profile and is rarely seen without a nondescript dark suit and starched white shirt. He always seems to be sweating as if he is late to a meeting. Most important for his clients, Sidoti doesn't do investment-banking work, which means he gets paid for making market calls that are right and alerting his clients to companies and stocks that will make them money.

Talk to his clients and they'll also tell you he's right most of the time.

During the first three months of 2009, Sidoti went out and began interviewing management at these small companies. The first thing Sidoti discovered was that of the six hundred "small" businesses he was researching, nearly all had survived the great recession in relatively good shape. He was pleased to tell his clients—mainly large institutional investors such as mutual funds and pension funds—that the stocks of these companies were looking pretty cheap. They had made it through the worst of the financial crisis with their balance sheets intact, and with economic growth now beginning to pick up, albeit at a tepid pace, their stocks looked cheap. (Just to recap, the Dow, after reaching an all-time high of 14,164 points in October 2007, a year before the financial collapse, eventually crashed a staggering 57 percent to only 6,626 points by March 2009.)

But the survival of these small businesses came at a larger price for the country: These companies were ensuring their survival simply by slashing jobs, tens of thousands of them, as they were doing now and would continue to do for the foreseeable future. Why were these companies shedding employment so fast? Sidoti discovered they were terrified of the higher taxes they were sure Obama was going to put in place, scared of his new "mandates" such as socialized health care, and simply full of disbelief that Obama's $800 billion stimulus bill would actually put people to work and so spur spending and consumption. Instead, these companies were maintaining profit margins simply by cutting costs, and their biggest cost center was jobs.

Sidoti had been in the research business long enough to extrapolate what the vast reduction in employment by the six hundred typical small businesses he covers meant for the wider economy. First he had to gauge the impact of the president's stimulus package, and he could sum it up in two words: a joke. The more he studied it, the more he realized that most of the money wasn't going into infrastructure spending—"shovel-ready jobs" was the phrase the president and congressional Democrats threw around so often in trying to drum up public support for the massive spending spree on top of the bank bailouts and the automobile company takeovers. Instead, most of the cash was merely being transferred to state governments around the country, some of them the most inefficient enterprises (after, of course, the federal government) known to mankind. This was so they could plug their budget holes without cutting their massive layers of bureaucracy—i.e., they could keep the various state government employees (and the Democrat-supporting unions who represented them) employed.

In other words, as unemployment rose to nearly 10 percent (and to around 23 percent in the construction business thanks to the near absence of those "shovel-ready" projects the president had promised with his stimulus plan), the economic stimulus that Obama and his economic team predicted was a huge failure. Sidoti knew it, and so did the vast majority of the men and women who ran the small businesses he was researching. And that is why they were laying off so many of their workers: Taxes were about to *explode*, not just at the national level but also at the state level, because the stimulus transfer provided nothing more than a onetime break (for governments) from the effects of the economic collapse. That money would eventually run out, and with the economy still in shambles, state and local government would begin a new round of tax increases.

So here was Peter Sidoti, a smart man who ran his own independent research firm on Wall Street that was decidedly not part of the Jamie Dimon/Larry Fink/Lloyd Blankfein economic elite, coming to the conclusion that the country was about to go through one of the most uneven and unfair economic recoveries in years. Thanks to its partnership with government, Wall Street had been allowed to gamble away almost everything, get bailed out, and because of this continued partnership, Sidoti heard through the Wall Street grapevine during the first three months of 2009, the big firms were beginning to make money once again. And all of this was occurring while the innocent bystanders of the financial collapse, the small businesses (and their workers), which now could not get loans from those same banks, needed to cut costs to survive and (they hoped) remain profitable during the great recession.

Sidoti, like most businessmen, believed that lower taxes often allow businessmen, those at both large and small companies, room to hire more people and get the economy rolling again. And yet, like the politicians in Washington, those in Albany, New York's state capital, were promising just the opposite: continued aid to the businesses that had caused the collapse and penalization of the businesses that had done the right thing. So these businessmen did what any rational person who is not protected by government guarantees and crony capitalism would do: They would hoard cash by cutting jobs and investments in plant and equipment. Sidoti estimated they would slash as much as a third of their workforce in 2009, which, if true, meant that the recovery the president promised after his Democratic-controlled Congress passed and he signed the $800 billion stimulus package wasn't really coming for a very long time, at least for average Americans.

As for Wall Street? Well, that's another story.

- - - - - - - - - - - - - - -

"It's total bullshit. He's bluffing," snapped Paul Miller, a veteran financial analyst for the Friedman, Billings, Ramsey Group. Miller was traveling through Fort Myers, Florida, on one of his ground assessments of the housing market. The beginnings of a recovery both for Main Street and Wall Street, according to the conventional wisdom, would start with a recovery in home prices, particularly in places like Florida, where housing speculation had reached astronomical levels during the bubble years. The reason? Like most Americans, Wall Street had invested heavily in housing. The bailout measures of 2008 and 2009 may have stabilized the financial crisis and prevented a complete collapse of the banking system, but those toxic housing bonds that had helped to cause the crisis in the first place were still on the books of the financial firms. If Wall Street were to recover, Miller and many others believed, those toxic bonds, filled with mortgages from places like Fort Myers, would have to recover first.

But what Miller was seeing wasn't a recovery at all: Houses were sitting on the market, unbought, offered at a large discount from their purchase price amid continued defaults by those who had invested in the market, either with hopes of flipping for a quick profit or because they had borrowed far more than they could afford with the "generous" assistance of the big banks and Big Government. From just looking around Fort Myers, Miller wasn't optimistic about Wall Street turning around anytime soon.

His profane reaction about bluffing came when he got an urgent message from his office: Vikram Pandit, the CEO of Citigroup, was saying that his company was about to make money again. Miller had long doubted the ever-optimistic statements from Wall Street CEOs; these CEOs, of course, were the same people who had plunged Wall Street into crisis with their bad bets in the bond markets and then spent 2007 and 2008 saying that the crisis was coming to an end, even as it nearly ended Wall Street.

The CEOs of the two major firms that went down in 2008, Bear Stearns and Lehman Brothers, were making positive statements about their firms' condition on financial TV and in the newspapers right up until the end. In the case of Lehman Brothers, this was especially dramatic: On September 10, 2008, then CFO Ian Lowitt boasted to analysts of the strength of the firm's liquidity; i.e., its abilities to meet its financial obligation with available funds. Five days later, on September 15, the firm collapsed and filed for bankruptcy. And as we've seen, Lloyd Blankfein of Goldman Sachs *still to this day* proclaims that his firm didn't need the government money during the financial crisis, that it was "forced" on Goldman, and that the firm had been doing just fine through the entire debacle.

So Miller remained unconvinced, particularly because the guy making the statement was Vikram Pandit.

Pandit had survived as Citigroup's CEO into the spring of 2009—but just barely. His bank, of course, was one of the largest recipients of government bailout money. In order to survive, Citigroup had needed not just one but two bailouts in the form of fresh capital from the federal government, and that doesn't count billions of dollars in government guarantees on its holdings of toxic assets. Pandit, to be fair, had inherited much of Citigroup's mess from his predecessors, Chuck Prince and Sandy Weill, the men who had created the Citigroup "empire" with the assistance of Bob Rubin.

"Vikram is the best person for the job, and we had several potential CEOs to chose from," Rubin nervously explained in early 2009, just before he was forced out of Citigroup, when asked whether his support for Pandit as CEO could be counted among the myriad mistakes that he made during his decade at the company, when it went from the most powerful bank in the world to a virtual ward of the U.S. government.

Rubin was defending himself as Citigroup was forced to take another dose of bailout money, one that made the U.S. taxpayer the largest single shareholder of the big bank. Shares of Citigroup, which had traded near $60 during its glory days, were now hovering around $1. Outraged investors had pushed for Rubin's ouster (he would leave in early January 2009), and they weren't crazy about Pandit sticking around, either.

And with good reason: When Pandit replaced Prince in early 2008, he had refused to sell off vast pieces of the unwieldy bank, despite pressure from his investors, who saw nothing but losses for the next year and had begun selling Citigroup shares. And now he was conducting a fire sale of assets to drum up much-needed cash as regulators like FDIC chief

Sheila Bair began threatening to end his short-lived career as CEO once and for all.

It was an odd decision for someone who had made it to the very upper echelon of Wall Street, not because of his personality (he's considered among the least inspiring and charismatic of Wall Street executives) but because he was considered one of the smartest. He came to Wall Street with a PhD from Columbia University, and during his many years at Morgan Stanley earned a reputation for understanding incredibly complex financial products, particularly details that eluded more senior executives. And he knew how to make money. In order to get him to join the company, Citigroup purchased his hedge fund for nearly $800 million, even though a year later Citigroup closed the fund due to its poor performance.

That's why it was so confounding that he started out by listening to Bob Rubin, one of the architects of Citi's massive and bloated infrastructure and, in many ways, of the financial crisis itself. Rubin's defense of Citigroup's absurd business model was unyielding. Now Citigroup had created a massive dilemma for the federal government: If it let Citi fail, the taxpayer would have to cover part, if not all, of the $800 billion in customer deposits (because of deposit insurance), not to mention the systemic damage to the financial system when traders had to unwind a balance sheet of nearly $3 trillion.

Rubin's miscalculation was based, of course, on the time-tested Big Government–Wall Street bailout recipe, where the government helps Wall Street by lowering interest rates, thus pumping massive amounts of liquidity into the system and reviving profits. Maybe a bank or two would fail; one immediately did, as Bear Stearns ended up imploding just a few months after Pandit was named CEO of Citigroup. But Citigroup would survive and eventually thrive in this difficult environment because it had a base of customer deposits to draw on if money got tight (a benefit that not even the mighty Goldman Sachs possessed).

By the time the financial crisis reached full force, neither Pandit nor Rubin seemed as smart as his advanced degrees and their reputation had suggested. Citigroup had so many stashes of toxic assets that even top company officials had no idea how much crap it had on its balance sheet. It held some profitable businesses that could have been sold off at a profit—like its brokerage business, Smith Barney—but the time had already passed for Pandit to get top dollar if he tried to sell them.

So, stuck losing money and with nothing to sell, Pandit came crawling to the federal government (Rubin would deny playing any role in the negotiations) for as much bailout money as possible. He nearly lost his job over it, and yet he survived because no one else wanted to run a bank whose symbol on the NYSE is the letter *C* for "Citi," but whose symbol among investors had become *S* for "shitty."

Then something happened—Citi was back in the black just like in the good old days, at least if you believed Vikram Pandit. He claimed that the first quarter of 2009 was Citi's best since before the financial crisis began to pick up steam. If Miller was skeptical, the market wasn't. Shares of Citigroup, which had been trading below $2 (less than the price of a copy of the *New York Times*), were now moving higher—close to $5. That's after the beleaguered banking behemoth logged five straight lousy quarters that produced a staggering $40 *billion* in losses.

And Pandit and Citi weren't alone. Two days after Pandit announced his results, JPMorgan Chase's Jamie Dimon, not to be outdone by his old bank, went on television and told CNBC's Melissa Francis that he was optimistic that his bank, also one of the biggest recipients of TARP bailout money, would be profitable in the quarter as well. The remarks sent shares up over 4 percent to just over $20.

Ken Lewis, the soon-to-be-ex-CEO of Bank of America, was under investigation by former Housing and Urban Development (HUD) secretary and current New York attorney general Andrew Cuomo for his role in the bank's controversial purchase of Merrill Lynch. I won't dwell on Lewis's legal problems here, but I will point out what he told the markets about the bank's postbailout progress: Bank of America, with hundreds of billions in bad loans, which inherited Merrill's portfolio of bad debt, made a profit in both January and February 2009, and it would continue to make money for most of the rest of the year.

How can all of this be possible? Miller thought. He considered the three banks in question: Citigroup was drowning in a sea of subprime loans. A few months ago it had been basically insolvent, and it was now a virtual ward of the state (the government took a 30 percent ownership in Citi in return for its bailouts). Bank of America, based on its holdings of toxic assets, wasn't far behind Citi in terms of the state of its balance sheet, and the government owned a piece of it as well. Jamie Dimon and JPMorgan Chase had escaped the worst of the subprime crisis, but even they weren't without their problem loans and issues. And then there was the fact that the future, at least on paper, didn't look too bright. Wall Street had gotten itself into the mess in the first place by holding onto bonds tied to the real estate market. And as Miller's tour of Fort Myers real estate revealed, housing prices showed little sign of recovering or even stabilizing.

Paul Miller is a good analyst, but like most analysts, he was rarely allowed to explore the inner workings of "the machine," as the trading operations of Wall Street are known. Among the reasons why the burgeoning financial crisis had escaped the notice of most Wall Street researchers (and of most journalists, as well) is that the trading desks are considered off limits to all but a chosen few. The reason for this is simple: The trading desks are the Fort Knox of Wall Street. Over the past thirty years, the trading desk, particularly the bond trading desk, was where the big money had been made.

The profit margins for creating and trading a mortgage-backed security dwarfed those of any other business on Wall Street. Why offer stodgy merger advice to a corporation or tell a small investor where to put his retirement savings when you can create a mortgage bond and basically print money? The result was that traders like Lloyd Blankfein were picked ahead of the bankers to fill the management ranks.

One of the big ironies of the financial collapse was that while the likes of Blankfein were making so much money for Goldman, they were also creating the situation that led to its demise. Bankers used to love to brag that the mortgage-backed security did so much social good, allowing people who couldn't afford homes access to loans so they could achieve the American dream. Maybe so, but consider the following: All the trading and risk taking with mortgage bonds, particularly bonds for which there was no public market and no way to truly gauge their value, had led to the financial collapse of 2008. Under Blankfein, Goldman had made a decidedly left-hand turn with its support of political liberals like the president and the Democrats who ran Congress, and Goldman was one of the top underwriters of mortgage debt. But that didn't stop the firm, when it saw the crisis coming, from shorting (betting against) the very bonds that Big Government fans touted as vehicles toward universal homeownership. The "big short," as it was known inside Goldman, had made the firm billions in profits. But Goldman wasn't the only bank that benefited. Indeed, another large benefactor of this process was Fortress Capital, the giant hedge fund that had hired former liberal presidential candidate John Edwards in 2006. It should be noted that Edwards, for all his lofty rhetoric as a U.S. senator from North Carolina, a vice presidential candidate, and later a presidential candidate, had something in common with his liberal soul mate Lloyd Blankfein: Both apparently saw nothing wrong with profiting off the demise of the American economy as Fortress, too, was making money betting against the subprime market.

And now, in another irony, it was that same trading that was returning Wall Street to the profitability that even informed skeptics like Paul Miller couldn't believe was happening.

The reason was simple: Miller and his colleagues weren't allowed anywhere inside the Fort Knox–like secrecy that surrounded the trading desks, because if they had been, they would have seen that the Wall Street money machine wasn't a function of brilliant bets on the bond markets (as the firms would later try to spin their return to profitability) but rather another, less publicized bailout engineered yet again by Wall Street's friend, Big Government.

The program was billed as a way to revive mortgage lending to consumers, which had virtually dried up. By purchasing an unbelievable *$1.2 trillion* in mortgage bonds and Treasury bonds (that's almost $4,000 worth of bonds, many of them near-worthless toxic assets, for every single person in the United States), the Federal Reserve would stimulate the lending markets by lowering interest rates, thus reviving the mortgage bond market that allowed banks to make loans to consumers. Forget the fact that the mortgage bond market itself was the reason why so many lousy loans had been made in the first place; it was fairly clear from the beginning that it would be Wall Street rather than consumers that would see the immediate benefits from the program.

"The government stepping in and buying mortgage securities accomplished two things for the banks," Miller later reflected, as he began making sense of the situation. "It not only gave them a trading partner for all these illiquid assets, but it essentially allowed them to reprice their balance sheet."

Prices for mortgage-backed securities had fallen to historically low levels during the height of the financial crisis and immediately thereafter, resulting in massive losses in the banking system. Meanwhile, no trading was occurring with these bonds because no one wanted to be holding illiquid mortgage debt—it was a multitrillion-dollar game of hot potato, as it were, and the big financial firms were caught with the bonds nobody wanted. But now, with Uncle Sam coming in and buying those mortgages, the bonds were no longer illiquid. They were being priced, and priced higher because the Fed was essentially bidding up the prices of the debt from their rock-bottom levels. As a result, the banks were able to mark up the prices of many of these assets and book profits.

"It diminished the possibility for more write-downs," Miller would recall, "and it turbocharged their trading business."

While the banks' trading business got roaring once the Fed started buying this near-worthless mortgage debt, the point of the whole exercise—to get banks making loans again to small business and consumers—was lost.

The reason the Fed cared about the banks' balance sheets and their giant holdings of toxic debt was that these massive losses on their balance sheets prevented the banks from making new loans: How could they give away cash when their own balance sheets were hundreds of billions in the red? Now that the banks' books were healthier, they would go back to lending money.

Or so the thinking ran. But what appeal does lending—which is time-consuming and carries risk even if it does provide a societal good—have, when trading, traditionally a riskier activity, could now be carried on virtually risk free courtesy of Uncle Sam?

The answer? None.

According to the *Wall Street Journal*, banks are nowhere close to meeting the borrowing needs of small businesses—only 50 percent of those polled say they received sufficient loans from their banks, compared with 90 percent just a few years ago. When asked about the paucity of bank lending, Jamie Dimon once told the president that as a result of the burgeoning recession, people and businesses weren't borrowing, while JPMorgan Chase needed to preserve capital because it was still saddled with lots of bad debt on its books, the legacy of the financial crisis that will take years to wash away.

The president, I am told, accepted Dimon's explanation, but maybe he shouldn't have, given all the special benefits Dimon and his fellow CEOs were receiving. Combined with near-zero interest rates and "too big to fail" protections, the Fed's mortgage buying spree made Wall Street trading a no-lose proposition. While small businesses were laying off workers and desperately hoarding cash to survive, Wall Street, just months after staring death in the face, was once again hiring traders. In the fourth quarter of 2008, Citigroup recorded over $8 billion in trading-related losses, according to SNL Financial. But by the first quarter of 2009, the battered bank had churned out over $3.5 billion in trading profits, lifting it to a $1.5 billion profit for the quarter—this after a record $17 billion loss just the previous quarter.

Bank of America's trading profits were even better. With the integration of Merrill Lynch, which it had acquired at the height of the crisis, combined with its existing force of fixed-income traders, Bank of America's trading force generated $7.5 billion in profits, lifting its total quarterly profit to $4.2 billion. But it was Goldman Sachs whose results in the second quarter of 2009 finally made Miller a believer: The company, even though it was smaller than many of its competitors, recorded an incredible $8.3 billion in trading profits.

This was no fluke. The government spigot pouring money into Wall Street's coffers had been opened up all the way.

"The government basically created an environment where Wall Street couldn't lose," Miller later remarked. "They bought product from the banks, and that buying not only helped their trading activity, but it also helped establish a higher price for many of these assets. It was a win-win."

It was the summer of 2009, and Lloyd Blankfein, the diminutive CEO of Goldman Sachs, was basking in the twin achievement of having not only saved Goldman Sachs from extinction but also returned the firm to the profitability that its partners had grown used to for so long. The firm was on its way to its best year ever—annual profits of about $13.4 billion. And that meant that bonuses would return to prebailout levels; at least, that's what Blankfein's senior staff began telling the big earners at the firm who would receive these multimillion-dollar bonuses.

It was once again a good time to be a Goldman Sachs executive. Blankfein himself, if the firm kept on its current pace, could make as much as $100 million in 2009, nearly double his record-breaking CEO payday of approximately $67 million for 2007.

That, perhaps not coincidentally, was the year when Goldman came up with the idea to short the housing market, while much of the rest of the Street kept drinking the Kool-Aid and buying and holding mortgage bonds that would eventually implode. Goldman's short sale of housing-related debt was fairly controversial on Wall Street. Competitors accused the firm of betting against mortgage bonds it sold to customers or, even worse, knowingly selling toxic mortgage debt to customers while it profited on the demise of the mortgage bond market and the entire financial system. (The SEC would eventually charge the firm with failing to disclose to its clients that it was peddling them toxic debt that was basically created to fail with the help of famed hedge fund manager John Paulson, who made billions of dollars also by shorting housing bonds in 2007.)

Goldman, of course, denied the charge and insisted its remarkable 2007 performance was nothing more than "hedging," or good risk management. (It would also insist, just a little later, that because of its savvy business practices, it really didn't need any bailout money but was forced to take it by those in Washington.) And now it was attempting another spin, saying its massive trading profits during in 2009 were once again the result of its exceptional abilities to trade better than the next guy.

Goldman's explanation was only half right. Yes, Goldman *was* an exceptional firm; in 2007 it foresaw the housing bubble's collapse while firms like Citigroup, Merrill, Lehman, and Bear Stearns continued to double down on the market. But in doing so, Goldman didn't just "hedge" its own positions; a growing body of evidence began to build that the firm relished making money by screwing those of its clients who were either too stupid or just too blinded by profits during the bubble years to see the looming collapse. Goldman did this by selling these clients, mainly large banks and other sophisticated investors, mortgage bonds and other derivatives of these bonds that its own traders had described as "crap."

Goldman had spent much of the end of 2008 arguing in the press that it had been forced to accept bailout money it really didn't need, including the $180 billion government bailout of the once-mighty insurer AIG. That bailout ensured that AIG could make good on insurance policies known as credit-default swaps, which covered the value of hundreds of billions of dollars' worth of near-worthless toxic debt on Goldman's balance sheet. Thus, the bailout of AIG was in effect a backdoor bailout of Goldman; without the government rescue, AIG wouldn't have been able to fully insure the debt held by Goldman, and Goldman would have had to take massive losses.

At least that was the opinion of the federal government, namely the men trying to stabilize the financial system during the meltdown of 2008, then Treasury secretary Hank Paulson and New York Fed president Tim Geithner. They argued that in order to prevent a complete meltdown of every bank in the world, the largest ones in the United States needed to be saved by pumping as much money into AIG as humanly possible.

The result was a windfall for Goldman—it was paid one hundred cents on the dollar for bonds worth far less. But Goldman was far less generous in thanking the American people. In fact, it thanked no one except itself. Goldman's PR chief, Lucas van Praag, a smart, sharp-tongued Englishman with a gift for biting remarks, became the main conduit of Goldman's campaign to make the bailouts seem like a nonevent and attribute the firm's good fortune to its own "risk-management" techniques.

By early 2009, having avoided the fate of Lehman Brothers and Bear Stearns and making gobs of money once again, Goldman and van Praag began to fine-tune their talking points to fit the changing times. They took the position that the near-zero interest rates and the too-big-to-fail status that meant Goldman was classified as a bank by the government rather than as the hedge fund it really was, not to mention the Fed's mortgage-bond purchases, really weren't the causes of the trading profits that kept piling up.

No, according to van Praag, Goldman was making money because it was really, really smart.

"We're simply good at what we do," he told me.

At Morgan Stanley's headquarters in Midtown Manhattan, the mood was less jovial. Morgan's CEO, John Mack, was widely regarded inside Morgan as having saved the firm from imminent collapse by securing a massive investment from the Japanese bank Mitsubishi, even if he had also needed the government bailouts to make it completely through the crisis. In the end, Mack had been shaken by the financial crisis and decided to step down by the end of 2009. He was, after all, the architect of the firm's foray into risk that had resulted in billions of dollars of losses, including a massive $8 billion loss from just *one trading desk,* possibly the biggest single trading loss in Wall Street history. With that, Mack vowed to change the firm's direction: Morgan was going back to its roots as a financial adviser to individuals through its brokerage (it was now in the process of buying pieces of Citi-group's brokerage business, Smith Barney) and to large companies through its investment bank.

The firm would deemphasize trading, which, along with the Citigroup deal, accounted for its first-quarter loss. Mack also wanted nothing to do with Goldman's spin. He had ordered his PR staff to do the exact opposite of what Goldman was doing; instead of laying the credit for its eventual recovery on its own brilliance, Morgan would thank the government and the American taxpayer at every chance it got.

The straight talk from Morgan Stanley's PR staff paid off—the firm remained out of the headlines as Goldman began to get crushed with bad publicity—but Mack's other edict seemed to backfire. While Goldman was killing the markets with massive trades and investments in esoteric bonds, Morgan's new approach resulted in a shocking first-quarter loss. That's when the spin at Morgan began: Executives blamed the loss on the expensive acquisition of the Smith Barney brokerage firm from Citigroup as Pandit began to unload assets to satisfy his new shareholders, the federal bureaucrats, who, because of the government's continued ownership stake in Citi (as of the writing of this book, the feds are still looking to sell their share and unwind their stake), were now practically running the daily operations of the big bank.

But inside Morgan, board members were seething. Mack may have wanted to do the right thing by leaving the gambling to Goldman, but it was costing the firm money. Within days of the announced losses, Morgan announced that it had gone out and hired a couple of hundred traders. And presto, the profits began to soar, as did the firm's bonus pool.

But by now, the press was on to a new angle in the continued drama of the financial crisis, and it was one that especially resonated with the general public: Only a year after the bailouts the very same people who were saved by the American taxpayer were now enriching themselves with huge bonuses. The biggest and most conspiracy theory–esque attack came from writer Matt Taibbi of *Rolling Stone*, who took special aim at Goldman Sachs, calling it a great "vampire squid" that had used its connection to government to make money when the markets tanked and was now making money while setting the stage for yet another meltdown. Among the article's shortcomings (and there were many hidden inside its well-written passages) was its insistence that Goldman was somehow more of a financial menace than its rivals. Taibbi asserted without much real evidence that Goldman stood at the center of nearly every financial scandal "since the 1920s," looting and pillaging its way to massive amounts of wealth and power inside the federal government.

But the article struck a nerve, mostly because Goldman couldn't spin the one essential truth: that the Big Government Goldman had helped to put in place with the rest of Wall Street was in turn helping it create the massive profits and bonuses it now enjoyed. Bonus money is set aside every quarter by the firms, and it didn't take long for analysts and the financial press to sniff out that 2009 would be a *great* year. Goldman was on its way to amassing some $23 billion in bonus money, which by past calculations meant Blankfein was on track to beat his 2007 compensation of $68.5 million and possibly earn as much as $100 million. The other big firms wouldn't match Goldman's performance, but based on the level of profits being amassed on their trading desks, 2009 was destined to be a great year all around.

"Someone making one hundred million dollars is taking too much risk, and that can't be tolerated under the legislation," Wall Street's "pay czar," Ken Feinberg, boomed after I asked him why he forced Citigroup to basically fire a trader who demanded what was due to him under his contract.

Feinberg, a voluble, straight-talking lawyer, had gained a degree of fame as the special administrator of the 9/11 victims' compensation fund, where he decided how much money victims of the terrorist attack received from the federal government.

Now he was earning a degree of infamy, at least on Wall Street, for being the special administrator of something else: Wall Street salaries. Under TARP, the president can appoint a "special master" to determine the propriety of bonuses doled out to top Wall Street executives.

As long as the firms remained in what they referred to as "the roach motel" of TARP, Feinberg was their master as far as the compensation of their senior personnel was concerned. And much of Feinberg's analysis on pay revolved around risk—he believed high compensation, even if it was subsidized by the federal government, indicated the taking of outsized risk.

"Andy Hall [the $100 million bonus Citigroup trader] was taking too much risk," he added, with his voice rising, "and that's not allowed under the law!"

Feinberg is one of the most engaging people I have ever met in government. He's smart, funny, and above all fair. But he also scared the daylights out of Wall Street, because he built his reputation on being above political influence and, as he showed he would do in the Citigroup case, he was willing to stand up to anyone, even the ultrapowerful Lloyd Blankfein and Jamie Dimon.

"He's out of his fucking mind!" an executive at JPMorgan Chase told me after hearing the news about Hall, one of the most prominent commodities traders on Wall Street. As it turned out, Citigroup was forced to get rid of not just Hall but his entire trading business because it made so much money.

And with that, the entire Street, Citigroup included, made a mad dash for the exits of the roach motel.

With so much money flowing in, the firms now demanded approval to repay the government's TARP money. Citigroup was the basket case of the banking system, but it too could repay its bailout money and began developing plans to do so before the end of 2009.

Just months after being saved by the government, Dimon, Blankfein, and Mack spent countless hours on the phone with people like Emanuel, Geithner, and many lesser bureaucrats explaining how strong their balance sheets had become, even if many analysts believed the financial system, just a few months after the meltdown, wasn't yet on firm footing.

At first the administration balked at all the requests; the system was too fragile, Geithner argued. The bank "stress tests" to determine the strength of their balance sheets hadn't been completed, even if the firms referred to them as "feather tests" for the low bar set to pass these examinations. Then the adminstration seemed to balk at every firm except Goldman, which was showing the strongest profits and, of course, was making use of its continued power inside the halls of government.

"If those bastards think they're going to let Goldman out and not us, they're crazy," said a senior executive at Morgan Stanley when word began to leak that Goldman had the green light to repay the $10 billion it had received under TARP. "Jamie Dimon is going to go bat shit."

And he did. In meetings with administration officials, including regular meetings with the president himself, Dimon turned up the heat: His firm just couldn't be competitive with Feinberg breathing down his neck. (More than that, how would he pay himself?)

When you meet with the president on a regular basis, it becomes rather easy to get what you want, as Dimon was now discovering. Obama may not have been the most economically sophisticated president in recent history, but he did lean on Dimon for advice from time to time, with Dimon making regular trips to the White House to dispense his economic wisdom.

It's unclear how the president's near-socialist leanings gelled with Dimon's liberal but more market-driven philosophy, but it appears Dimon's advice on compensation hit home.

Along with Goldman and JPMorgan Chase, Morgan Stanley was among the first firms to repay the TARP money, and therefore it was free to pay its bankers and traders any way it saw fit. But there was little celebration; Mack made sure of that. While Lloyd Blankfein and his inner circle were counting their winnings and the days before they could once again cash those big bonus checks, Mack saw the coming tsunami of bad publicity and was busy trying to figure out how to act. He began calling up Blankfein, asking how he would handle the PR firestorm when it came—and it was only a matter of time before it came. Blankfein, Mack would later remark, either didn't know or didn't care about the fallout.

It was around this time that Mack took a trip down to Washington to meet some friends in the Obama administration. In mid-2009, the

administration was preoccupied with issues other than Wall Street bonuses, namely the economy, which continued to lose jobs, the twin wars
in Iraq and Afghanistan, and the president's falling poll numbers. Even so,
Mack worried about an increase in the attention being paid to the inequality of Wall Street's resurgence, with Wall Street pay surging while Main
Street suffered from 10 percent unemployment.

At one point he asked Larry Summers, Obama's chief economic
adviser, for advice. Summers wasn't as attached to Wall Street as was his
mentor Bob Rubin, who had just retired from Citigroup after becoming
the target of populist ire over his role at the bailed-out bank, but he wasn't
an innocent bystander, either. Before joining the administration, Summers
had worked for D.E. Shaw and had walked away with $8 million for stra-
tegic advice and speech making before joining the Obama team. Not bad
for a couple years' work.

Mack's question involved Wall Street's bonus pool, namely what the
Obama administration wanted firms like Morgan Stanley to do. Mack was
asking for guidance now instead of waiting because the press attention to
the issue of bonuses and bailouts was starting to grow.

But Summers, according to what Mack has told people, didn't seem
fazed by the prospect of massive Wall Street bonuses, as the firms began to
repay TARP money to the government. When Mack asked him for guidance, Summers shot back, "How would it look for government to be giving private businesses guidance on something like compensation?" Other
than the so-called pay czar, Ken Feinberg, who was mandated by Congress
to regulate the compensation of the top twenty executives at firms that
hadn't yet repaid TARP money, the administration wanted nothing to do
with the issue. At least that was the impression Summers left with Mack.
Wall Street, as far as Summers and his boss were concerned, could just do
what it liked when it came to bonuses, the few people subject to the TARP
restrictions aside.

In other words, Wall Street really *did* have a friend in one of the most
liberal presidents since FDR.

6

DOING GOD'S WORK

By the end of 2009, the outrage over Wall Street's evil ways seemed to be growing by the day. Much of it was fueled by anger over the Street turning into a profit machine (funded by the American taxpayer) just over a year after the record taxpayer bailouts. Then add on top of that the reports that the firms were getting ready to hand out record bonuses to their bankers and traders. In another era Lloyd Blankfein would have been showered by love letters from his clients and shareholders. He was running the most successful firm on the Street, having turned a loss in the last quarter of 2008, the peak of the crisis, into four consecutive quarters of massive profits. Goldman had earned about $13.4 billion in 2009, projected to do at least that much or even better in 2010, and was now setting aside $23 billion for company bonuses to its bankers and traders.

But Blankfein had to hold off on the celebration. With the bailouts of 2008 still fresh in the public's mind, Goldman had come to embody all that was wrong with the American economy and the president's approach to it. Unemployment remained high—the "official" unemployment rate (which most economists agree understates the actual level of unemployment) hovered around 10 percent, even as economic growth (as measured by the nation's GDP) was signaling that the great recession was nearing its end. But the GDP didn't reflect the true state of the country, where the president's plan to revive Main Street—an $800 billion stimulus program of so-called shovel-ready jobs—had been a colossal flop, unless of course you worked in government, where unemployment continued to remain low. Or unless you worked on Wall Street, which just a little more than a year after the 2008 collapse and bailout was flourishing, thanks to its ties to Big Government and the myriad benefits that government doles out—but only to the politically connected. Citigroup, JPMorgan Chase, Bank of America, Morgan Stanley, and Goldman Sachs in particular were printing money, mainly on their trading desks, where they could borrow at next to nothing and invest risk free in bonds because they were "too big to fail."

How on earth has Goldman Sachs (as well as one of its chief competitors, JPMorgan) managed to amass so much in profits so soon after the financial system nearly collapsed? We've explored some of the answers already, but here's one we've haven't yet discussed: Technically, Goldman Sachs is a commercial bank. A commercial bank is the kind that you and I keep our money in, with ATMs, tellers, and the rest, as opposed to an investment bank, which arranges for the flow of massive amounts of money between governments and corporations and undertakes highly risky trading activity for profit.

Try opening a checking account at Goldman or Morgan Stanley or finding an ATM in the lobby of their headquarters in Manhattan. Good luck. And by the way, neither bank is offering debit cards anytime soon, at least as far as I know. Even so, during the height of the financial crisis both Goldman and Morgan Stanley became bank holding companies, and with that earned not just the protection of the Federal Reserve but also all the benefits that come with being a bank, including access to the Fed window for emergency borrowing and government guarantees on the firms' long-term debt, which allows the firms to borrow cheaply.

The classification was designed to stave off panic in the financial markets—lines of credit were drying up, and without access to capital to trade and invest, Goldman would have followed Lehman and Bear into extinction. But now that the crisis was over, these benefits amounted to nothing short of a huge taxpayer subsidy for the firm's shareholders, as their stock started to climb back to its pre–banking crisis levels, and the bankers and traders at the firm, who would be entitled to big bonuses at the end of the year.

By the start of 2009, Obama began to sense the public's growing anger and said of bankers' pay: "[There's a time] for them to make profits, and there will be time for them to get bonuses. Now's not that time. And that's a message that I intend to send directly to them." If Obama ever intended to send that message, he clearly never followed through, because just a year later, Goldman has used all the taxpayer-subsidized benefits allotted to the firm—in effect a taxpayer subsidy—to amass enormous riches.

Executives at the Wall Street firms were now admitting that behind the eye-popping numbers was the growing likelihood of the mother of all paydays. Barring the Fed's raising interest rates (Bernanke vowed he wouldn't, and based on that pledge, Obama was eager to reappoint him and push for his Senate confirmation) or the Treasury removing the banks' protected too-big-to-fail status, Wall Street seemed to be on course for a record year. The firms would be more than able to repay the TARP money, their executives bragged, which meant they would not have their salaries capped by Obama's executive pay czar, Ken Feinberg, and could dish out bonuses any way they saw fit.

How did the banks justify this publicly? Goldman continued to argue that it was the first firm to repay the $10 billion loan it had received during the financial crisis (it would be followed by JPMorgan, Morgan Stanley, Bank of America, and finally Citigroup) and that it was the firm best prepared to withstand the financial meltdown in 2008—both of which are undoubtedly true—and, of course, that it didn't really need all those billions in bailout money.

The others went to the public with the standard line that they were no longer wards of the government, that they weren't being bailed out anymore, so what was the harm in compensating the people responsible for their trading profits?

Word of the spin even caught their best friend in the White House by surprise. Barack Obama, as well as key members of his cabinet, owed the

big Wall Street firms many things, including their tireless support during
the campaign. But as he heard the PR spin repeated on business television
and on the business pages of major newspapers, even Obama and key cabinet members were blown away by the arrogance, people close to him say.

Obama's reaction to the bonus news and Wall Street's spin may have
been best chronicled by journalist Jonathan Alter in his book *The Promise.*
"Let me get this straight," Alter quotes Obama as saying as he heard the
big firms rationalize making so much money so soon after the bailouts and
while the special privileges continued. "They're now saying that they deserve big bonuses because they're making money again. But they're making
money because they've got government guarantees."

Obama might have projected verbal outrage, but actions speak louder
than words, and his policies all but ensured that the banks would make so
much money through 2009 that bonus pools would swell to astronomical
levels. Those policies, combined with the banks' PR chiefs' spin, only compounded the public's distaste for Wall Street and the double standard the
president privately recognized but did little to correct.

The biggest beneficiary of the bailouts and the postbailout environment once again was Goldman Sachs, which has a long history of figuring
out ways to profit beyond its competitors. No matter how many times the
firm attempted to say that the bailout money was forced down its throat
(in reality the firm digested $10 billion worth without a hiccup) or that it
hadn't benefited from the AIG bailout, a simple question remains unan-
swered: If Goldman didn't need handouts to survive 2008, why didn't it
just return the cash to taxpayers?

That was because, thanks to the various rescues, Goldman eked out
a small profit for 2008, around $2.3 billion. As a small sign of contrition,
Blankfein, whose net worth is at least $1 billion, chose not to take a bonus
that year, but others at the firm did: Goldman handed out nearly twice
as much in bonus money as it made in taxpayer-induced profits. Yet the
firm's profits in 2009 were now likely to be six times larger, and based on
prior bonus calculations tied to the firm's performance, the CEO's compensation could approach $100 million, 50 percent more than his $67 million

bonus in 2007. That's right, Lloyd Blankfein was on track to earn nearly $100 million as Goldman's government-supported profit making grew to new heights.

Those in Goldman's orbit benefited as well. Consider the windfall received by Warren Buffett, the legendary investor who had sunk $5 billion into Goldman during the dark days of the financial crisis, literally a week after Hank Paulson began handing his crony capitalists the bailouts that wouldn't end for the next four months. The deal gave Buffett the option to buy Goldman Sachs stock at $115 a share, and as Goldman shares headed toward $180, Buffett had earned nearly $3 billion.

Buffett, like Blankfein, was a big supporter of President Obama, and for all his folksy charm and past appreciation for fiscal prudence, he never once commented on the irony of the fact that he, one of the greatest capitalists of all time, was benefiting not just from the bailout money but also from the continued largesse of hardworking Americans, whose taxpayer dollars were being showered upon the big banks. Even so, Buffett, safely ensconced in Omaha, escaped being a target of the populist ire, but Blankfein and Goldman did not.

That populist ire—and how it's being played by various politicians—is something that Goldman truly hates. There is an interesting irony with Goldman; investors believe the firm is the most ruthless of the big Wall Street investment houses in terms of trading against their customers' best interests. And yet inside Goldman, top executives, led by Blankfein, believe theirs is the most ethical of the big firms. To them, being called a crook is a deadly slur, as Democratic senator Harry Reid discovered one afternoon when Goldman president Gary Cohn cornered him at a fundraiser at Goldman's headquarters in Manhattan and said, "Who do you think you are, coming here asking for money while you trash us?"

Reid was now in a particularly tight spot: Like most Democrats, he was taking his cues from the White House, and banker bashing was one of his election-year talking points (2010 being a year when many House and Senate seats were up for grabs). At the same time, he needed money, lots of it, because his support of the president's unpopular heath-care plan and other measures gave him a Wall Street–like approval rating in Nevada, a moderate- to conservative-leaning state he had represented for two terms.

In other words, if Reid was to win a third term, he needed Wall Street money nearly as much as he needed to bash Wall Street bankers and traders.

What's even more ironic about this episode is that Cohn himself had invited Reid in to Goldman to visit with the firm's bonus-stuffed traders a couple of weeks earlier. Part of the reason why Cohn agreed to the request was that the Goldman president was a committed Democrat—one of the Street's earliest supporters of Obama. But Cohn had his reasons too, and he wanted Reid and the rest of the Democratic Party to understand that Wall Street, Goldman in particular, was pretty tired of being used and abused.

"We're getting sick of the bullshit!" was the message Cohn relayed to Reid, who mostly sat back and took the abuse, according to a person with knowledge of the meeting. It's unclear if the abuse was worth the trip to New York for Reid, who took home $40,000 in donations that day. Nonetheless, the episode made it clear to those on Wall Street that no matter how much people like Cohn cried, Reid's silence during the event spoke volumes. The attacks would keep coming.

In the end, Reid, like Obama and other Big Government politicians, is perfectly willing to put up with a few Wall Street tantrums if it means getting reelected.

The growing anti–Wall Street populism had John Mack, now the chairman of Morgan Stanley, concerned. Normally, hate mail rarely makes it to the desks of Wall Street's top executives, as underlings intercept and deal with it. But as the public was growing increasingly frustrated with Wall Street, Mack began occasionally reading some of the more vitriolic letters, in part because it helped him gauge the public's foul mood toward the industry and anticipate what politicians might do in response.

In the fall of 2009, after reading a particularly nasty piece of hate mail that was addressed to both him and Lloyd Blankfein, Mack called the Goldman CEO to express his concern.

"That's nothing," Blankfein replied. "I get seventy-five to a hundred of those a day." Goldman now disputes the magnitude of the hate mail, but what it won't dispute is that around this time Blankfein was resigned to the fact that Goldman was being unfairly singled out as the great villain of the great recession, much as J. P. Morgan had been during the Great Depression a generation earlier. He had directed his press staff to keep telling reporters that Goldman hadn't been bailed out at all or, to be more precise, never needed a bailout.

But Mack, himself a recipient of government money, knew the argument could never hold water, not with the public, not with Wall Street's new masters in the federal government like the banker-hating Congresswoman Maxine Waters, and not with unemployment hovering around 10 percent while Morgan Stanley, Goldman, and the rest of Wall Street were feasting on the benefits of the 2008 financial rescue that President Bush had enacted as an emergency and that President Obama had left firmly in place.

While John Mack was continuing to take the high road, the partners at Goldman were acting as if they were entitled to the vast riches they had received on the backs of taxpayers, which brought even more attention and further condemnation. Maybe it was because the firm believed its own mythology of Goldman as something special, the elite of the elite on Wall Street. In the world of Goldman Sachs, its partners were special because they are, after all, plucked from the best schools, and they deserved (well, they believed they deserved) those multimillion dollar salaries, having survived in a corporate culture that demanded nothing short of success.

This Goldman myth is best exemplified in Blankfein's already famous interview with the *Times* of London, in which he defended Goldman's success and executive bonuses by saying, "As the guardian of the interests of the shareholders and, by the way, for the purposes of society, I'd like [my bankers] to continue to do what they're doing." He concluded by saying he was simply "doing God's work."

The Goldman myth is just that, a myth, because it ignores or at least downplays some very important facts. First, Goldman had been far from infallible; the firm owned much of the same toxic housing debt that took down Merrill, Citigroup, and the rest, even if Goldman had hedged its bets better than most. (Note that as I write this in mid-2010, Goldman is under assault even for that. Evidence is mounting in SEC and Justice Department investigations that Goldman was shorting the housing market—i.e., betting that housing prices would plunge—while encouraging its clients to do the opposite and buy the toxic housing bonds it was trying to sell them. More on this later.)

Mostly, however, the Goldman myth ignores the incredible amount of entitlement that fills the halls of its opulent headquarters in lower Manhattan. As the feeling there runs, Goldman Sachs makes so much money because it *deserves* to, even if it *was* the recipient of bailout money (bailout money it insists it was forced to take even though it would have survived without it). Likewise, executives at the firm truly believed they could put forth such nonsense without worrying about accountability because they had bought the right friends in Washington. Goldman executives were among President's Obama's largest contributors for his 2008 election and gave twice as much money to Democrats in Congress as they did to Republicans, who, thanks to Goldman's donations to the Left, were firmly in the minority. Records show that Goldman executives contributed almost $1 million, but that figure doesn't count the amounts of money raised by these partners from their wealthy, blue-chip friends and families. No Wall Street firm gave as much as Goldman did to Obama and the Democrats. It was an unprecedented show of support because in the past Goldman had split its donations pretty evenly between Democrats and Republicans.

But that was before the reign of Blankfein, a committed Democrat, and his number two, Gary Cohn.

Lloyd Blankfein looks a little like the character Gollum from *The Lord of the Rings*. He's balding, with wide eyes, which also gives him the (false) appearance of being perpetually confused. In public he can be stiff and seem arrogant and is prone to gaffes.

Yet his friends say he's charming in private, and don't let that dopey look on his face fool you. Blankfein is one of the savviest players on Wall

Street. After graduating from Harvard Law School, he went to work for a big law firm, Donovan, Leisure, Newton & Irvine, and then decided to make his fortune on Wall Street, which he did nearly from the moment he joined Goldman's commodities trading unit, then known as J. Aron, as a gold salesman in 1981. Over the next thirty years, Blankfein became one of the richest men in America, with an estimated net worth of close to $500 million.

But for all his wealth and pedigree of success, Blankfein's story is about as Horatio Alger as you can get: He grew up working class in a Brooklyn housing project and worked his way through Harvard, just as he worked his way through the brutal meritocracy at Goldman Sachs, where professionalism, teamwork, and most of all, making money for the firm, are the keys to success.

And under Blankfein, Goldman flourished like never before. When Blankfein and his trading-desk associate Gary Cohn took over Goldman in 2006, they did two things: First, they transformed the firm from a place that coddled its blue-chip clients—mainly large companies, big pension funds, and the superrich—into a casino. While the firm won't disclose exactly how it makes its money, some analysts estimate that nearly 70 percent of its profits come from trading, often, it is charged, against its own clients. For instance, one of Goldman's clients might want to take a given position, say, buying some housing bonds betting that prices would go up. If Goldman's internal research indicated the opposite, rather than tell the client to watch out, Goldman might sell the client those bonds— and take the opposite position itself. That way it would profit twice: first from the fee on selling the client the position it wanted, and second from the trade itself, which it hoped would decline in value. Thus, Blankfein and Cohn made Goldman more profitable than ever before, thanks to an aggressive, almost Darwinian trading style, where a firm that had once relished its strong relationships with clients openly and brazenly began taking advantage of those same clients in the markets.

Second, even though the firm had always tended to give a bit more to Democrats, under Blankfein Goldman has moved even further to the left.

In 2009 Goldman gave nearly four times as much to Democrats as to Republicans, and its support for Obama was particularly strong. People who know Blankfein will tell you he was doing what he loves to do: pick winners. But those same people will also say that being a Democrat is in his blood, both because of his humble background and because of where he has put himself on Wall Street, which flourishes when Big (and Bigger) Government becomes the law of the land.

And that strategy was paying off, at least for a while, as Obama took office. Wall Street even managed to dole out some $20 billion in total bonuses for the bailout year of 2008. Seated with Wall Street's favorite Treasury secretary, Tim Geithner, President Obama, known during the campaign as "No Drama Obama" for his calm and cool demeanor, even managed a little righteous indignation, calling the payouts "shameful."

If Geithner was sending strong messages to Wall Street about its post-bailout behavior, no one seemed to care.

During the first nine months of Obama's presidency, Blankfein had Goldman's flacks and lobbyists spread throughout Washington, focusing mainly on the Democrats, who were in power, to push the Street's agenda, which focused on limiting whatever "reform" legislation Congress and the president were now promising and making sure that the firm could continue to pay its bankers and traders as it had in the past. Goldman, which plucks the best and the brightest for its trading desk, plucked the most politically connected people to run its lobbying department. Politics had become just as important as interest rates for its—and any Wall Street firm's—bottom line. Whereas in the past Goldman would make sure it had contacts on both sides of the political aisle, now many of its top lobbyists were former staffers for lawmakers like Barney Frank, the Massachusetts Democrat who served as the powerful head of the House Financial Services Committee, which, given all the subsidies flowing to Wall Street from Washington, could make or break the firm with a single edict.

Or to be more precise, could divert the firm from its scheduled massive taxpayer-supported bonus bonanza.

As early as January 2009, just weeks after the worst of the financial crisis had ended, Goldman began to take full advantage of the programs that had been set in place during the Bush and now Obama administrations, and it began to develop its press strategy to mask the true source of these profits.

As Lucas van Praag and Goldman's other media handlers (it also relied on a PR firm named Public Strategies, with connections to the Bush administration, for advice) continued arguing, the myriad bailouts and benefits that Goldman had received (which included everything from being declared a bank, thus protected from failure by the Fed, to being lent billions in bailout money, receiving near-zero interest rates, getting a backdoor bailout via the AIG bailout, and having its debt guaranteed by the federal government) were really beside the point. It was Goldman's tradition of excellence that allowed the firm to profit so handsomely just a couple of months after being bailed out.

Despite the growing backlash, Blankfein is said to have ordered van Praag to continue spinning (some would say lying about) the source of the firm's enormous wealth: Goldman made money because it was smart, van Praag would smugly counter anyone who questioned the firm's business practices, and it took the bailout money because it had to. End of story.

What was odd about Goldman was that it didn't stray from this spin even when it became clear it wasn't working. People close to the firm blamed the strategy of Blankfein, who might be smart when it comes to trading but knew almost nothing about the press, the media in general, or its shifting role in the financial business. Blankfein was running Goldman as if it weren't 2009 but 2006, when the firm never had to care about Middle America or the press because its clients—the megarich, big institutional investors, and Fortune 500 companies—didn't care how the firm made money. But that was before the bailout, and before Goldman made its vast fortune through government handouts. Now Middle America *did* matter for Goldman; the same Ohio construction worker who could never have his small savings managed by a Goldman broker could now influence his local congressman to call Lloyd Blankfein to testify before his committee and demand to know why he should be paid $100 million while the construction worker remained out of work.

But that wasn't all, and not by a long shot. Goldman had moved from the financial pages to be a mainstream story. The firm was now the subject of story after story in local newspapers and on local television stations. From coast to coast, in small-town America and in major cities, Goldman Sachs had become the very face of an inequitable system that rewarded the bad guys with government grants and guarantees while most of the country suffered.

To be fair, Goldman wasn't the only bank to take advantage of the system, but it did push the limits in using these measures to bolster its bottom line. While other firms, like Morgan Stanley, were cutting back on risk after the financial collapse and lowering their profit margins as they refined their business models to provide more advice to clients, Goldman, in the face of growing public unrest, did just the opposite as executives like Blankfein discovered that the various government protections and guarantees were a traders' dream.

Goldman could go out in the market, borrow at next to nothing because of the Fed's low-interest-rate policy and its protected status as a bank, and simply buy everything from Treasury bonds to mortgage-backed securities, which were now enjoying a little-known renaissance because the Fed had been supporting the market with purchases of the same bonds that Goldman had been buying and holding, and that sent prices soaring.

For all the populist fervor in the country today, most Americans believe in free markets and don't begrudge the wealthy their money—it's the fact that anyone, even a humble gold salesman who grew up in the projects in Brooklyn, can make their fortune here that has brought this country so much success.

But the big financial firms aren't racking up most of their profits by financing the next new cancer-fighting drug or finding seed capital for a new business that will employ thousands of workers. They're doing it by trading bonds and borrowing huge sums of money to enhance their winnings, a practice known as leverage. Historically, the big banks have been addicted to leverage—it's a drug they can't stop using, because at any given time their balance sheets contain enormous amounts of stocks, bonds, and more exotic financial instruments that were all bought with borrowed money. That money is borrowed from the firms' customers—big financial institutions, pension funds, hedge funds, and so on—with the understanding that the customers can call in their loans if they desire.

So when firms start to lose access to that money—when the customers start to pull their lines of credit because they've lost faith in the firm—that's the beginning of a death spiral for the financial firm in question. It's what brought down Bear Stearns and Lehman Brothers at the height of the crisis, and as much as Goldman likes to insist this wasn't the case, it's what was beginning to happen to Goldman, JPMorgan Chase, Morgan Stanley, and the other firms after Lehman went down.

It was only the bailout money provided by hardworking American taxpayers that kept those firms from following Bear and Lehman to the grave.

And after a brief spell following the financial collapse, the firms were borrowing and trading just as in the good old days. They say they're borrowing less (instead of borrowing $30 dollars for every $1 of cash on hand, they tell me they borrow just $15), and that might be true. But they are still borrowing, still using leverage to enhance their esoteric trades, and still counting on the federal government to bail them out when they lose.

"Who the fuck do these guys think they are?" said Steve Davis, a cop turned private investigator.

It was early February 2010 and we were eating dinner at a Manhattan restaurant called Campagnola, a place, incidentally, where many bankers and traders conduct their after-work schmoozing and socializing. Davis spent three decades in the New York City police department. He retired a captain, and he understands a thing or two about con jobs. The tip-off for most cons is that the phony investment being offered is too good to be true.

Steve Davis would have smelled a crook like Bernie Madoff a mile away.

When Davis exploded with profanity (expressing what so many Americans were thinking and feeling) that night at Campagnola, his point was that just a year after being bailed out, publicly shamed as riverboat gamblers playing on the public's dime, Wall Street was enriching itself again, just as it had before the crisis. To him it seemed like an impossible feat—a crime.

I said that while it might *seem* illegal and certainly might feel morally suspect (at best), much of the profit taking was entirely legal. The Obama government had propelled Wall Street earnings by leaving in place nearly all the bailout mechanisms created by Bush and his Treasury secretary, Hank Paulson, the former CEO of Goldman Sachs, right down to their support of Federal Reserve chairman Ben Bernanke and his policy of keeping interest rates near zero.

This, combined with other government guarantees—and the all-important too-big-to-fail status—gave Wall Street benefits that small businesses and entrepreneurs could only dream of. Wall Street could borrow nearly free of charge to conduct its business of trading and brokering, while small businesses couldn't get a loan.

An avid reader of the financial press, Davis was pissed off by all of this. He lives in a place where taxes are out of control (for a middle-class New York City resident the combined federal, state, and city taxes can easily reach 40 percent—and go up from there the more you make) and are likely to rise higher given New York's budget mess. His business was in decent shape, but because of the great recession not as decent as it once had been. And yet there he was, surrounded by all these Wall Street bankers and traders, standing around him drinking $20 martinis or sitting at the white-linen-covered tables in the swank restaurant eating expensive pasta and guzzling costly wines and making out like bandits.

What Steve Davis couldn't understand was the same thing millions of Americans were grappling with as well: a system that rewarded the miscreants at the expense of those who played it straight. As most Americans were taking care of their families, starting businesses, working in factories, and trying to make ends meet, Wall Street was gambling like mad, and now those gamblers were being given a second chance to gamble, a fresh bankroll from the taxpayers, with few, if any, personal consequences.

And instead of addressing the problem—instead of cutting off the umbilical cord that allowed this inequality to exist in the first place, the politicians chose to play upon the public's fears to gain cheap political points.

"She's such an asshole," muttered a CEO from one of the big banks as he sat stone faced before one of their money inquisitors, according to a person with direct knowledge of the matter. The "she" the CEO (all the executives present publicly deny they were the responsible party) was talking about was Maxine Waters, the passionate far-left congresswoman from California, as she laid into the gathering of nine CEOs from the largest U.S. banks testifying before the House Financial Services Committee about the financial crisis. Waters had just derisively referred to the CEOs as "captains of the universe" before badgering them on whether they continued to make loans and whether they raised their credit card rates.

The irony of Waters's vitriol is that she, with other class-warfare types, was maybe just as responsible as the Wall Streeters for starting the crisis she was now investigating. Waters was a huge proponent of the Community Reinvestment Act and other measures that forced banks to lend to poor communities for housing. Those loans, of course, made their way into subprime housing bonds, which eventually went into default, thus igniting the great financial collapse of 2008. (Another irony: As this book was going to press, the House ethics committee was investigating whether she influenced the federal bailout of a bank her husband owns stock in.)

Aside from the "asshole" comment, Dimon Mack and the other CEOs in attendance either kept their mouths shut during the grilling or dutifully answered the committee's often inane questions because they knew the inquisition was just the beginning. With the public outraged at Wall Street's recovery, Big Government needed to show it was on the case by scoring political points through "investigations," i.e., public hearings like this one, designed to do little more than embarrass Wall Street CEOs. And of course, through something the president and his supporters increasingly began referring to as "financial reform."

Goldman, for all the reasons listed above, became a familiar target. The SEC referred its case to the U.S. attorney's office for the Southern District of New York, the gold standard in white-collar prosecutions, which launched a preliminary investigation of its own. Even overseas regulators began to act. The British equivalent of the SEC, the Financial Services Authority, launched its own probe into the firm's business practices. Even the securities industry's self-regulator, the Financial Industry Regulatory Authority, launched a probe into why Goldman hadn't alerted investors that it faced so much regulatory scrutiny. And not to be left out of the action, New York attorney general Andrew Cuomo, who was announcing his candidacy to succeed the scandal-plagued David Paterson as the state's governor, joined in the Goldman bashing as he announced an investigation into whether Goldman and other firms pressured bond raters to hand out high ratings on mortgage bonds that ultimately turned toxic.

Name-calling from a president is particularly unbecoming, yet Obama increasingly began referring to the bankers who were his supporters as "fat cats" (without mentioning their past support of him, of course). The names of the various committees and subcommittees that began holding hearings soon began to blur, but not their primary target. Lloyd Blankfein made for a particularly enticing object of scorn, not just because he ran Goldman, or because his argument that Goldman hadn't been bailed out was so absurd, but also because he was so bad at public speaking. His various facial contortions, his deer-in-the-headlights gaze when asked tough questions, all seemed to make him a favorite punching bag for politicians eager for their time on camera.

And the hearings seemed to run on with no end in sight, primarily because Congress had so much material to deal with, particularly when it came to Goldman.

In private meetings with top Goldman executives, these same politicians, men like Senators Harry Reid and Carl Levin, continued to assure Goldman's lobbyists that their interest in the firm wasn't personal. On the contrary, the politicians liked Goldman and (it was understood) especially liked the money the firm handed out.

The media circus, with the name-calling, the hearings, and the investigations, was simply the price of doing business in the new world, and when all was said and done, it wasn't such a high price to pay given all the money Wall Street was making.

Meanwhile, just as Blankfein finished trying to explain to various committees just how on earth his traders could tout and sell to their best customers investments that they privately labeled as "shitty" in e-mails inside the firm, Goldman's role in another international debacle was slowly being uncovered as Greece—a country that seemingly has no direct ties to Wall Street—fell into a financial panic.

For decades, Goldman Sachs, especially its derivatives desk, had been working with the government of Greece. According to the *New York Times*, in November 2009 a team of bankers led by Goldman president Gary Cohn traveled to Athens to pitch the Greek government a type of transaction that would hide its obligations and allow it to push out its liabilities to the distant future. This wasn't the first time. In 2001, right after Greece gained entry to the European Union, Goldman had helped structure another complex deal intended to make Greece's finances appear to be in compliance with the strict rules for membership in the EU. For around a decade Goldman's derivatives desk—through the hocus-pocus of modern financial technology—was able to mask just how much the Greek government was borrowing, until, of course, it couldn't be masked anymore. In essence, the firm was able to use the same kind of financial wizardry that had allowed the banks that had gone under, like Lehman Brothers and Bear Stearns, to keep billions of dollars in bad debts from showing up on their balance sheets (until the very end), wizardry for which Greece had paid Goldman at least $300 million in fees over the years. These deals were essentially gimmicks designed to do nothing more than make a country that needed to borrow heavily to support its welfare look like it was fiscally sound. But like all such gimmicks, it didn't last forever.

By midspring of 2010, Greece had to fess up to decades of wild spending, heavy borrowing, and generally living beyond its means. If civil servants in the United States are sometimes perceived as getting fat off the public trough, it's nothing compared to Greece, where government employees (and a huge chunk of Greece's economy was run by the government) got paid fourteen months' salary for every twelve months of work. The country was a fiscal basket case—it owed money to everyone, with the British and the Germans at the top of a very long list of creditors. The country's economy was in such bad shape that it couldn't raise taxes (no one had money to pay them) and no one was crazy enough to lend it any more money. In other words, Greece was broke, and it was looking for a bailout to keep the country functioning.

But how did it get so bad? Greece was part of the European Union; it had given up its own currency, the drachma, years earlier in order to gain entry and use the euro. It had needed to meet the EU's quality standards to gain entry, which meant it couldn't just borrow to pay its bills, because the EU imposed public debt limits on its member nations. To be more accurate, Greece couldn't simply disclose how much it was borrowing if it was both to maintain those EU debt limits and fund its literal welfare state at the same time. So it turned to Wall Street for help, much as Orange County had back in the early 1990s.

What the slick salesmen who peddle these deals don't tell their clients, whether corporations or governments, is that such transactions can't actually eliminate the borrowing and debt payments to creditors, only conceal them for some time, and even when done with the best of intentions—e.g., staving off potentially crippling economic cutbacks until business conditions improve—derivatives are dangerous. A sudden change in interest rates can set off a chain reaction that turns those investment gains into losses, making the debt payments on already high levels of borrowing seem exponentially great.

Many government officials I have come across during my career make easy targets for investment bankers. They are largely unaware of these dangers because they're political appointees and as a result aren't schooled enough in the fine points of high finance to really know what they're buying. Even if they are savvy, like the finance officials in New York City who have been balancing budgets on gimmicks for years, they probably don't care about the long-term ramifications of their actions because they are serving a higher purpose, at least in their own minds. Their main goal is to keep government functioning—even in its often dysfunctional state.

In many ways, the officials in Greece who bought what Goldman and, to a lesser degree, JPMorgan Chase were selling them were almost no different from all those homeowners in the United States who helped instigate the financial crisis by taking out subprime loans on homes they should have known they couldn't afford and then defaulted when the payments came due. In other words, they were content to remain blissfully ignorant in the present even if it meant their future was threatened.

By the spring of 2010, Greece was broke and threatening to default on billions of dollars of its debt. Riots were breaking out in Athens as the Greeks, accustomed to the free health care and the incredibly generous benefits of a welfare state they couldn't afford, realized that the gravy train was coming to an end.

As of the writing of this book, Greece's finances are still is disarray, and Goldman, along with the other Wall Street firms, I am told, is still running around the world giving "advice" to countries on how to "manage" their finances, which usually means offering up ways to hide their largesse and postpone the inevitable payment that comes after a spending spree. Goldman makes sure, of course, to collect its own fees well before the collapse occurs.

It would be nice to think that this sort of stuff doesn't go on here in the good old U.S. of A. But so it does. As I previously mentioned, New York City has been finagling its books, often when Wall Street goes into a temporary downturn, for years. And as we saw in chapter 2, Orange County, California, was brought low by Wall Street just as Greece would be later. Is the United States heading down that same path? While the U.S. government is hardly Greece, or even Orange County, there's no doubt that fiscal conservatives—on the left and the right—are starting to look at the nation's debt relative to its GDP and wonder: Where *are* we going to end up?

FAT CATS AND FAT BONUSES

With the election of Barack Obama, Wall Street thought it had everything it could want in a president, and the results rolled in with profits and paychecks. Meanwhile, the middle-class Americans who had voted for Obama were facing increased unemployment and higher taxes. The college students and young adults who had served as a driving constituency in Obama's campaign were facing one of the worst job markets in decades. For these Americans, Obama had failed to deliver on his promises of hope and change, and they were demanding answers.

As the anger continued into late 2009, Obama and his hand-picked team of Wall Street-supported advisers (Robert Rubin, Larry Summers, Tim Geithner) and those with strong Wall Street connections (Rahm Emanuel, Valerie Jarrett, and others) woke up and realized that unless the president somehow addressed the public's outrage, it would be more than just those annoying Tea Party activists who would be voting against him and his buddies in Congress when the midterm elections came around the following year. And so Barack Obama, who had sounded so moderate, so reasoned, to Larry Fink, Jamie Dimon, and Tom Nides, all of a sudden began sounding like the guy who'd palled around with Bill Ayers and Reverend Wright for all those years back in Chicago. Instead of trying to work with them as promised, the president started using the bankers who had put him in office as his whipping boys the minute he needed them to advance his faltering political agenda.

The real change occurred in late 2009, around the same time the White House conducted a poll that showed Obama's approval ratings were slipping. The same poll found that nearly 90 percent of the people surveyed, on both the far left and far right, had a negative opinion of Wall Street, much higher than the president's number.

The polling came as Obama had been holding frequent meetings with Dimon over the state of the economy. In those private meetings, Obama sounded like a man from the Robert Rubin school of Wall Street–friendly economics: The best way to help the economy flourish is to help Wall Street banks succeed. The two met so frequently that the speculation about whether the president was considering appointing Dimon to replace current Treasury secretary Tim Geithner began to feel like a done deal in Washington and on Wall Street. Despite the rumors, the president has unswervingly supported Geithner, and his political adviser David Axelrod has even dismissed talk of a Dimon appointment by chalking the relationship up to nothing more than mutual admiration. "Don't these people realize," he said of the rumormongers, "they [Dimon and Obama] have a man crush on each other?"

Robert Rubin had been meeting with Obama as well, and the worst thing he could say about the new president wasn't that he seemed to hate Wall Street. Quite the contrary: He seemed to appreciate what a strong banking system could do, namely advance the liberal agenda by packaging mortgages into bonds so the government could grant home loans to people who couldn't afford them.

No, the worst thing Rubin thought about Obama was that he relied too heavily on advice from relative neophytes when it came to economic and financial matters. Among those people was Valerie Jarrett, a longtime Chicago attorney and lobbyist and friend of Obama's who was now ensconced inside the White House and influencing many of Obama's economic decisions.

At least that's what Rubin learned one afternoon when he cautioned Obama that despite his talent for politics, he was relatively unsophisticated when it came to economic matters.

"That's why I have Valerie," Obama shot back.

Larry Fink was coming to the same conclusion. BlackRock, his massive money-management concern, had benefited enormously, much to the envy of the rest of the Street, from the various postcrisis bailout payments, including $45.3 million to manage the assets of Bear Stearns following its collapse and government bailout, $33 million to manage the assets that the Fed purchased from AIG, and $12 million to value the assets on Citigroup's troubled balance sheets, as well as other business opportunities too numerous to quantify. Of course, those fees are relatively small. The real value in managing the government's money is much greater: "Being in the flow of information—pricing information, knowing who's buying and selling, will ultimately be more important than actual fees," analyst Charles Peabody told Bloomberg News. Except for Goldman, no one had better knowledge of the markets than Larry Fink's BlackRock.

Critics would point to Fink's early and unabashed support of Obama for his success at winning government contracts, while others with a more nuanced view would point to Fink's financial acumen; he was a perfect choice to manage the Fed's portfolio of bad debt from bailout victims like Bear Stearns because he'd been trading in these securities for years.

But by late 2009, Fink was worried, and not just about the populism that had begun sweeping the country. According to friends and associates (Fink declined to comment), Larry Fink was having second thoughts about his support for Obama. The same guy who had promised moderation now promised an endless array of entitlements—from a government-run healthcare system and hundreds of billions of dollars more in stimulus to supplement the failed one Obama had pushed earlier in the year, had Fink concerned.

"How are we going to pay for all of this?" Fink began asking friends. Fink knows a lot about how the government pays for stuff because he made his fortune as a bond trader. But he also knows that in order to spend so much, the government needs to borrow more, and there's only so much borrowing our creditors, most prominently China, will allow before they start demanding concessions over and beyond much higher interest rates.

All those promised entitlements demonstrated how few people inside Obama's inner circle had real business experience. To be sure, Summers and Emanuel had spent some time on Wall Street to make a few bucks before they went back to government, but that was about it.

"It's really shocking," Fink remarked, before reminding himself that as bad as Obama might be, the McCain/Palin ticket would have been worse.

Past presidents like Bill Clinton, George W. Bush, and, of course, Ronald Reagan had run large states before ascending to the presidency, so they knew how to balance a budget and otherwise govern; George H. W. Bush went into the oil business, becoming a millionaire by the age of forty before becoming vice president and president. His son George W. Bush had been both the governor of Texas and a businessman before his election.

Barack Obama, in contrast, had been a politician for a relatively short period of time and had never before held an executive position. He was a legislator first and foremost, and his work outside of politics had been as a community organizer, where he fought against businesses rather than working with them.

Yet as absurd as it may be for Valerie Jarrett—a political fixer from Chicago—to be determining how best to run the U.S. economy, she wouldn't be the first or the last lobbyist to hold sway in the Oval Office. In fact, Jarrett may have never run a real business or started a company from scratch, but in reality neither had Bob Rubin or the other Wall Streeters who found themselves in positions of power as aides to various presidents, Republican and Democrat alike. She was simply doing what Bob Rubin, Hank Paulson, et al. had done for years: straddle the line between Big Government and Big Business. Not unlike Rubin and Paulson, she knew how the game was played because she had seen legions of politically connected bankers doing the same thing for years.

And so, apparently, did Obama, as he plotted his vast expansion of government predicated on the notion that his economic policies were beginning to take hold. In March 2009, the Dow Jones Industrial Average reached its low point and began a steady climb that would total more than four thousand points by the end of the year. Wall Street was getting beaten up in the court of public opinion, but it was also feasting off Obama's policies and making money as if the financial crisis had never occurred. Prosperity, according to the president, appeared to be right around the corner, and Obama had big plans that began to solidify as 2010 approached: a massive expansion of the welfare state, free health care, cap-and-trade energy limits, and who knows what else.

The president even sounded giddy at times. At one point, he urged Americans to start buying stocks because, given all the stimulus he had pumped into the economy, they looked cheap—an unprecedented move in the eyes of some on Wall Street, who couldn't believe a president was making investing recommendations to the American public. He touted the marginal increases in economic growth as if they were proof positive of the vision of his policies, even as unemployment remained alarmingly high through the year.

And the press bought the spin as the nation's GDP began mimicking the stock market, rising quarter after quarter through the end of the year.

Even the great conservative TV economist Larry Kudlow proclaimed a "*V*-shaped" recovery to be in the works, meaning that after a sharp decline, all the cheap money and pent-up demand for business would sooner or later lead to massive economic growth and hiring once again. These optimists were more worried about inflation than anything else.

And yet the upward part of the *V* in the recovery never came, at least for the millions of people out of work. During the course of 2009, the GDP did begin to improve and the recession was officially over. But Peter Sidoti's research had held up better than the predictions of the president's economic team. Obama's stimulus package had failed to simulate private-sector employment, even if Wall Street was making money again.

Small business continued to cut costs and cut jobs. Construction remained in a depression. Even states that had kept their workforces fat and happy began to cut, particularly places like New Jersey and Virginia, where

Republicans tapped into the voters' growing discontent with Obama's policies and were able to defeat Democratic incumbents for governor by vowing to rein in runaway state spending.

The president, reading from his teleprompter, assured the country that jobs would return—he would make sure of that—while reminding Americans of the mess he had been left by the previous administration. But by the end of 2009 and into early 2010, the blame game had become tiresome to most Americans and Obama's once-lofty poll numbers began to fall.

Obama had now been in office for nearly a full year, and even though his voters were beginning to reconsider their support, Obama still had the backing of the Democrat-controlled Congress. With its help, he had rammed through a stimulus package that didn't work. And now he was vowing to ram through health-care reform that polls showed most people either didn't want or didn't understand well enough to have an opinion about. That's because average Americans understood what the president couldn't or wouldn't: Both measures did little to help Middle America recover from the worst economic disaster since the Great Depression, and the Big Government programs only ensured a huge increase in the nation's already massive deficit.

A growing majority of the American people were coming to realize that the president, for all his political savvy, knew very little about how the economy works. Why nationalize health care when getting a job means getting health insurance? Why stimulate the economy through massive amounts of government spending when businesses usually begin to hire workers when government cuts their costs through lower taxes?

They also realized something else: While they were still suffering, Wall Street was living it up again. If you came to New York and hung around the city's swankiest bars, you could see it happening: twentysomething traders once again ordering bottles of Cristal and bragging to their friends about the killing they made in the markets. In the executive suites of Goldman Sachs they were partying as well; senior Goldman executives weren't bluffing when they promised bankers and traders that 2009 would be a very good year for them if they stuck around through all the political noise as the firm began doling out bonus money to its senior executives.

Blankfein, despite his humble beginning, saw nothing wrong with the subsidized paychecks.

But many Americans saw it differently, and now they were looking for blood.

"We're the only thing separating you guys from the pitchforks," a very excited Rahm Emanuel told Tom Nides one afternoon, using a line he'd actually borrowed from the president. Emanuel had been fielding telephone calls from his Wall Street buddies with great regularity by the end of 2009 and into 2010, as the public perception of Wall Street sank to new lows and the impression that Obama was in the pocket of the fat cats grew.

The political advisers like David Axelrod believed Obama and a wary public needed a common enemy, and Wall Street was it. And with that, the name-calling reached new heights. During an Oval Office meeting in February 2010, the president seemed to slip, referring to Blankfein and Dimon in particular as "savvy businessmen" when asked about their bonuses, only to cause the White House to issue a statement suggesting that he didn't mean what he said when the complaints came flooding into the White House.

Emanuel was caught in the middle. Despite his long political résumé, he had been a creature of Wall Street himself, serving as a consultant for Goldman Sachs in the early 1990s and later in the decade as an investment banker heading the Chicago office of investment boutique Wasserstein Perella, where he earned close to $16 million for just two years' work.

And now he was hearing his Wall Street buddies talk as if the past two years of bailouts and subsidies hadn't happened. Nides, for his part, was in a particularly nasty mood about the attacks coming from the White House.

A longtime political adviser and confidant of Morgan Stanley CEO John Mack, Nides had just been promoted to chief operating officer (COO) of the big brokerage firm, and his ascendancy spoke volumes about the changes on Wall Street in the era of Obama, featuring unprecedented government intervention. Nides had very little, if any, real Wall Street experience—he had never sold or traded a bond and never served as an investment banker. But with vast experience in greasing the wheels of Big Government on behalf of his Wall Street clients, Nides now found himself at the top of one of the biggest Wall Street firms. He was an invaluable commodity on the new Wall Street—one that would be more dependent on government handouts than ever before.

But what made Nides unique was his relationship with Emanuel. The two had been friends for nearly twenty-five years, having worked in politics since the mid-1980s while making periodic stops on Wall Street to make money. Recently, Nides had made Wall Street his more permanent home, while Emanuel had chosen Washington.

That didn't stop the two from being frequent dinner companions when they were in New York or DC, or from speaking on the telephone almost every day. In addition to his senior role at Morgan Stanley (he reported to new CEO James Gorman), Nides moonlighted as chairman of Wall Street's chief lobbying group, where he could put his relationship with one of the most powerful men in Washington to good use on behalf of the entire securities business.

But now Nides was on the hot seat. The attacks by the president, not to mention the new financial regulations Obama promised in mid-2010, sent Wall Street, particularly the CEOs who had so enthusiastically supported Obama, into a tizzy. And Nides was on the receiving end of many of the complaints. Inside Morgan and among his vast network of contacts across Wall Street, he had implored both Democrats and Republicans to vote for Obama, telling anyone who would listen that the same guy who had palled around with Bill Ayers and Reverend Wright was actually a moderate at heart and would surround himself with moderate advisers.

Nides had seemed to deliver on the advisers part when Obama appointed Geithner, Summers, and Emanuel to key positions in his administration. No one could argue with the president's policies toward Wall Street, which experienced a massive boom in profits and bonuses just months after the big firms nearly evaporated.

But now the full reality of Obamanomics had set in. The Republicans he had convinced to endorse Obama worried about exploding debt levels and the unprecedented government intervention in the economy, soon to grow even greater as the president began plans for his financial-services overhaul. Meanwhile, the Democrats on Wall Street couldn't understand why Obama was bashing them at every chance he got. Mack, now the chairman of Morgan, never seemed to miss an opportunity to walk into his office to remind Nides what his "friend" was saying.

Just as Nides became the target of anti-Obama anger inside Morgan Stanley, Larry Fink became the target inside Wall Street hot spot San Pietro. The BlackRock founder's favorite restaurant had become ground zero for anger that couldn't be directed directly at Obama but could be directed at one of his biggest and earliest supporters.

"Are you talking to your fucking friend in Washington yet!?" billionaire financier Ken Langone bellowed one afternoon as he held court along the famed chairmen's row of tables in the restaurant and pestered Fink about his association with the president. Fink just put his head down and sheepishly said, "No."

More recently, Joe Perella had been telling everyone he knew that the Wall Street crowd had ignored his advice and voted for Obama, despite his proving to be a socialist.

"I told everyone about this guy and no one wanted to listen!" he screamed at Fink one afternoon while lunching at San Pietro.

The difference between Perella and Langone and the heart of the Wall Street establishment is that they are entrepreneurs: Perella runs a boutique investment bank and Langone a small brokerage house after he was a founding partner of The Home Depot. They don't rely on Big Government to shower them with riches, at least not on the scale of Fink and the rest of Wall Street.

While Fink just brushed off the criticism, the daily drumbeat of complaints was starting to take its toll on Nides. He often complained that he felt like a "piñata" at work, getting beaten up every day from all sides—by the Democratic liberals at the firm and by the Republicans who had backed

Obama out of firm loyalty. Even people outside Morgan began to chime in with complaints, stating that he wasn't doing enough in his job as head of the Wall Street lobbying group known as SIFMA.

Nides's response to them mirrored what he was told by Emanuel: The special programs given to the banks by Obama had been controversial, and the president had taken his lumps in public opinion over them, but he hadn't backed down.

Moreover, the alternative would be worse, he repeated and repeated. The Republicans were increasingly enchanted with the Tea Party activists, who hated Wall Street more than the Maxine Waters left wing of the Democratic Party hated the bankers and traders. If the Tea Partiers and their friends in Congress had their way, Wall Street would be a ghost town. So Rahm Emanuel's message to Nides and Nides's message to the rest of the Street was pretty simple: Watch what Obama does, not what he says.

Nides could only hope.

In December 2009, Obama was planning his second meeting of the year with his campaign contributors on Wall Street. But before he did so, he needed to draw a strong rhetorical distinction between himself and the men who had destroyed the economy. The venue chosen by the president was the television news show *60 Minutes*, which was viewed by millions of Americans. Reporter Steve Kroft asked for and received permission to air the interview the Sunday before the president's meeting with his bankers–cum–fund-raisers.

Obama, whose policies had allowed the firms to make so much money almost immediately after the crisis, sounded as if he were as perplexed and angered as anyone about the turn of events. He attacked firms like Goldman for paying themselves huge bonuses while the nation suffered through nearly 10 percent unemployment (though he never mentioned that his stimulus package had failed to actually stimulate the economy and job market). He railed at the bankers for their greed, which had caused the financial collapse (though he never mentioned the millions of dollars in campaign checks those greedy bankers had produced for him). And he said he didn't get elected to help "fat cat" Wall Streeters make money while the rest of the country suffered (though he never mentioned his regular meetings with those very same fat cats, nor their close ties with key members of his administration).

It's funny what a little name-calling can do on Wall Street. Obama's "fat cat" description of the bankers and traders he was set to meet the following day wasn't quite the "shot heard round the world," but it *was* an interesting wake-up call that the friendship Wall Street had enjoyed with the president was morphing into something more like a business relationship, where two sides use and abuse each other for mutual gain.

It's easy to understand why Obama decided to resort to banker bashing. His economic policies had produced clear winners and losers. While the big banks shelled out multimillion-dollar bonuses to the same people responsible for the recession, those in more blue-collar industries suffered. What Obama couldn't escape was the continued reality of the disaster of his stimulus package and the dual economy it created: Massive unemployment in many industries, such as construction, continued largely unabated, while government bureaucrats—the real beneficiaries of the stimulus package—remained comfortably employed.

Also remaining comfortable and employed were the people who had plunged the economy into the mess (and helped elect Obama), the Wall Street bankers and traders. By early 2010, the big firms made plans for a big expansion in their workforce to keep up with mounting profits that showed no sign of slowing down. With superlow interest rates promised by the Fed for the foreseeable future, and too-big-to-fail status making it easy and cheap to borrow, all the firms were earning big money and finalizing plans to shell out record executive bonuses. The firms argued that they were actually showing restraint, paying bonuses that were a smaller percentage of overall revenues than in previous year, with more than half of the money coming in company stock. But the argument failed to impress once the raw numbers were disclosed: JPMorgan Chase led the pack, paying $29 billion in total compensation—even more than it had paid out in 2007, the year before the meltdown. The unyielding press attention on Goldman overshadowed the fact that Citigroup handed out more money in compensation than its more successful rival, $23.6 billion compared to $21.5 billion for the evil empire, and that Bank of America, despite its massive bailout, was getting ready to shell out $31 billion in total compensation. Morgan Stanley, in keeping with Mack's austerity plan, paid just $16 billion, though people inside rival Goldman Sachs groused Morgan paid out a higher percentage of its revenue in compensation than any other big bank. Mack, it should be noted, earned a salary of a little less than $1 million.

This, naturally, caused the class warfare that had been brewing at Tea Party rallies, among union workers (not the still-employed civil service unions, of course), and in other fringe groups to spread to the mainstream.

That's why Obama's old friends—Jamie Dimon, John Mack, Larry Fink, Lloyd Blankfein, and Gary Cohn—made such enticing targets. With Obama's own poll numbers dropping and the country in a foul mood, the one thing he knew of that united the Left, Right, and Center was hatred of Wall Street. It didn't matter that Obama was about to meet with the very individuals he was now bashing or that they had been largely responsible for helping him win the presidency in the first place. When you've bought and paid for a politician at this level, as the bank chiefs were slowly coming to realize, you have to take such attacks in stride.

But that didn't mean they had to like it.

It was around 8:00 A.M. New York time, and John Mack was seated in first class for his flight to Obama's much-touted bankers' meeting. He was still digesting the *60 Minutes* interview that had aired the night before, when he received a call from Blankfein. Mack was taking off from the Westchester County Airport in Purchase, New York, Blankfein from LaGuardia. Both had decided to fly commercial, rather than take their respective corporate jets. Earlier that year, several auto executives had flown to Washington on their private planes in an attempt to beg for government assistance in helping their companies get back on their feet. The move had solidified the CEOs' reputation as insensitive and greedy businessmen, out of touch with reality, and after a year of getting killed in the press, the last thing Mack and Blankfein needed was to be compared to the morons who had run GM and Chrysler.

But now they thought they had outmaneuvered themselves. "We're being delayed because of fog," Blankfein said. Mack said his flight was delayed as well. Mack and Blankfein had become close over the course of the past year, which was odd given that Goldman and Morgan were longtime rivals. But they had come to realize that they now shared a mutual dilemma. They were both among the most despised businessmen in America, although with Matt Taibbi's conspiracy theories about Goldman still making news (remember his "vampire squid" comment?), Blankfein was clearly sitting in the hotter seat. That hot seat would get even hotter in the days and weeks ahead.

As they sat in their plane seats and chatted on their cell phones, the president's *60 Minutes* interview came up. Mack remarked how much "everyone hates us" and that even the guy who billed himself as the first "postpartisan president" was getting in on the act. Mack said he was prepared for the worst during the meeting, expecting the president to pick up where he had left off in the *60 Minutes* interview and begin badgering the banks over bonuses and their lack of lending. One of the staple criticisms of Wall Street over the past year had been that despite taking taxpayers' bailout money, the banks weren't recirculating the cash to small businesses in the form of loans. And why should they? It was far more profitable to take all that cheap government cash and make easy trades with it than to lend it out.

Of course, Goldman Sachs and Morgan Stanley aren't commercial banks, so they don't make loans. But that's part of the absurdity of the bailouts. The casinolike firms that made all their money trading were treated the same as the real banks, like Citigroup, JPMorgan Chase, and Bank of America. These commercial banks are supposed to fuel the economy by safeguarding customer deposits and using that money to extend loans to companies looking to do business and to people looking to buy homes. But now these commercial banks were taking a page from Goldman's investment-banking playbook, and instead of extending credit to cash-strapped small businesses or consumers, they were either hoarding the cash or trading bonds just like Goldman, by borrowing at superlow interest rates supplied by the government, buying up bonds on the open market, and pocketing the difference between what they paid to borrow and what their bonds were earning.

And since all the banks were now considered too large not to protect, they had a limitless supply of funds available to them. Creditors—the cash-rich hedge funds and pension funds that were lending in this market—had no problem lending money to the banks because if worst came to worst they were guaranteed to be paid back in full by the American taxpayer. As for the small businessmen who needed loans and credit to make ends meet (and to stop laying off workers), they were out of luck.

So as Blankfein prepared for the meeting, he expected a tongue-lashing at the hands of a president who, if nothing else, has proven to be adroit at sensing the public's foul mood. Blankfein had finally realized just how much Goldman—the most successful of the big firms—made an enticing target. It had become the postbailout poster child for everything that was wrong with Wall Street, which for a time thrilled its competitors, like Morgan Stanley. "Better Goldman than us," is what one Morgan executive told me at the time. But Mack was actually beginning to feel a little sorry for Blankfein as the Goldman CEO lamented the endless negative press coverage, the massive amounts of hate mail he received, and the vilification by public officials the firm had once supported. That's when they both received an announcement that their flights were being canceled because of heavy fog.

Now Mack was pissed: "How the fuck am I supposed to get to this meeting?" he muttered as he dialed his assistant back at company headquarters to come up with an alternate plan. Blankfein did the same and they came to the same conclusion: There was no time to jump on the Amtrak, a three-hour ride to the White House not counting the time it would take to get to the train station. So they decided to phone it in—literally. They would "attend" the meeting by conference call. Later in the day, when news of their nonappearance hit the wires, Mack and Blankfein (along with Citigroup chairman Dick Parsons, who also didn't attend) were criticized for not taking the meeting seriously enough and leaving earlier.

All Mack could think was that neither he nor the rest of Wall Street could catch a break.

Unlike Mack and Blankfein, Jamie Dimon continued to ride a fairly strong wave of positive publicity, so he felt perfectly comfortable taking his corporate plane to meet the president and arrived in Washington with a few hours to burn before the meeting. "Fuck it," he would later snap in his characteristic who-gives-a-crap style, "that's why we have the jet in the first place." Dimon's staff was actually given a heads-up about the topics in advance (one of the perks of being the reigning king of Wall Street): Obama would politely ask the banks to make more loans, keep bonuses under control, and try to work with the administration to make the world a better place.

Knowing the topics ahead of time helped Dimon plan his response. Unlike Mack and Blankfein, he wasn't nervous or particularly worried about the president's reaction; rather, he was almost praying for a bit of a confrontation. Over the past year he and Obama had grown close during his many White House visits, close enough that Dimon believed he could tell Obama that his anti–Wall Street attacks might win him a few more votes, but they weren't good for the country. Dimon, like all the heads of the big firms, hated class warfare, even if he had voted for and supported maybe the biggest class warrior to hold the office of president in modern times.

And yet for all the premeeting drama, the event itself was fairly routine. Obama stuck to his script as it had been supplied to Dimon: He argued that the banks should lend more and said he was worried about bonuses. Despite Blankfein's worst fears, the president didn't engage in name-calling, nor did he single Goldman out in anyway. He even cracked a few jokes.

When it was over, the mood was still tense, as some of the CEOs and their minions said they were annoyed about being used as props in a photo op by the president.

"The guys at Goldman, JPMorgan, Morgan Stanley—anyone working at a major firm—hate being called crooks," said one senior executive at Goldman as the nasty comments from Democrats and the president continued unabated for months through the winter and early spring of 2010.

"The public might hate us; they may consider the typical Wall Street executive a greedy gambler living large while the rest of the country suffers," the executive continued, "but most of us are family people. We all went to the best schools. We give a lot of money to charity. We've worked hard our whole lives. And now we're considered the worst that society has to offer. On top of that, the guys we helped put into office, including the president, remind the country of this every day. It just ain't right."

That's one way to look at it. Another way was "Let's just take the punishment and keep making money." That was the general attitude inside JPMorgan in early 2010.

Dimon, of course, was still considered everyone's favorite CEO, including the president's, and, as most of the firms' senior executives concluded, for all the name-calling, it was Obama's policies that led to the firms' massive profits in 2009 and into 2010. And it was his advisers, people like Geithner, Summers, and several others, who were still preventing financial reform from taking a dangerous turn as it simmered on the desk of its chief author, Senator Chris Dodd, for most of Obama's first year in office.

By early 2010, none of the legislation being discussed proposed to break up the banks by bringing back Glass-Steagall, as many in Obama's own party had called for. Such a remedy wasn't advocated by the lefties alone; none other than Nouriel Roubini, the NYU economist who had predicted the housing collapse and Wall Street implosion, was advocating such a solution as a way to make the financial system less prone to excessive risk taking. Smaller banks would be forced to take smaller risks, Roubini argued, and if Glass-Steagall was brought back commercial banks wouldn't be taking risks at all—that would be left to the Goldman Sachses of the world, which would no longer be protected by the federal government.

But Obama resisted, choosing instead to deal with Wall Street through words and limited action. That's why, when early word came back to Wall Street from the White House that there would be financial reform in 2010, Wall Street wasn't overly concerned. There would be things in the package that Wall Street wouldn't like, but the protections and benefits of a partnership with Big Government were here to stay. The president, for all his class-warfare talk, knows how important Wall Street profits are to the economy and thus to him. Like any good politician, he wants to get reelected.

So while some bankers grumbled about being called a bunch of fat cats, others saw the bright side: It could have been worse, possibly much worse. Were it not for the financial crisis, John McCain might have been president, and what would that have meant? Would the old fighter pilot have surrounded himself with policy advisers close to Wall Street and the big banks? Almost certainly not.

Would McCain have allowed banks to get away with buying bonds instead of making loans to small businesses, the engine of any real recovery? Doubtful.

And would he have supported Ben Bernanke's continued stewardship of the Federal Reserve after he famously missed the signs of the financial collapse, and allowed him to keep interest rates near zero (the driving force behind Wall Street's profits) for yet another year? Again, doubtful at best.

So okay, Obama had called them fat cats, and Blankfein, Dimon, and Mack, like all of us, hate being called names, but the equivalent of a little schoolyard ragging was a small price to pay for being saved and allowed to make record amounts of money. And maybe, they figured, by not confronting them directly during his meeting, Obama was signaling that deep down he really wanted to "repair the relationship" with his old friends: "He knows he needs us if he wants to get reelected," said a high-ranking public relations executive at JPMorgan Chase.

"If you get a pet rattlesnake, expect to be bitten."

That's what Congressman Spencer Bachus, a sophisticated, genteel southerner who represents the suburbs of Birmingham, Alabama, told a long line of Wall Street lobbyists and a few CEOs, including Dimon himself, who came to his office in the late winter and early spring of 2010 complaining about the man they'd helped elect a little more than a year earlier.

Bachus, a free-market conservative Republican, is the ranking Republican on the House Financial Services Committee. He's also the counterweight to the famously liberal, and volatile, committee chairman, Barney Frank. Yet while Frank might gain headlines for his caustic style, Bachus's understated tone belies a toughness that can spring at a moment's notice, as he did during hearings on the troubled bond insurance business in the early days of the financial crisis in early 2008.

Back then, the star witness was Eliot Spitzer, the New York governor, whose office was supposed to be overseeing these companies. Spitzer became governor based on his record of cracking down on Wall Street abuse as New York's attorney general. But Bachus asked Spitzer a simple yet direct question: Where were you when the insurers were taking so much risk? Spitzer could have answered the question in about a dozen different ways. But instead, he exploded, angrily blaming the problems of a New York–based insurance company on the lack of regulation coming from Republicans in Washington. It was vintage Spitzer: his hands flailing, saliva oozing from his mouth as he attacked what was a fairly innocuous question. Needless to say, his message was lost in the psychodrama. When it was over, Bachus simply remarked that Spitzer looked like he hadn't gotten enough sleep the night before and was jacked up on too many cups of coffee.

He might have been right. It was later revealed that the night before, Eliot Spitzer brought a prostitute to his room in Washington's upscale Mayflower Hotel. A few months later, Spitzer was forced to resign when "Hookergate" became front-page news.

Bachus still chuckles at the antics of Spitzer, now the disgraced former governor trying to make a comeback as a cable news talk show host, as he does over Wall Street's grumblings about the "rattlesnake" known as Barack Obama. Of course, Bachus doesn't really consider Obama a rattlesnake, just a committed liberal who was able to hide his radical agenda during the campaign. That was back when the financial crisis was threatening Wall Street. Bachus initially wasn't in favor of the bailouts—he voted against the initial proposal by Hank Paulson because he believed all the money spent to save Wall Street's bad investments would come out of the pockets of Main Street (as it eventually did). But in the end, the bailout bill passed as the crisis worsened, with Bachus and many other Republicans ultimately supporting the plan once they were convinced the financial system would collapse otherwise.

It was a bitter pill for him to swallow. He's likely to get a primary challenge this fall from a conservative businessman and pastor, Stan Cooke, who has been endorsed by Sarah Palin's brother and who no doubt will attack him on his vote, which Bachus ultimately viewed as necessary to save the banking system. What he doesn't view as necessary was what happened next: the near-zero interest rates and other guarantees that have made Wall Street trading a no-lose proposition and the feckless fiscal policy of the Obama administration, which has increased spending, expanded government, and done little to actually improve the economy.

But as we've seen, even those responsible for these Wall Street–friendly policies changed their tune when they realized these programs were increasingly unpopular.

And with that realization, the Republican "rubes" in Congress, like Bachus, noticed something odd: The sophisticated Wall Street lobbyists and CEOs had suddenly become their friends. Lobbyists who had stopped by once a month now came by once a week. People like Dimon and Blankfein, who didn't have time in between meetings with Rahm, Barney, Nancy (the Wall Streeters always seemed to refer to the Democratic leadership by their first names), and Obama himself, now fit Spencer Bachus and John Boehner into their schedules (though it is unclear if these executives feel comfortable enough to call Bachus by his first name).

Boehner, himself, wasted little time telling Dimon during one Capitol Hill visit that, if he wanted new friends, he better act like a friend and support the Republicans as the midterm elections approached. Jamie Dimon, the king of Wall Street, lifelong Democrat, proud liberal even from the seat of his limousine, suddenly began to feel powerless. It was such an odd feeling for Dimon. He had been able to call the shots through most of the financial crisis. He had been the go-to guy for advice when the president needed some.

Now he was abandoned by the people he had helped elect, who in his mind owed him so much. He couldn't even turn to the New York delegation for help. Senator Chuck Schumer, once one of Wall Street's biggest supporters, had joined the banker bashing, as had Senator Kirsten Gillibrand, who replaced Hillary Clinton when she became Obama's secretary of state.

Gillibrand explained her position this way: "Seventy percent of New Yorkers hate Wall Street."

Maybe the biggest disappointment was Representative Carolyn Maloney, who represents Manhattan's Upper East Side, also known as the "silk stocking district" for its wealthy residents, including many Goldman Sachs executives who have given to her many campaigns. Yet Maloney had toyed with the idea of holding hearings on how Wall Street and Goldman Sachs in particular had helped Greece hide its massive debt through derivative transactions, setting the stage for the financial collapse of the country in early 2010. She backed off her Goldman focus, but only after Goldman lobbyists begged her to consider the ramifications for the firm of facing yet another congressional investigation.

Dimon was a Democrat, but he was also a pragmatist, and as the Left abandoned the Street, he led the Street in abandoning the Left, and began to write checks to politicians on the right. People close to Dimon say when he returned to JPMorgan Chase headquarters in New York following his meeting with Boehner, the word was out that the Republicans needed money, and fast.

While some Republicans felt giddy about Wall Street's reversal and the campaign contributions it began to produce, Bachus saw it as part of a bigger pattern: Wall Street loves Big Government because it can feast off its programs, make money off its "infrastructure" spending, and earn its fees selling government bonds to finance deficit.

And yet "they always come calling here whenever they feel threatened," Bachus said.

Aside from banker bashing, health-care reform became the president's other obsession. As Obama used name-calling to prop up his faltering poll numbers, he was also using the notion of deficit reduction to legitimize his plans to socialize health care, which makes up 16 percent of the economy accounted for by health care. If you believe the administration and the Congressional Budget Office, "Obamacare" would cut the deficit by $136 billion over the next decade by reducing costs, particularly the costs of government subsidies already in place.

Most of the mainstream media barely questioned the analysis. On Wall Street, there was a different reaction.

"We have to do something, but not this," remarked Tom Nides. Unlike most business reporters, Nides understands that even if you buy the CBO's analysis, the $136 billion in savings over ten years comes out to around $13 billion a year, a drop in the bucket given the size of the U.S. economy: $14.2 *trillion* in 2009, as measured by GDP. Those much-touted promised savings would amount to only about one-tenth of 1 percent of that GDP.

But more than that, in the relative blink of an eye, Obama had created a massive new government entitlement, which, given the history of entitlements, will almost certainly cost more than originally thought.

Others on Wall Street were becoming petrified. Privately, people like Larry Fink, who ran investment funds tied to the bond market, worried about the burgeoning budget deficit and, of course, what that might do to the bond markets, BlackRock's specialty. "When [Obama] was making the rounds in 2007 and 2008, you never heard him talking about new entitlements, just how we need to get costs under control," Fink commented to a friend about Obama's new health-care initiative.

The word "privately" is important here: Fink's BlackRock investment fund was among the biggest recipients of the administration's postbailout largesse, receiving contracts to manage the bad debt of failed firms like

Bear Stearns and AIG and an assortment of other programs. Nor was he alone.

The trillions of dollars in new debt needed to pay for Obamacare, and for everything else the president had and has in store for the nation, barely registered a peep of caution out of Wall Street's biggest players—many of whom, after all, were making money financing Obama's Big Government agenda. (One noticeable exception was Bill Gross, the CEO of mega-fund PIMCO.) Should the clients of Bank of America, JPMorgan Chase, Citigroup, Goldman Sachs, or Morgan Stanley be snapping up Treasury bonds in light of the massive amounts of debt needed to pay for the president's agenda? Not one of Wall Street's most powerful executives would venture a guess. In fact, for all his "concern" over the deficit, Fink proudly declared during a CNBC interview that the Obama administration had done a great job with the economy.

Will the economy take a hit as interest rates rise on bonds to attract buyers, meaning higher interest rates on everything from mortgages to credit cards? Don't ask Jamie Dimon, Vikram Pandit, Brian Moynihan, Lloyd Blankfein, or any of the other members of Wall Street's brain trust.

The smartest, most powerful men in American finance and their firms remained largely silent on the biggest financial issue of the day—the economic impact of Obamacare—even as a national debate was raging on talk radio, cable television, and the editorial pages of the country's biggest newspapers.

The rating agencies, Moody's, Standard & Poor's, and Fitch, after the embarrassment of failing to warn about the housing bubble were almost equally silent, unless, of course, you count their tepid remarks assessing the slightest possibility that the spending of Obamanomics could cause them to downgrade the status of the U.S. government's triple-A rating someday long in the future. After all, who at the rating agencies is going to risk offending the entire U.S. government, not to mention all the agency's clients, the big banks that provide the vast majority of their business while they feast off government handouts?

It's just another example of what "bought and paid for" is all about.

At bottom, the Street knows that the profits it reaps from its relationship with Big Government are worth being called names. Much of the negative populist rhetoric from the general public and from politicians is recognized by Wall Street as just that, rhetoric.

Likewise, the heads of Goldman Sachs, JPMorgan Chase, Morgan Stanley, Citigroup, and Bank of America—the survivors of the 2008 crash—were coming to the conclusion in late 2009 and early 2010, as the broad outlines of the president's Wall Street regulation began to take shape, that they might not like *everything* that appeared in the new financial reform legislation (which, as this book goes to press, was recently signed by the president), but they liked most of it—around "80 percent" of it, according to an executive at JPMorgan.

Why so much? It's quite simple. The president may want the banks to give a little more back in the form of higher taxes (that they will just pass on to consumers) or better disclose their trades of the complex securities known as derivatives, but the bill all but assures that the mutually beneficial relationship between DC and Lower Manhattan remains largely untouched.

In the end, both Wall Street and Washington are getting what they wanted: Obama counters the public's perception that he's too soft on Wall Street while being careful not to offend his rich banker friends too much, so he can still tap their campaign cash for the 2012 presidential election. And Wall Street suffers a little in the form of tightened regulation, but even the most free-market of Wall Street kingpins acknowledge, at least in private, that *some* bill was going to have to be paid after they nearly brought down the global economy. In the meantime, they've had two years (or more) to reap many tens of billions of dollars in profits (in that sense, the financial crisis has actually been a net positive for Wall Street), while most important, even though some reduction in profit from the financial reform bill will certainly take place, the key mechanisms that have been the drivers of their historic profits (and bonuses) will remain to generate future returns.

For Goldman, JPMorgan Chase, Citigroup, and the rest, that special too-big-to-fail status is tantamount to the power to print money—because they are guaranteed such protection, they can borrow cheaply to make the risky trades that have returned the firms to record profits.

What better way, if you're the president of the United States, to pay off your largest supporters?

For all the press coverage of the administration's attacks against Wall Street, of Obama's call for more new regulations (did the president ever meet a regulation he didn't like?), there is much that Wall Street would like in the bill and a *lot* more that they like in Barack Obama.

And while Wall Streeters like Gary Cohn, with his assault on Harry Reid, and Jamie Dimon, with his increasingly negative feeling toward the Democrats, have made no secret of their distaste for the rhetoric coming from Washington that paints the typical Wall Street executive as a greedy tycoon, they, like the rest of their staff, can fully appreciate what the president is doing: using Wall Street as a whipping boy for an outraged public but doing little to disturb the status quo as he looks for the same support for his 2012 campaign that he received for his 2008 effort. As one senior JPMorgan Chase executive told me as this book goes to press: "He's already cutting back on the name-calling and soon will be looking for money."

Exactly so: Being bought and paid for means that you serve the needs of your benefactor, whatever those needs may be.

8

MONEY WELL SPENT

"There's no guarantee we're going to be paying that much in bonuses," explained an increasingly exasperated Lucas van Praag. "Trust me."

The problem for Goldman's expensive mouthpiece was that no one was trusting either him or his employer much these days. The firm had basically bragged it didn't need the bailout money it had been given, something that even Obama found offensive, not to mention Goldman's former CEO Hank Paulson, who had written the initial bailout check when he was George W. Bush's Treasury secretary. Now Goldman was once again trying to downplay the obvious: The firm set aside $23 billion during 2009 in bonus money.

And somehow, according to van Praag, not all of that money would find its way into the pockets of Goldman's risk-taking traders. Or Blankfein himself, who was making van Praag defend the absurd to the point that the flack's reputation among reporters had fallen to Nancy Pelosi–like levels of unpopularity. Stories began to appear that chronicled his various equivocations. A fake Twitter account was created in his name, mocking his British-accented defenses of the firm, and the press attention began to unnerve Van Praag.

"I would just love to be on an island somewhere and forget about all of it!" he moaned to a couple of friends one afternoon just after the Mc-Clatchy news service published a lengthy exposé raising questions about how the firm had "benefited from the housing crash" while the rest of the nation suffered.

The story was basically a rehash of much of what was known about how Goldman had profited off the housing collapse. While Americans were being foreclosed on, Goldman traders in 2007 were getting rich, in some cases shorting, or betting, that mortgage bonds would decline in value even as it sold similar securities to its clients. Goldman officials, including CFO David Viniar, one of the key people at the firm who had devised this strategy, kept assuring reporters, analysts, or anyone who would listen that it was nothing more than a hedging technique to reduce risk. Ironically, while the firm was reducing risk it was also mysteriously increasing profits, so much so that Blankfein walked away with a record bonus that year.

The McClatchy story didn't have the gravitas of a *Wall Street Journal* exposé or the sensationalism of the one from *Rolling Stone*, but it hit a nerve. The McClatchy news service was decidedly Middle American, with thirty newspapers in fifteen states reaching over two million people. Bashing Goldman Sachs suddenly became a mainstream sport as the article was picked up by television and radio shows across the country.

Despite the fact that they had become the most hated people in America, by early 2010, Wall Street bankers and traders and the posh restaurants in New York that catered to them were flourishing. It was standing room only at the expensive eateries—Campagnola, San Pietro, and the Four Seasons— where the bonus babies were spreading their wealth. As predicted, 2009 had been a really good year, at least for Wall Street. In fact, it had been its fourth best ever in terms of overall compensation and on par with what Wall Streeters had made in 2004, when the markets were raging.

The joy extended not just to the partners at Goldman, with its titanic bonus pool, but also to Morgan Stanley, which despite its near-death experience at the end of 2008 found it could easily pay its new CEO, James Gorman, $15 million for 2009, even as it boasted that John Mack, now the chairman and the man who had saved the company during the crisis, would forgo his bonus for a third year in a row. (The firm later disclosed that Mack earned a "salary" of about $1 million, or $939,000 to be exact.)

Even lowly Citigroup, which because of its size and the fact that the government still owned 27 percent of the firm in spring of 2010, was not doing as well as the other banks, still found ways to pay its people handsomely. And a near revolt among traders and brokers at Merrill Lynch who hated working for the Charlotte, North Carolina–based executives at still-wobbly Bank of America was quelled by generous bonus packages—the vast majority of them in cash despite the media-publicized myth that firms were handing out their bonuses in restricted stock that couldn't be cashed in for a number of years as a way of incentivizing their traders toward long-term goals. The final 2009 bonus tally appearing during the first quarter of 2010 went something like this: With all eyes on Goldman's money making, Bank of America seemed to escape media attention as the firm that paid out the most money to its executives in 2009. Blankfein and company, who were obviously hypersensitive to being singled out not only as the great Satan of Wall Street but as its most highly paid devil worshippers, came in midrange while the real shocker was Citigroup, which topped the bonus payment charts.

The most bailed out of the big firms was making money again (who couldn't in this environment?), so much so that at the end of 2009 it joined Bank of America as the last two firms to officially repay TARP. Now, breathing a small taste of freedom (the government was trying to unwind the stake it had taken in the company as part of the bailout), the bank was free to pay its people like real Wall Streeters again.

While other firms paid more than half of the bonus grants in stock, Citi handed out much more generous cash awards, signaling that for all the improvement Pandit was boasting about, its shares weren't likely to trade much higher than the $3.50, at least for the foreseeable future.

When Wall Street had doled out some $20 billion in cash bonuses just months after the bailouts the previous year ($123 billion in overall compensation), the president had described it as "shameful." Now he had even more choice words for his Wall Street friends. But they, at least for the moment, seemed not to have a care in the world. And they traded that way. For all the PR talk about how the big firms had learned their lesson and scaled back on risk, just the opposite seemed to be the case: Goldman Sachs took more risk in 2009 than it did in 2008, allowing it to earn a profit of $100 million per day in 131 trading days—a Wall Street record. Its results so far in 2010 meant it would likely meet or surpass that record, and the rest of the banks weren't far behind.

They weren't far behind in their arrogance, either, as they brushed aside suggestions that their firms' profits and their traders' bonuses were primarily the result of Big Government. Goldman, meanwhile, continued to offer the most brazen defense of its success, as Lucas van Praag and the firm's PR staff trotted out their tiresome reasoning that the traders at Goldman were just better and smarter than the rest of the Street.

That may be true, but it's also like bragging you're the tallest midget in the room. The reality for Wall Street was something the bankers either didn't want to admit or couldn't bring themselves to concede: that in the era of Obamanomics they were now in a sense reduced to highly paid bureaucrats being bailed out by Big Government, granted enormous wealth because of government handouts and certain to face more regulation from Washington.

But they were still highly paid, and on Wall Street that's often all that matters.

"This has been a very good year—very good," boasted one investment banker at Merrill Lynch who specialized in getting municipalities to issue more debt, which they were doing, at Wall Street's behest, like never before. Tax revenues were going down because of the great recession, but borrowing had skyrocketed, and not just for municipal projects. The shell game of municipal finance was that all that bond money got thrown in a big pot, and much of the financing went to plug budget gaps.

While bankers at Merrill Lynch (now part of Bank of America) were making money feeding the needs of Big Government, bankers at Goldman were both counting their massive year-end bonuses and trying to ignore the company's notoriety, which seemed to grow by the day among average Americans thanks to the McClatchy wire service story and many others.

"Why the fuck should we care?" a senior Goldman executive asked me at the time. "Our clients don't read the fucking McClatchy wire service."

He was right—the typical Goldman client read the *New York Times* and the *Wall Street Journal.* McClatchy, with its newspapers in South Carolina and Sacramento, was beneath Goldman Sachs, which had former CEOs who were Treasury secretaries and cabinet members, the kind of people whom Fortune 500 CEOs looking to hire an investment bank care about.

But as Blankfein and his team were starting to discover, Goldman's "clients" were no longer the guys paying the bill—they were the public officials who were making the rules about how much money the firm could make and whether the subsidies it had feasted on during the past year would continue.

Barack Obama didn't create the financial crisis in 2008, but he certainly created the uneven economic situation of 2009 and 2010 that allowed Wall Street to make so much money while America had to suffer through another dismal year of low employment.

Was Obama just tone deaf when it came to the economy, or just plain financially incompetent? Or was he so ideological in his approach to government that he ignored the suffering of average Americans who were out of work to spend his time pushing for a health-care entitlement and promising higher taxes on individuals, entrepreneurs, and small businesses while the jobless rate remained steady at around 10 percent?

No one will ever know, except maybe Obama himself. One thing is certain: The guy who appeared so smart and poised during the campaign couldn't seem to get his arms around some simple economic facts, namely that his policies offered none of the massive incentives to most businesses that they offered the favored few, namely the banks and brokerage firms (and a few large companies like General Electric that embraced his social agenda of "green jobs"), no matter how many times he called them names. A factory in South Carolina won't hire additional workers if management expects more taxes (as Obama was promising), bigger entitlements (like health care), and higher energy costs.

But on Wall Street the incentives were everywhere, including, most prominently, low interest rates and increased government protection. By the spring of 2010, Wall Street was doing what it had done in the post-meltdown period: trading even more mortgage debt and racking up monster profits. At Goldman Sachs, so much of the firm's profit was derived in one form or another from bond trading that even executives inside the firm compared the situation with the firm's precrisis heyday, the only difference being that Goldman, like the rest of the Street, was feasting off a market that was being directed almost solely by the very visible hand of government (even if every major bank had by now boasted that it had repaid the bailout money given to it during the dark days of 2008 and early 2009).

In early 2010, President Obama's Treasury Department proudly announced that Citigroup's repayment of its TARP money and the government's planned sale of its 27 percent stock ownership of the firm would net the American taxpayer some $8 billion. But like most things involving Obamanomics, the devil is in the details. The Treasury's analysis ignored the costs of hundreds of billions in "ring-fenced" assets (a term used mostly to describe the billions in toxic mortgage debt) that Citigroup held and that the American taxpayer had guaranteed against failing, as well as other programs designed to make life easier for the bankers. For the bankers, ignoring Obama's radical past while demonizing Sarah Palin at their Manhattan cocktail parties had its benefits. The technocrats at the Obama Treasury Department and at the Fed—whose chairman, Ben Bernanke, was a Bush appointee who had earned the support of his new left-wing boss—would say that this program was needed to remove the toxic debt sitting at depressed prices on the banks' balance sheets. They will tell you all the government programs were freeing up capital so businesses could borrow and expand. But the average American small businessman would tell you the programs weren't working and that despite positive economic growth, the banks were still nearly as tight-fisted with their money as they were during the financial crisis.

Election years bring lots of surprises, and none bigger for Wall Street than the resurrection of Paul Volcker as the 2010 midterms approached. The aged former chairman of the Federal Reserve was supposed to serve as nothing more than window dressing for the Obama administration—his early support had given Obama much-needed assurance in economic circles that the candidate wasn't the flaming liberal that his detractors tried to portray him as.

Volcker, a committed Democrat, had, after all, first been appointed as Fed chairman by president Jimmy Carter, had been reappointed to run the Fed in the early 1980s by conservative icon Ronald Reagan, and is credited with taming the economic malaise of the late 1970s and early 1980s—so-called stagflation, the lethal combination of high unemployment and high inflation. Volcker squeezed inflation by raising interest rates to historic highs, and he did it with brass balls. When called before Congress to answer for the 20 percent interest rate he had imposed and the consequent economic despair it was causing, he rolled a cheap cigar in his mouth and calmly but firmly explained that it was the necessary medicine for years of excess. And he was right. The short-term pain of high unemployment ultimately gave way to long-term economic gain. Once inflation fell, so did interest rates, and when combined with the Reagan tax cuts the economy took off on a decadelong boom.

Volcker had since left the Fed and continued on as a consultant, but one that was decidedly anti–Wall Street. Unlike his successor, Alan Greenspan, he hated the newfangled financial alchemy that spread though the banking system in the 1990s, the newfangled bonds, and most of all the newfangled banks—and he constantly and continuously let the world know it. He showed particular contempt for Citigroup. By commingling investment banking, risk-taking traders, and customer deposits under one roof, Volcker thought Citi had become a disaster waiting to happen, no matter how much its founders, Sandy Weill and Bob Rubin, were initially celebrated. And based on the events of 2007 and 2008, he was right.

For being right about the financial crisis, Volcker was offered what was thought to be an easy job with the Obama administration, something that was more or less a "thank you" for his early support for the young and economically inexperienced candidate. The president's economic inner circle of Geithner and Summers and their senior staff regarded Volcker as someone who had to be tolerated but not taken seriously.

There was only one problem: Paul Volcker didn't see it that way.

"I hear about these wonderful innovations in the financial markets, and they sure as hell need a lot of innovation," Volcker said in his trademark no-nonsense, almost monotonic style of speech, "and I can tell you of two—credit-default swaps and collateralized debt obligations—which took us right to the brink of disaster. Were they wonderful innovations that we want to create more of?"

Volcker was speaking at a December 2009 *Wall Street Journal* conference that focused on the banking crisis and Wall Street's role in creating the massive risk that upended the financial system. During his speech and in answering questions, Volcker attacked Wall Street on everything from its massive compensation packages based on short-term trades to its corporate governance system, where boards of directors barely understood the business of risk that the banks had adopted.

Despite the creation of all those funky derivatives, CDOs, and the like, Wall Street actually lacked innovation, Volcker claimed. The massive amounts of derivatives designed to limit risk only caused more of it. Many of the high-tech companies the firms brought public paid them massive investment-banking fees to downplay their shortcomings in research to investors and ultimately became insolvent. In fact, the greatest innovation that he could come up with from the banks over the past two decades was the ATM—the automatic teller machine, because it "really helps people and prevents visits to the bank and is a real convenience."

"More of the same," was how one banking executive who heard of the speech described it to me. That's because for years Volcker had attacked big banks like Citigroup and JPMorgan Chase as "bundles of conflicts," in other words, for being so big that they often served the interests of corporations at the expense of depositors and people who bought stock through their brokerage channels.

What made Volcker's commentary so searing and accurate was that he couldn't be bought, and wouldn't be. His post-Fed job was with a small but prestigious investment advisory firm rather than a large bank. He didn't engage in the corrupt and conflicted banking practices that were so lucrative and evil at the big firms. As a result, he was free to opine on Wall Street's aberrant behavior, particularly when it came to the business model du jour, the large universal bank where millions of small investors, many of them buying stocks for the first time to save for retirement as 401(k) plans replaced old pension funds, constantly got the shaft because they were prodded by the firms' brokers to buy shares of companies that the banks had underwritten. The stocks of these companies were further enhanced by conflicted analyst research reports issued by people like Henry Blodget of Merrill Lynch and Jack Grubman of Citigroup. Critics charge that these analysts promoted the shares of the companies they analyzed because they weren't necessarily paid to steer clients to the best investment but rather to help their firms get more underwriting business from those same companies. Paul Volcker was one of those critics.

Now Volcker wanted to rein in what he saw as Wall Street's other sin, namely its addiction to risk. But for a guy who wasn't supposed to have much sway inside the Obama administration, Volcker worked as if he had a lot of it. I ran into more than a few former top executives at Wall Street firms who told me in mid- to late 2009 that they had spoken to Volcker, who was planning something big to reduce Wall Street risk taking once and for all. For a time Volcker toyed with the idea of bringing back Glass-Steagall, which would have forced a separation of JPMorgan, Citigroup, and Bank of America into separate investment and commerical banks. Based on what I know about these meetings, I believe he decided against that measure because putting the genie back in the bottle was much more difficult than it appeared. Moreover, not even the great Paul Volcker was prepared to tell Jamie Dimon that he had to spin off his commercial banking business.

So in the end, Volcker called for some pretty inconsequential reforms— soon to be collectively dubbed the Volcker rule—which would prevent all banks, from Goldman Sachs to those that handle customer deposits and are thus protected by the FDIC, from risking it all by speculating in the markets with company capital. No more so-called proprietary trading, no more hedge funds or private-equity funds for banks, if the federal government was to back up their deposits in the event of massive losses.

And now, as the public outrage over Wall Street profits grew louder amid burgeoning unemployment, the president began to listen to his most anti–Wall Street economist. Had Obama come to understand that the massive protections he continued to offer the banks while they gambled should finally come to an end? Probably not. Did he understand that the public was beginning to associate him and his administration with the fat-cat bankers? More likely.

The wake-up call for Obama was when Republican Scott Brown, a little-known state legislator, won the Senate seat held by liberal icon Teddy Kennedy, even after Obama spent time in Massachusetts campaigning for the Democrat, Martha Coakley. Obama, the man who made women swoon when he ran for president and packed stadiums filled with admirers to hear his pearls of wisdom, was getting a taste of reality. Americans loved his personal story but had begun to hate his policies. His poll numbers were now cruising lower, mostly the result of the struggling economy but also because the public was fully digesting the inequity of Obamanomics: Bankers make bundles while everyone else suffers.

Amid this tailspin, Obama began to embrace the original anti–Wall Street economist, Paul Volcker, and the Volcker rule got a new lease on life in a new financial reform law Obama promised to get done before the end of 2010. As Obama began to unveil his plan to reform the financial markets, which included new proposals to limit risk Volcker had advocated, there was the six-foot-six-inch Volcker standing right to his side, hovering over the president like a giant tower while the diminutive Geithner stood meekly in the background.

The spectacle sent a chill through Wall Street. The consequences for JPMorgan Chase of the "new Volcker rule," as it became known on Wall Street, were not life threatening though they were still pretty stark and they made Jamie Dimon seethe: Depending on the final language, the firm might have to spin off its massive hedge fund, known as Highbridge Capital, which had $21 billion in assets under management. Goldman Sachs not only owned a bank in Utah (not the biggest part of its operations but a nice moneymaker) but the firm was officially designated as a bank, meaning the rule would squeeze its lucrative business of "proprietary trading." (It turned out not to be that easy for Goldman, since the firm had been deemed a bank after the 2008 financial collapse.) Who knew how Citigroup would be affected, as the bank traded commodities all across the world even in its current shape as a near basket case.

Blankfein, of course, never saw it coming. The Volcker proposal appeared on its face to hit the banks hard, but Citigroup and JPMorgan had somewhat curtailed their proprietary trading activities. Goldman, on the other hand, was in essence one large hedge fund that was only technically a bank; it didn't matter whether or not it offered checking deposits; the Fed still regulated the firm as it did Citi and JPMorgan.

As one JPMorgan executive put it, "Goldman is now in the roach motel with the rest of us, and the poison will be worse for them than anyone else."

When news hit that the rule was being strongly considered as part of the legislation, Goldman's lobbyists, many of them former legislative staffers who had worked for key Democratic lawmakers like Barney Frank, fanned out across Capitol Hill. David Viniar, the firm's CFO, scheduled a conference call and assured analysts that the rule was no biggie; proprietary trading accounted for just 10 percent of the firm's revenues, he said. Dimon's flacks offered the same spin—the rule would get modified down to almost nothing, they told reporters, even as Dimon privately worried that JPMorgan might have to spin off its massive private equity holdings and hedge funds when he read the fine print of the Volcker rule.

One of the ironies of the rule is that neither proprietary ("prop") trading nor hedge fund investing was the major cause of the 2008 financial collapse. Wall Street's massive losses largely stemmed from the firms' creating mortgage bonds and other complex investments for clients, so in essence the

Volcker rule was meaningless. It did nothing to prevent the possibility of another financial collapse and it still allowed the banks to be "too big to fail."

"Volcker has no idea how the financial crisis began," Larry Fink remarked after he heard that the president was beginning to take Volcker seriously. Fink, as we've seen, had made a killing from the various bailouts and mechanisms offered during the postbailout months. And yet by early 2010 he had begun telling friends that he was no longer a fan of the president. Obama, Fink complained, had lost his way. Not only was the president listening more to Volcker, whom he considered crazy, but the Wall Street–loving guy he knew on the campaign trail had morphed into a class warrior. Fink told people he had voted for Obama as a change toward moderation—change from the big-spending ways of George W. Bush and the nation's cowboy image overseas, particularly in the Middle East, where BlackRock managed money for wealthy Arabs—and because he couldn't bear to vote for a ticket that included the superconservative and, in his eyes, incompetent Sarah Palin.

What he got instead was a doubling down of Bush in terms of spending and a heaping dose of class warfare to boot. The guy he had thought was a moderate turned out to be a lefty.

And he also received a doubling down of abuse. Ken Langone, who had supported Rudy Giuliani's failed presidential run, never let Fink forget that the man he had helped elect had turned out to be a disaster, according to people who overheard their conversation over lunch at San Pietro.

Lloyd Blankfein had initially supported Hillary Clinton for president, but had gravitated toward Obama with the rest of Wall Street. Now, like Fink, he wished he hadn't. The pressure on Goldman mounted through the spring of 2010 at an unrelenting pace, with verbal attacks and more congressional hearings. Despite estimates of a $100 million bonus, Blankfein ended up taking just $9 million. Goldman presented the award—all of it in company stock—as a sign that Blankfein was doing the right thing, walking away from money he had rightfully earned but couldn't take because of the public's distaste for the firm's success.

The PR victory, such as it was, barely registered with the general public, which believed that even $9 million to a banker that feasted off the taxpayer was far too much. Private polling done by the financial firms showed Wall Street's standing sinking even lower, with Goldman leading the downward trend.

The prickly Blankfein, it should be noted, isn't a beloved figure inside Goldman as, say, the charismatic John Mack is within Morgan Stanley. But oddly enough, his plight—and now the plight of the firm—brought Goldman's many warring factions (the bankers never really got along with the traders) together for the first time in years.

The consensus inside the firm, even among bankers who hated both Blankfein and Gary Cohn, was that the firm was the victim of a witch hunt. Many even believed that Goldman's woes could be traced to latent anti-Semitism in the public, ironically inflamed by the relentless coverage of the firm by the *New York Times*.

Goldman, of course, traced its roots to German Jews who after the Civil War couldn't work at the WASP-owned banks, and that identity remained part of the firm's cultural fabric for years. After the firm's being run for the past fifteen years by WASPs (Jon Corzine and Hank Paulson), Blankfein was a throwback to the early days, and according to people at Goldman, several top executives believed the critical press coverage, particularly some of the most stinging rebukes published in the *New York Times* by acclaimed investigative reporter Gretchen Morgenson, carried anti-Semitic overtones and as absurd as such a charge might be, the firm should register the complaint with *Times* management.

But it's hard to play the victim when you're making so much money (Goldman earned $3.5 billion during the first quarter of 2010), and the firm's war-weary flack Lucas van Praag cautioned that such a press strategy would ultimately backfire.

For a change, Blankfein and company listened to him.

Meanwhile, Wall Street's best friends in the administration, Treasury secretary Tim Geithner and chief economic adviser Larry Summers, had continued to signal to Blankfein, Dimon, and the rest of the Wall Street ruling commission that they shouldn't worry too much about Obama's financial reform rhetoric, assuring their friends on Wall Street that they had all but killed the most pernicious parts of the Volcker proposal, namely the call to end proprietary trading and the provisions to limit how much the firms can place of their own capital in hedge funds and private equity.

It had been a hard-fought battle, they said. Obama, after all, was actually beginning to *listen* to Volcker after about a year of ignoring the most experienced economist in his administration, and Volcker hated Wall Street. But a sharp drop in the stock market had made Obama think twice, and the Volcker rule, in its current form, was dead, at least until the next financial crisis.

With that, the firms began feeling good about themselves as they partied on more than $140 billion in bonus money for 2009, doled out during the early part of 2010. It was as if 2008 had never happened, and in the minds of most of Wall Street, it hadn't.

But it did happen, of course, and just about as soon as word leaked that the Volcker rule was out, it was back in.

"Volcker is crazy" was the assessment of just about every banker on Wall Street when they heard the latest: The old man somehow reclaimed the president's attention.

Volcker, as it turned out, might be crazy, but he wasn't stupid. For all the push-back from Geithner and company on Volcker's proposal (Geithner through a spokesman denies that be opposed the final product), the plan somehow received a second life when Wall Street started buzzing as to how Volcker made his plea directly to the president. Soon his political aides, particularly David Axelrod, who was credited with devising Obama's successful campaign strategy, began to support the measure as well. The public, Volcker argued, wanted something done about the risk taking that had proved so dangerous. More than that, by doing nothing to rein in the banks, Obama, the candidate of hope and change, was being associated with the most hated entities in America.

For all the rule's faults, its political value couldn't be underestimated. Obama's association with the big banks, combined with his far-left agenda, had begun to crush his once-lofty poll numbers and threatened Democratic control of the House and Senate. Among the most vulnerable was Senate majority leader Harry Reid, the same Harry Reid who had gone begging to Goldman for campaign cash and gotten screamed at by Blankfein's enforcer, Gary Cohn. Many in Obama's own party would have supported a breakup of the banks, something the public probably would have supported as well. But that would have assured a war with the likes of Jamie Dimon, and all the Wall Street cash would have begun to flow to the Republicans.

So Obama settled for the next best thing, a compromise: the Volcker rule. Thanks to Summers and Geithner, Volcker and his rule languished inside the Obama White House for months, Wall Street executives with direct knowledge of the matter say—that is, until it became clear that Obama's presidency depended on doing something that took on the banking system that he had protected for so long and that had allowed the hated Goldman Sachs to boast record-breaking profits, which were on track to beat bonuses earned in 2009.

With that, Paul Volcker, eighty-three, who was for most of his time in the Obama White House considered nothing more than an ornament, a rare antique to be marveled at for a brief moment before going about your business, became a star once again. The man who had raised interest rates in the late 1970s and early 1980s and argued that high unemployment for a time would be good for the country had now found relevance in the populist anger that was sweeping the country and in Obama's decision to tap into it by attacking his old friends on Wall Street.

Geithner, people at the firms tell me, was livid and so scared about his own relevancy that he began cutting ties with many of his closest contacts on Wall Street. Summers, for his part, kept those contacts but told them he was so frustrated by his diminished status that he might leave the administration at the end of the year. Emanuel, meanwhile, explained to his Wall Street friends that given the anti–Wall Street mood of the nation, the hatred that was palpable from the lefties who read the *Huffington Post* blog and the right-wingers attending Tea Party rallies, the banks should be glad they had friends in high places.

The Volcker rule, despite assurances from Emanuel, Geithner, and Summers to the contrary, wasn't merely in the new financial reform bill; it had become the centerpiece of the entire package being adopted by Chris Dodd, the Democratic senator from Connecticut, not just to rein in Wall Street but also to curry favor with the public as the 2010 midterms drew closer.

Despite funneling substantial sums of campaign cash his way because of his senior position on the Senate Banking Committee, Wall Street had always considered Chris Dodd a fair-weather friend. Since he was from Connecticut, his base of support wasn't Wall Street but the giant hedge-fund industry, which had its offices in the swanky areas of Greenwich and Stamford and competed with the New York–based banks for talent.

The first sign Dodd wasn't in the banks' corner had come when he proposed pay caps for the bailed-out firms back in 2009, a move shot down by Wall Street's friends in the administration, namely Geithner, according to people on Wall Street. But now Dodd had been given a broader mandate as the primary author of the new financial reform legislation, to be known as the "Dodd bill" on Wall Street because he took such a direct interest in the legislation and the president handed him so much control. In other words, Chris Dodd had Wall Street's future in the palm of his hand, and that had the Street on edge. The big question was just how far he would go. Would Dodd embrace not just the Volcker rule in its most strict interpretation but also some of the more loony proposals that had cropped up during the last two years? Or would he play ball with Geithner and Summers?

Inside JPMorgan Chase, Dimon weighed the odds: Politically, Dodd was finished, thanks in large part to his association with the subprime lender Countrywide Financial, run by the controversial Angelo Mozilo. Dodd had received sweetheart loans from the bankrupt mortgage company, whose loans were responsible for the financial crisis, and he had been a major recipient of campaign cash from the disgraced mortgage lenders Fannie Mae and Freddie Mac. With his poll numbers dropping, Dodd had announced that he wasn't running for reelection.

But he wasn't going anywhere fast (his term ended in 2010), and his aides let it be known that after a long and distinguished career (nearly thirty-five years in public office), Dodd wanted a grand exit, something that he could point to as his legacy. That something, they said, was financial reform, and that made Dimon and the rest of the Street nervous.

As for banker bashing, that was here to stay as well. The Democrats, even ones whom Wall Street had considered real friends, like the usually pro–Wall Street senator from New York, Chuck Schumer, liked the idea of running against Wall Street and trying to tie the Republicans to the greedy bankers, even if those bankers were themselves Democrats.

Financial reform became their weapon of choice. It didn't matter that the so-called proprietary trading that Volcker wanted to outlaw and the banks' ownership of hedge funds and private-equity accounts weren't at the heart of the financial crisis. Obama didn't really care, several senior Wall Street executives told me, and he didn't need to. It was the message that mattered to Obama and the rest of the Democratic leadership as the midterms approached, and that message was all about banker bashing in public while his lieutenants continued to assure Wall Street everything was just fine—even if it wasn't.

The attacks on Wall Street, with particular emphasis on Goldman, kept coming, not just from the pols or from *Rolling Stone* or the McClatchy newspapers, but also from liberal documentary film producer Michael Moore, the *New York Times*, the *Wall Street Journal*, and all the cable news shows. Even the *Wall Street Journal*'s right-of-center editorial page took aim. "Goldman will surely deny that its risk-taking is subsidized by the taxpayer—but then so did Fannie Mae and Freddie Mac, right up to the bitter end," the *Journal*'s editorial writers opined. "An implicit government guarantee is only free until it's not, and when the bill comes due it tends to be huge. So for the moment, Goldman Sachs—or should we say Goldie Mac?—enjoys the best of both worlds: outsize profits for its traders and shareholders and a taxpayer backstop should anything go wrong."

The stories had legs because (a) they were true, but (b) they were also prodded and pushed by an unrelenting political attack. Goldman wasn't the only firm to feel the heat: In fact, they all did. But as the rhetoric heated up from the president and his minions in Congress, the firm that had given the most to him and, of course, made so much money from his policies, remained public enemy number one.

In a sense, Goldman was crying all the way to the bank. It was making more money than ever. Its stock price was soaring. But the firm was in crisis as its success brought greater scrutiny and greater outrage from the public. Citigroup was a far greater culprit in the financial crisis, and cost taxpayers far more to save, than Goldman, which for all its faults had done the smart thing as early as 2006 when it began betting against the same housing bonds that two years later took down the system.

But somehow that logic failed to convince the growing ranks of Goldman's detractors. The firm's legendary access to politicians, even the Democrats it embraced with massive amounts of campaign cash, was now being cut off. "Goldman Sachs is radioactive" was the message the firm's high-powered team of Washington-based lobbyists delivered to Blankfein back in New York.

"I never thought I would say this, but the Democrats are killing us. It's a betrayal," said one senior Goldman executive who was a lifelong Democrat.

Many of Goldman's problems were self-inflicted. The firm's latest media campaign, in which for the first time Blankfein had begun to field questions from reporters, backfired big time. Blankfein may have been the least media savvy of all the CEOs. In front of reporters he appeared stiff and highly scripted, as if he were trying to hide something. But the bigger problem was that Blankfein, as hard as he tried, couldn't spin the obvious: that while the firm was the best of the lot, Goldman had also made the most of the vast handouts given as part of Big Government's protection of

Wall Street, and with every disclosure of the firm's profits or its growing bonus pool, the public seethed.

By early spring of 2010, Blankfein had become obsessed with two issues: the prospect that the Dodd bill and the Volcker rule would become law and the name-calling from politicians looking to tap into the public's distaste for Wall Street. As bad as it felt, Blankfein, like his cohorts on Wall Street, could take being called a fat cat every now and then, but by early 2010, he had realized that the name-calling was having a substantive impact.

The vilification made it that much easier to ram the Dodd bill and the Volcker rule through Congress, and that would mean Goldman would have to make some significant changes in its business model unless, of course, it could find a way to change the legislation before it became law.

It owned a bank with several billion dollars in deposits, so that might have to be sold, but even worse, Goldman would face stiff restrictions on its bread-and-butter trading business. Blankfein ordered his legal staff to study the matter. The result wasn't good. If the Volcker rule was interpreted broadly, Goldman would have to scale back on its trading activities dramatically. The profits that had powered Goldman Sachs shares nearly to where they had been before the banking crisis began would decline by as much as 20 percent.

The legal analysis showed that there was a gray area in the legislation: It was unclear that all so-called proprietary trades were covered by the rule. Trades that began with a customer order might be exempt, depending on the rule's interpretation. And interpretation was key: Would it be Geithner or Volcker himself interpreting the rule? No one knew.

It was one of the downsides of being too big to fail: The government control of trading might extend to Goldman because it was too big and too important to run free. And that's why Blankfein was, according to one banker, "obsessed" with the looming Dodd bill. The only thing worse than running Goldman into the ground, as he nearly had in 2008, would be if he were the CEO who allowed the great institution to become a ward of the state. And that's where the firm was heading.

In the past, Goldman's words had carried a certain weight. Former Goldman executives have for years been littered throughout the government regulatory apparatus (the controversial decision to give Goldman one hundred cents on the dollar to cover its AIG liabilities and save the firm tens of billions of dollars was made by a Treasury Department bureaucrat who had worked at Goldman and held its stock, according to the *New York Times*). Even those bureaucrats in Treasury or the Fed or working for any of the Senate or House committees that provide oversight who hadn't worked for Goldman probably wanted to in the future. Meanwhile, there was always the threat that if Goldman didn't get its way there would be repercussions: Campaign contributions would disappear.

But times had changed. The pleas from the firm's lobbyists carried less weight and more desperation. That's because Blankfein believed that the name-calling had now spilled over into the policy arena; the public's hatred of the bank was giving Dodd and the Democrats the ammunition they needed to push an anti–Wall Street bill.

More than that, Goldman was dealing with that potentially messy investigation into its business dealings during the bubble years: the "big short," or how the firm had bet against the housing bubble by shorting certain toxic assets while it was selling those same assets to its customers in late 2006 and early 2007.

Now it wasn't just pain-in-the-ass reporters at McClatchy who were turning the screws on the firm once lauded for its brains and guile as a market maker. The focus in Congress wasn't about how smart Goldman had been in shorting the housing market but rather how scummy the firm had behaved in selling those securities to its clients.

Lloyd Blankfein has many skills: He's one of the best risk managers on Wall Street, and if you talk to people he used to work for, like Bob Rubin when he ran Goldman in the 1980s, they will tell you that Blankfein worked extremely well with clients. But those skills don't necessarily translate into being the public face of a major company that is under constant scrutiny, and that's what many at Goldman were discovering as Blankfein began attracting more and more attention from the multitude of congressional committees and other public investigative bodies (the former treasurer of California, Phil Angelides, was heading something called the Financial Crisis Inquiry Committee, which was supposed to produce a report to Congress by the end of 2010 on the causes of the financial crash) delving into Wall Street, its abusive practices, and the banking collapse.

Inside Goldman, Blankfein's team tried to spin their boss's uneven performances in 2009 and one particularly uneven piece of testimony in early 2010 before Angelides's committee as the best of a bad situation. There were no major gaffes, even if in one instance, while being grilled by Angelides about why Goldman had sold faulty mortgage-backed bonds to investors it was actually betting against, Blankfein appeared confused, adding that the firm had sold the toxic debt to "the most sophisticated investors who sought that exposure. . . . There were people in the market who thought it was going down and there were others who thought these prices had gone down so much they were going to bounce up again."

Angelides's response was significantly more coherent.

"Mr. Blankfein himself never admitted that there was any responsibility of Goldman Sachs to make sure the products themselves were good products. . . . That's very troublesome."

If Blankfein thought his attempt to cash in on the class-warfare mood of the country would work, he was wrong. The lame response only heightened the tension. Retired partners of the firm, powerful because they held so much Goldman stock, began grousing that Blankfein, with his odd looks and lack of public-speaking skills, shouldn't be the public face of the company; the firm should reassign the chairman role to someone better suited to being grilled by angry politicians, as Morgan had done when it made the photogenic and articulate John Mack chairman while leaving the day-to-day management chores to the new CEO, James Gorman, a former McKinsey partner.

Blankfein angrily refused to budge, but the calls for him to at least give up part of his job (later there would be calls for him to step down altogether) intensified as more hearings followed. The Angelides committee made Goldman one of its prime targets. With anti-Goldman sentiment heating up, the commission let Goldman know that Blankfein or his number two, Gary Cohn, might be called back to better explain how the firm had made so much money while everyone else suffered so much.

Blankfein was doing a lot of explaining as 2010 wore on. Goldman was once again on a path toward record profits and bonuses. Its stock was soaring. But instead of telling the world how great the firm was, or how his management was making investors rich, he spent much of his time explaining how he wasn't running the functional equivalent of a criminal organization.

That's what Blankfein also tried to do in his annual letter to shareholders, when he began to portray a kinder, gentler Goldman. He and the sharp-tongued Gary Cohn, who mixed left-wing politics (he was an original Obama supporter) with a nasty streak (he has been known to tell colleagues to "fuck off"), appeared in a soothing photo together, smiling, as if they had just gotten done doing God's work. This wasn't the Goldman Sachs that clients complained about for its Darwinian trading culture of selling faulty investments during a mortgage bubble or the one journalists were now portraying as a wild gambling den that used its vast power to escape scrutiny for its wild ways. In the letter, Blankfein explained how much Goldman gave back to the community (certainly, he thought that would score points with the guys in Washington) by "investing in people and communities," and how a Warren Buffett–inspired program to donate $500 million to small businesses was doing so much good (I couldn't find a single small businessman who said the effort represented anything more than a drop in the bucket in terms of financing growth). He even managed to thank Big Government for aiding and abetting Goldman's success over the past year. "By the end of 2009, owed in no small part to actions taken by governments to fortify the system, conditions across financial markets had improved significantly and to an extent few predicted or thought possible. Equity prices largely rebounded, credit spreads tightened and market activity was revitalized by investors seeking new opportunities, all of which imply renewed optimism, if not the beginnings of a potential recovery," he wrote, while assuring the markets that Goldman's focus wasn't on screwing its clients but "on staying close to our clients and helping them to navigate uncertainty and achieve their objectives."

Blankfein used the word "client" fifty-six times in the letter, compared to just seventeen times the year before. He could have used it a thousand times. It would have made no difference to the Securities and Exchange Commission, which believed Goldman's contempt for customers was great enough that the staff of the commission sent "Wells notices" to the firm in March 2010.

The Wells notice is named after attorney John Wells, who created a formal process of alerting targets of SEC probes that they're in the agency's crosshairs. This one alerted Blankfein that the SEC's enforcement staff had recommended to the full commission that a case be filed against the firm and a midlevel executive regarding a particular sleazy deal. The transaction in question was called Abacus: Goldman sold some highly toxic mortgage debt to two of its clients, withholding, according to the SEC staff, several key disclosures, including the fact that the brains behind the deal was a man named John Paulson, an investor who would make a name for himself by betting against housing debt. By not alerting customers to Paulson's involvement, the SEC asserted, Goldman had duped the clients into thinking the deal was better than it really was.

Goldman's lawyers were outraged. "Your case sucks!" was the message delivered to the SEC staffers and the commission, which was now weighing whether to approve the filing of civil charges. The case certainly had its flaws; for starters, Goldman might have screwed people, but it sold the deal to sophisticated investors and provided full disclosure on the type of collateral of which the Abacus debt was composed. If the two clients, a German bank and a large U.S. investor, didn't know that the mortgages used in the deal were toxic, it's because they never cared to check.

But at the commission, the case took on a life of its own. For all its holes, the case had some obvious merits: The casino that Wall Street had turned into was aided and abetted by some of the borderline sleazy business dealings Goldman had become famous for, namely dishing out investments its traders viewed as "shitty" (a word found in company e-mails regarding such investments) to clients, which for all their size and alleged sophistication had no idea what they were buying.

The case also had obvious political merits. The SEC, known as Wall Street's top cop, is supposed to be an apolitical arm of government that enforces the nation's securities laws. And yet its leaders, including the chairman of the SEC, are appointed by the president and often enforce the laws within the context of the White House's political agenda.

Running the SEC in 2010 was a lifelong Democrat named Mary Schapiro. After the black eyes the agency had taken for missing both the Bernie Madoff Ponzi scheme and the subprime crisis, Schapiro had vowed to turn things around. According to people close to the commission, investigators viewed charges against Goldman as a way to repair the commission's battered reputation after these failures.

To be sure, Obama had given speech after speech attacking his predecessor, George W. Bush, for the lack of regulations that had allowed Wall Street to run wild and destroy itself and the economy. It didn't matter to the president that his Treasury secretary, Tim Geithner, had been part of the same regulatory apparatus as president of the New York Fed or that Schapiro had been part of it as head of Wall Street's self-regulatory organization, FINRA (the Financial Industry Regulatory Authority), where she earned $3.3 million in 2008 and took a $7.3 million "retirement" package when she left to join the SEC as its chair.

What mattered to the president was that, like Geithner, who dutifully carried out Obama's plans to increase spending and raise taxes on small businesses to astronomical levels, Schapiro would carry out the president's agenda in regulating Wall Street and attacking corporate America for political gain, which she did with gusto. Despite her own massive compensation as head of FINRA (Schapiro was paid millions to regulate firms that paid her salary through their annual dues), she began to mimic her boss's criticism of high executive pay.

That conflict of interest didn't seem to concern the Obama administration, nor did the president and his economic team seem much interested in FINRA's lousy record of cracking down on Wall Street abuse. Schapiro was seen as a loyal soldier, someone willing to carry out the president's wishes, as she did on so-called proxy access, when she fought for new rules that allowed Big Labor to have a greater say in who sits on corporate boards.

Now, at least as far as Goldman's attorneys were concerned, Schapiro was gearing up to use the case against Goldman to once again achieve the administration's larger aims, namely forcing Wall Street to accept financial reform (which the president was now actively pushing following his health-care reform victory and while he was at it trying to score points with a general public as he geared up for the 2010 midterms.) The SEC's broadside would do wonders to inoculate Obama against the growing impression that he was too cozy with the likes of Jamie Dimon and Lloyd Blankfein.

Even so, Goldman's lawyers assured Blankfein that they had a strong case and could get the SEC to back off before it went before the full five-member commission (which includes Schapiro). But Blankfein wasn't taking any chances. He wanted the firm out of the news, and that meant begging everyone in Washington who had ever received a dime from the firm to turn down the Goldman hating.

But it wasn't that easy. Goldman's lobbyists reported back to company headquarters in New York that the firm's reputation in Washington had itself become so toxic that the firm, which for most of its existence had had the ear of every major decision maker in Washington, was now persona non grata.

Now no one in Congress or, even more so, in the White House wanted to be seen near a Goldman banker. Blankfein, a savvy commodities trader with a degree from Harvard Law, had been a master of the universe for a long time, having his way whenever he wanted, but he finally understood what it meant to be used. Perhaps for the first time in his life, Blankfein was getting a taste of what it's like to be on the wrong side of a trade.

Wall Street, which was also so used to getting everything it wanted, had finally discovered that there's a price to be paid when you're bought and paid for, as the big firms had been for the past year. Like spoiled children, CEOs like Dimon and Blankfein began to seethe as the Volcker rule remained in place and their friends in the administration, Geithner, Summers, and Emanuel, appeared powerless to prevent other measures from sneaking into the plan.

Senator Blanche Lincoln, an Arkansas Democrat and no expert on the finer points of the risk taking that led to the 2008 collapse, introduced an amendment she believed would make Wall Street and the world safer. Lincoln's plan was to force the firms to spin off their businesses that dealt in derivatives into separate units that must be capitalized with costly new stock. It didn't matter that many derivatives, such as interest-rate swaps, are used by corporations and municipalities to hedge risk rather than take risk, and thus her move would put the squeeze on cities, states, and, of course, businesses already burdened by the soured economy.

But the notion that she was screwing Wall Street sounded good, and the president's political staff (as opposed to his economic team) told Dodd that the amendment should remain. If Dimon was livid over the derivative plan, he went nuclear over another measure: an amendment to create a new consumer protection agency designed to protect bank customers from unscrupulous lenders. Goldman couldn't care less about the measure, but for JPMorgan, with its massive Chase banking unit, the move would cost countless millions in the way of extra compliance staff.

Dimon and his team now attempted to assess the damage the various measures packed into the still-formulating bill would cost his bank. The consumer protection agency would mean much higher legal and compliance costs; the derivative spinout would mean extra money to capitalize a new entity that would sell those products to JPMorgan's clients. JPMorgan didn't do much proprietary trading, but it did own a massive hedge fund and private equity unit that, at least for now, appeared to be something the firm might have to sell.

There were so many moving pieces to the bill, and language that still needed to be written, that no one, neither Dimon nor some of the smartest minds at JPMorgan, could estimate a real cost, which in the world of Jamie Dimon, an executive who demanded to know everything about anything, was a fate worse than death.

"What the fuck are you guys doing for us?" Dimon screamed into his telephone at JPMorgan headquarters in New York one afternoon after hearing about the mother lode of new amendments being inserted in the bill. "You guys are worthless!"

Part of working for Dimon, who is alternately brilliant and hotheaded, is managing his moods. His senior management team—most of them longtime associates—have been schooled in how to deal with Dimon's more than occasional expletive-laced outbursts. It's part of the deal: You want to work for the best, be prepared to get screamed at once in a while.

On the other end of the receiver was Kirsten Gillibrand, who, though not a JPMorgan employee, had grown close to Dimon since she had been chosen to replace Hillary Clinton as New York's junior senator. So close, in fact, that JPMorgan had held a series of fund-raisers for Gillibrand, a former corporate lawyer whom Dimon had met while she worked at the white-shoe law firm Davis Polk. Gillibrand was now up for reelection and sure to be challenged for her inexperience and connections to the Clinton HUD department, which, as we saw earlier, greatly contributed to the housing crisis. But she appeared to have the king of Wall Street firmly in her corner. When asked about Gillibrand by the *New York Times*, Dimon said she was "hard-working, constructive and understands the issues."

That was before the Dodd bill began to take shape. Now, according to people with knowledge of the conversation, she was a "sellout" and "good for nothing," "letting down her supporters."

Gillibrand knew Dimon's temper, but she had never seen it on display like this and responded simply that there was little she could do because the country wanted Wall Street to be held accountable.

Gillibrand later complained to a Goldman executive that she had "never been chewed out" like that before. She wasn't alone. Dimon, I am told by people at JPMorgan, had similar choice words for New York's senior senator, Chuck Schumer, once Wall Street's most reliable protector (and biggest recipient of campaign cash), who was now playing the class warfare game himself, attacking his contributors as if he had never received a dime from Wall Street during his long political career and letting the least Wall Street–friendly planks of the reform bill remain without much push-back.

While the Democrats ran for cover, several prominent Republicans began to raise serious issues with the bill. U.S. Representative Peter King, a fiscal conservative and the son of a New York City cop, represents a district on Long Island, outside of New York City. King is one of Congress's few straight shooters (he refused to apologize for calling Michael Jackson a "pervert" and criticizing the coverage of the pop singer's death as "too politically correct"). So when politicians like Gillibrand and Schumer cowered amid the anti–Wall Street hysteria, King was blunt about the legislation: The costs associated with implementing all the so-called reforms would be passed on to consumers, he said. New York State, which needed all the tax revenue it could drum up from the banks, would suffer if Wall Street profits declined, as even the most rosy cost estimates showed that they would. The New York region would be placed at a competitive disadvantage in terms of jobs if, for example, derivatives must be traded on a public exchange, because the only public exchanges that could handle such trading are located in Chicago.

But all of this wouldn't be so bad if the legislation had some teeth to prevent another financial meltdown. Dimon, for his part, is the type of Wall Street executive who simply hates to lose anything, which contributed to his growing disgust with the bill. But as the various amendments and their proposed language started to make their way to the corner offices of the big firms, an internal JPMorgan analysis showed that if the worst things in the legislation became established law, it would shave a mere $3 billion off JPMorgan's annual earnings of close to $12 billion in 2009—significant, but hardly catastrophic.

That was even before the bank began saddling its depositors and customers with higher fees and surcharges, and before JPMorgan's savvy and well-connected lobbyists figured out how to work their away around the bill's various edicts and orders. In the end, the JPMorgan brass, like the rest of the banking system, know how to bend the rules. They've done it before, and as angry as they were with the Obama administration, they would kiss and make up so they could do it again.

And that's exactly what happened, because for all the hand-wringing over the Volcker rule, the legislation as it was taking shape included no requirement to break up the banks, no mandate to force Citi and JPMorgan Chase to spin off their trading businesses to protect depositors from excessive risk taking (a mandate that some had called for after the crisis and that Volcker himself had toyed with but in the end backed off from). Under the bill, the Fed would still regulate banks and Wall Street firms, giving them access to emergency borrowing power when they screwed up. The feckless SEC would still be the investment business's chief cop.

There would be "systemic risk regulators" and other government agencies that would both weigh risk taking at the banks and force the government into the financial system in an unprecedented manner. The firms would have to hold more capital to cover trading activities, but there would be loopholes for those that played ball with Big Government: Banks would be given breaks on the capital standard for so-called community-based or socially responsible lending. It didn't matter that years of such lending practices—pushed by the Community Reinvestment Act (CRA) and other government edicts—had helped bring the system to its knees in 2008.

Shockingly, Fannie Mae and Freddie Mac wouldn't be touched by the reform. In fact, as I write this, the Obama administration and Congress are feeding the monster once again, trying to revive the agencies, which are now completely wards of the state, with a bailout estimated at $1 trillion.

The Federal Reserve was looking like the big winner in the developing legislation, having gained near complete top-line regulatory control over the big banks with new and expanded powers to prevent another meltdown, the theory being that it didn't have enough authority already to stop some of the mindless risk taking. It did, of course. The Fed, for example, could have prevented Citigroup from keeping all those toxic mortgage bonds off its books, neatly tucked away in so-called structured investment vehicles that were moved back on the firm's balance sheet when they began losing money.

But it didn't, which raises the question of why the agency and its feckless bureaucrats deserve a second chance. The answer, at least according to

Obama and his economic team, is that there is no limit to the amount of good the government can do.

Did Wall Street really care about this unprecedented government intrusion into what is supposed to be the free-market system? Not really. At bottom, the Dimons and Blankfeins, of course, cared about some of the costs associated with this intrusion—the Volcker rule being high on Wall Street's hit list—but not all that much about the ideology of having the government be the final arbiter of capital in a system that bills itself as the greatest free market known to mankind.

That's why, as the bill neared passage, when Goldman Sachs spent its last dime on lobbyists to water down the Volcker rule (the firm nearly doubled its lobbyist spending in the first quarter of 2010) and Jamie Dimon threw his last hissy fit, Wall Street threw its full support behind the bill. What the CEOs know and what most people don't understand is that Wall Street loves regulation—regulation may have costs, but it also serves and protects the rich and powerful, who have the means to mold the regulatory system as they see fit.

The trade-off for all this regulation is, of course, government protection, which is what makes the crony capitalism of the modern banking business really work. Despite assurance that the government would step in and "wind down" banks that took too much risk and were losing too much money to survive, implicit in just about every facet of the bill was that "too big to fail"—the notion that Citigroup, Bank of America, Goldman Sachs, JPMorgan, and Morgan Stanley are so large and intertwined in the global economy that they need to be monitored and propped up no matter how much money they lose—was here to stay.

Not only are the banks staying, but so are some of their worst managers. "Believe it or not, Vikram will survive," was the assessment of Larry Fink one afternoon as he sat in San Pietro eating lunch and for a change not having to defend his support of the president. The concept of "too big to fail" has benefited every major bank, but none more than Citigroup and its ineffectual CEO, Vikram Pandit.

After being named CEO of Citi in early 2008, Pandit did little more than steer a sinking ship—one burdened by hundreds of billions of dollars' worth of toxic debt and loans—right into the ground, defying calls to sell pieces of his sprawling, ill-conceived financial empire.

"I had nothing to do with it," remarked Robert Rubin when asked whether he used his connections in Washington to secure the mother of all bailouts for the firm he had helped create. Rubin made the statement to me nearly a year later and just weeks before he resigned in disgrace from Citigroup in early 2009, but people close to the firm say his influence was never far away when Citigroup was involved.

Rubin, these people say, played an advisory role in the bailout plan and continued to advise Pandit as he sought to remain in the CEO position for the rest of the year. If Rubin was to somehow preserve even a small part of his corporate legacy, he would have to preserve Pandit, whom he had helped make CEO in the first place. While investors saw a worthless CEO at the helm, Rubin argued that Pandit had made the most of a bad situation, and that's what he argued to policy makers in Washington, according to people close to the matter, when the bank's masters in the Obama White House had to decide if Pandit was up to the job.

Robert Rubin's reputation may have been toxic on Wall Street, but in Washington it continued to carry weight, particularly with his fellow travelers Geithner and Summers, who became Pandit's advocates to remain in the job even over the objections of other banking regulators, such as FDIC chief Sheila Bair.

Pandit helped his own cause through a combination of luck (as it turned out, not a lot of people on the Street really wanted the job), his vow to finally begin to unload pieces of Citigroup's massive bureaucracy (after initially resisting, Pandit sold Citi's brokerage unit to Morgan Stanley to help cover some of the losses that had accrued under his watch), and some skill at the art of sucking up to the Obama administration. Indeed, through 2009 and 2010, the Obama administration had no better ally in corporate America than Vikram Pandit, though GE CEO Jeffrey Immelt, whose company was making a killing off Obama's so-called stimulus infrastructure spending and green initiatives, was a close second.

Immelt, who friends say was absolutely giddy at the prospect of all those government checks going to GE, was now walking around company headquarters saying how "we're all Democrats now." Pandit did one better. He simply chose to endorse every so-called banking reform advocated by the Obama White House, from caps on executive pay to the Dodd bill, proclaiming that the president could "count on me and the entire Citi organization" to support the new banking law no matter how ugly the process or the final product turned out to be.

As Dimon and Blankfein paid lip service to the need for financial reform, Pandit became the bill's Wall Street cheerleader, something that earned him the enmity of just about every CEO on Wall Street. "Citi supports prudent and effective reform of the financial regulatory system," he told a congressional subcommittee in one of the most obvious suck-ups in modern American finance.

By now the Wall Street CEOs understood that it was their job during these hearings to bend over, take it in the rear, and get out of town as soon as possible. John Mack used to laugh that it had become an art form for him to keep his mouth shut and contain his anger and emotion while being grilled by lawmakers who didn't know a market maker from a ham sandwich. Even the notoriously hotheaded Jamie Dimon managed to play it cool when he gave testimony about the banking crisis.

But Pandit just didn't take his grilling—he all but begged for more. Jamie Dimon's JPMorgan took tens of billions of dollars in bailout money, but he continued to fly on the corporate jet and refused to apologize about it even when he was meeting President Obama. It was the cost of doing business, bailout or no bailout, Dimon told his senior staff. Pandit, on the other hand, apologized for using a corporate jet when asked about it by Congress. Not only did he "get the new reality," which meant no more company jets, he meekly explained, he vowed to take nothing more than $1 in compensation until he returned Citi to profitability.

After this performance, several of his competitors likened his groveling to the scene in the movie *Animal House* when the inductees to the Omega frat shouted, "Thank you sir, may I have another?" as they were being spanked during a bizarre hazing ritual.

For all of that, Vikram Pandit, the worst CEO in banking, survived and, as this book goes to press, is likely to remain Citi's CEO for the foreseeable future.

Meanwhile, people who know him say being bailed out and nearly dethroned as the bank toppled hasn't chastened Pandit. Citigroup's stock continues to hover below $5 a share. Though the bank is profitable, it's hardly the global powerhouse it was during its glory days earlier in the decade. Even so, Pandit clings to the notion that Citi will return to its precrisis glory of cranking out an annual profit of around $20 billion. And in the meantime, he never misses an opportunity to prostrate himself before Congress or plead with Geithner and his masters at the Obama White House about how great things are at his lumbering giant of a bank if only it is given a chance, and to beg them to please get his one nemesis, FDIC chief Sheila Bair, off his back.

Rubin may have influenced Geithner and Summers to support Pandit, and the firm's return to profitability (it earned $4.4 billion during the first quarter of 2010), seem to have given him job security. But to this day, FDIC chief Sheila Bair cannot bring herself to accept Pandit as someone who can adequately lead Citigroup, with its massive size and still billions of dollars in problematic loans and investments, completely back to health. More than any other bank, Citigroup's recent good fortunes, Bair has told people, were the function not of good management but mainly of a combination of factors beyond its control, such as record-low interest and the bailout mechanisms created during Bush's last term and extended under Obama.

Pandit never sold much of the vast and unwieldy pieces of the Citigroup empire that he promised; thus he still manages a huge mess of a bank. What happens once the Fed begins raising interest rates and Citigroup's traders can't make up for losses on loans and other investments? What happens if the economy, which based on GDP is slowly improving but based on unemployment of nearly 10 percent is struggling, takes a

dramatic turn for the worse and falls once again into recession, as some
economists (including Alan Greenspan) began predicting in mid-2010?

The FDIC, after all, is ultimately responsible to cover all those deposits at Citi, some $800 billion worth, if it faces another crippling crisis
where out-of-work consumers fail to repay their loans and the bank once
again faces steep losses.

Vikram Pandit, no matter how many times Bob Rubin comes to his
defense, simply isn't up to the task, Bair believes.

Maybe worse, Bair has never forgiven Pandit for a conversation the
two had back in 2008, at the height of the banking crisis, when Citigroup
believed it had managed to bail itself out by joining forces with Wachovia,
a troubled but deposit-rich bank headed by former Goldman vice chairman and Bush administration Treasury official Bob Steel. To make the deal
work, the federal government said it would guarantee some of the losses
on Wachovia's holdings of toxic loans and other securities, and Citigroup
would benefit from a cash cushion of tens of billions of dollars in customer
deposits that it could borrow from in a pinch.

Without telling Pandit, Bair gave the green light for another bank to
step in and buy Wachovia. That bank was Wells Fargo, which not only
outbid Citigroup for Wachovia but agreed to do the deal without government assistance.

Pandit was woken up in the middle of the night with the news, just
days before his deal with Wachovia was supposed to become official. One
person with knowledge of his reaction described it as "bat shit," in his
subsequent conversations both with Steel and with Bair.

Inside Morgan Stanley, Pandit's old firm, the rumor began to spread
that Pandit had lost his temper with Bair in an expletive-laced conversation,
something Bair won't deny (Pandit described it as "testy"). Whatever was
said, throughout 2009 and into 2010, Bair went on the offensive against
Pandit, forcing him to remove his CFO and placing his own job in jeopardy
were it not for his support from Geithner and Summers.

As I pointed out earlier, Pandit may not be a talented CEO, but he is lucky; Bair's power in regulatory circles has receded of late (she's expected to step down at the FDIC after the end of the year), and he knows how to grovel. Pandit continues to speak openly about the need to pass financial reform and how much progress his masters in the Obama White House and in Congress have made in crafting legislation that will protect the financial system.

But no amount of kissing up to Congress and bowing to the Obama economic team can change the fact that Pandit's Citigroup is still a monumental mess—too big and lumbering to make the type of money he's promising and, of course, too worrisome for the regulators just to let die.

"Tom, you care about your relationship with Rahm Emanuel more than you care about Morgan Stanley!" That was the analysis of an increasingly desperate Michael Paese, a lobbyist at Goldman Sachs who was imploring Tom Nides to use his considerable clout with the White House to get the president and the Democrats to ratchet back the class warfare and some of the more onerous aspects of the financial reform package as it neared completion in the spring of 2010.

The financial reform legislation as it came together in mid-July 2010 was a Rube Goldberg contraption containing more than two thousand pages of amendments and rules that the senior executives at the top banks had a hard time figuring out.

One of the great things about Wall Street is that even as it said it accepted the broad outlines of financial reform, it continued to fight over the very important details—in Goldman's case whittling down the Volcker rule as much as possible, particularly its provisions on prop trading, and, it hoped, receiving a respite from the political attacks, which had hit Goldman and Blankfein harder than anywhere else.

These days Paese, a former top aide to House Financial Services Committee chairman Barney Frank, was on speed dial from Blankfein, who wanted constant updates on his efforts and the politics surrounding the firm's image problems, and how that was shaping the new reform legislation. Paese, who has long experience working on Wall Street and in government positions that influence Wall Street, was particularly valuable to Goldman because of his ties to Frank, who was now emerging as the principal coauthor of the banking bill, along with Chris Dodd.

But Paese was increasingly powerless, as was the rest of the Street, in getting the people he had most power with—the ruling Democrats—to back off not only financial reform's harshest rules but also the anti–Wall Street talking points, which almost always began with some Goldman bashing.

What was particularly hard for Paese, Blankfein, and the rest of Goldman's senior management to accept was how Goldman was being used by the administration. Every political attack on the firm and the numerous investigations into its business practices had a single objective: to squeeze not just Goldman but also the rest of the Street into submission and force it to accept financial reform's most onerous provisions.

Paese had reported back to Blankfein that he suspected Dodd was being prodded by the president's political advisers to keep the Volcker rule in place, though it was unclear whether it would make the final cut. As for the name-calling, the only thing he could do was lobby against it or convince people like Nides, who had a direct pipeline to people like Rahm Emanuel, to lobby against it.

That's what he was doing today.

Nides said he would do all he could, and not just because someone at Goldman was telling him to do so. He was under fire from his boss as well to do something to turn down the volume of the attacks. John Mack had retired as CEO of Morgan Stanley effective January 1, 2010, turning over the top job to his number two, James Gorman. He was still chairman of the firm and still powerful. He traveled the world helping Morgan win investment-banking deals, and he spent a lot of time talking to people in Washington.

Mack earned kudos from people like Warren Buffett for saying things that most Wall Street executives wouldn't: that the pay packages of the past decade (which he had benefited from) were too high and that Wall Street was addicted to risk taking. In fact, Mack had gone without a bonus for the past three years of the financial crisis and while Blankfein had been trying to convince the world that Goldman hadn't been bailed out, Mack had been thanking the taxpayers for the bailout. And in that context, he couldn't fathom taking a bonus this year.

And yet, as Mack was finding out, it wasn't enough. "People just fucking hate us," Mack told Nides, before reminding Nides that the public's hatred of Wall Street was growing because "your friends are fucking us," meaning his Democratic Party pals, who seemed to relish holding Wall Street responsible for everything from the financial collapse to the influenza epidemic at the turn of the century.

Mack and Nides had been friends for twenty years, and yet if there was anything that created a small degree of tension in their relationship it was, first, that Nides began to immediately kiss up to Mack's replacement, Gorman—"I'm amazed how fast Nides had his head up James Gorman's ass when he took my job," Mack remarked—and second was the notion that somehow Nides's friend, the man whom Nides had implored Mack to jump party lines and support, President Obama, was "fucking" Wall Street and Morgan in particular. The firm wasn't in Goldman's league in terms of lopsided support of Obama in campaign contributions, but Mack had been one of the first of the CEOs who supported Bush to throw his support to the Democrats back in 2007, initially to Hillary Clinton and then to Obama.

And he didn't just say a couple of nice things about the Democratic agenda on the PBS television show hosted by his friend Charlie Rose. Mack opened up the firm to Obama fund-raisers—not an easy thing to do at white-shoe Morgan Stanley, which had often leaned Republican. He went before Congress, apologized for the firm's risk-taking activities, spoke out against executive pay, and kept his mouth shut (not easy for Mack, given his own rep for having a sharp temper) when he was being called a fat cat.

Nides initially corrected Mack—he wasn't friends with the president. Rather, he was friends with the president's chief of staff, Rahm Emanuel, whom he spoke to constantly on this very subject. He then reminded Mack of Emanuel's response: They say they're the only ones standing between us and the angry mob of pitchfork-carrying Tea Partiers.

Mack's own response, I am told, went something like this: With friends like these, who needs enemies?

That's what Blankfein was saying as he was sitting in his New York office when word came from his attorneys that the case Goldman had thought it could convince the SEC not to bring had been brought.

Without even a warning, the SEC had filed civil fraud charges against Goldman for, on behalf of a client, packaging a toxic security derived from a mortgage bond, shorting it (betting the security would decline), and then selling the same investment to other unsuspecting clients. The announcement sent Goldman's stock down more than 12 percent—wiping $12 billion out of the firm's market value. By the end of the day, the Dow Jones Industrial Average had lost 125 points on trader speculation that the case against Goldman was just the beginning of a larger assault on the Street to hold the bailed-out firms accountable for the financial meltdown of 2008.

On its face, the case itself seemed like a microcosm of why the public so hates Wall Street: greedy billionaires screwing each other and then screwing themselves so much that they needed to be rescued by the average taxpayer. Specifically, Goldman, the SEC said, had caused investors to lose as much as $1 billion by failing to disclose that the bonds it was selling were constructed in such a way as to be doomed to fail, and that failure was one of the contributing factors in the entire banking system meltdown.

Back in late 2006, the now-famous short seller John Paulson came to Goldman with an idea: to create an investment (a collateralized debt obligation, or CDO, that would come to be named Abacus) that would help him make money if housing prices fell, as he predicted. The rest of the Street, still drinking the Kool-Aid and believing that housing prices would never fall, either didn't grasp the potential or saw ethical conflicts that made them shy away.

In fact, of all the firms Paulson approached, it would be the one with the reputation for being maybe the most ethically challenged player on the Street, Bear Stearns, ironically enough, that said no for ethical reasons, as

Greg Zuckerman describes in his book *The Greatest Trade Ever:* "[Bear Stearns] worried that Paulson would want especially ugly mortgages for the CDOs, like a bettor asking a football owner to bench a star quarterback to improve the odds of his wager against the team." Bear's Scott Eichel would tell Zuckerman, "It didn't pass our ethics standards; it was a reputation issue, and it didn't pass our moral compass."

But Goldman's moral compass pointed in only one direction: toward cash. In typical Goldman fashion it (correctly) smelled a huge payday: Goldman was the only large Wall Street firm to short all those esoteric housing bonds that would doom the rest of the Street, which hoarded them on their balance sheets. More than that, Goldman began peddling the flip side of Paulson's investment to its clients, telling them to buy the security because it would rise in value.

Of course, it didn't, and Paulson became a billionaire several times over and Goldman made a mint in 2007. Blankfein walked away with a paycheck of nearly $70 million.

But now Blankfein was paying the price. As the charges hit the wire services and the television screens, Goldman executives could hardly believe what was happening. Work basically stopped as bankers and traders turned up the volume on their television sets to hear the breakdown of the charges. Goldman, meanwhile, ordered extra security in and around the firm's Lower Manhattan headquarters to protect employees from possible angry protests.

The worst thing about the day, as far as Blankfein was concerned, was that he knew that in the past, Goldman's lawyers would have found a winning argument. The one they were using, of course, wasn't half bad. It was Goldman's contention that it didn't matter whether or not Paulson had helped pick the investments going into the bond—he couldn't be sure of their true toxicity, as no one was. Remember, this was taking place in late 2006 and early 2007. The financial crisis hadn't yet begun, and many smart people believed the housing market would continue to flourish.

In selling the bonds, Goldman argued, the firm had been dealing with smart people who knew all the risks (the types of mortgages involved had been disclosed in the bond's lengthy offering document), even if Goldman hadn't told them a savvy short seller had been involved in creating the secutiy.

With the white-shoe law firm Sullivan & Cromwell putting all that together, the SEC would have caved and moved on to its usual fare of backlogged cases against small penny-stock operators while allowing the big Wall Street firms to do what they pleased.

But as Lloyd Blankfein and the rest of the Street were discovering, times were changing. The public wanted Wall Street blood, and Goldman, the most hated firm on the Street, was as good a target as the SEC could get for another reason as well. It was hardly a coincidence that the day the SEC announced its Goldman case, Obama held a news conference stating emphatically the need to reform sleazy Wall Street practices by pushing the still-formulating Dodd financial reform bill through Congress, where just about every Republican in the House and the Senate was opposed to much of what the reform package offered, largely on the grounds that for the sound and fury, it accomplished very little. The banks still had a sponsor in Big Government and that protection meant the mindless risk taking that led to the financial crisis would return someday.

That didn't stop Obama from publicly pushing the legislation. In fact, he seemed to be growing bolder by the day in his insistence that the reforms were necessary and in his Wall Street attacks, even if his poll numbers didn't rebound. It seemed that the mild-mannered politician who had said all the right things to his buddies on Wall Street during the campaign, and benefited from their campaign contributions, had gone back to his roots as an aggressive community organizer, a Robin Hood looking to take from the rich so he could spread the wealth to everyone else.

But a careful examination of Obama's deeds, rather than his words, shows just how much Wall Street has gained from his brand of economics. Despite turbulent markets, JPMorgan reported nearly $5 billion in second-quarter profits in 2010, Bank of America more than $3 billion, while Goldman earned $613 million, but that takes into account onetime charges for a regulatory settlement and changes in UK tax law. Without those charges Goldman would have earned closer to $2 billion, even as it accumulated $9 billion for 2010 bonuses.

Putting aside the nasty names and the Volcker rule, the list of benefits the Street has received from Obama are amazing: guarantees on firms' debt; active participation of the government in the bond markets, propping up the prices of debt still held on the firms' books; and, of course, the continuation of "too big to fail."

For all the bankers' obsession over the name-calling and worries about the pending Dodd bill a key point was lost on everyone. The whole reason financial reform was even discussed was because banks were making so much money at a time when average people were out of work. While Obama's plans to save the banks were doing wonders, his plans to revive the economy weren't. The Main Street employment numbers, as bad as they are, like many government statistics, were also inaccurate (especially when the government in power has an incentive to misrepresent them). For example, the spring 2010 unemployment numbers are distorted by the creation of countless temporary jobs for the 2010 census. Just how many is impossible to say, as the *New York Post* discovered: The Census Bureau has been "hiring" and "firing" the same workers many times over; each time a given worker is "rehired," it counts as another job in the employment numbers. Meanwhile, for Wall Street there's a hiring binge as the firms seek out experienced bankers, traders, and brokers. The cheap money and the bank bailouts have fueled the stock market to remain well above the ten thousand barrier as measured by the Dow through the first half of 2010. Goldman, for all the bile directed its way, is quietly putting aside enough money to match or possibly surpass its titanic 2009 bonus pool. Blankfein, Dimon, and their counterparts really are crying all the way to the bank, as Obama uses his old friends on the Street as a foil to pass his agenda and keep the Republicans from gaining control of the House and the Senate. Hollywood couldn't have written a better script.

"They're going to keep calling us names all through the midterms, but why should we care?" a senior executive at JPMorgan Chase advised Dimon one afternoon after being briefed by his sources in Washington about how the White House is expected to play the financial reform bill as a necessary check on Wall Street.

Jamie Dimon is an imposing man—he's about six feet tall and broad shouldered, and to complement his ruggedly handsome features he has what's best described a boxer's nose. He works long hours, tries to hit the gym several days a week, and demands the same from his senior management team.

He has a temper that matches his physique. While at Citigroup years ago, Dimon once almost punched out another senior executive at a company party, a prelude to his ultimate dismissal. He's known as a "screamer," in part because of his legendary shouting matches with his old boss Sandy Weill while Jamie was still a young executive at Citigroup. "I did plenty of things wrong while I was at Citigroup," he would later concede.

Since then, Dimon has learned to control his temper, though at times it can't be contained. This was one of those times.

"This is complete bullshit!" he screamed as he received the latest report coming from Washington from a slightly frightened senior aide who had watched Dimon grow increasingly incensed over the course of 2010.

JPMorgan was the premier bank in America (some would say the world) and Dimon the premier CEO in the banking business. It was that reputation that had made him so valuable to Obama early on and paved the way for his White House visits and pull inside the administration and with key members of Congress.

Yet for all his accolades and triumphs, by the late spring of 2010, Dimon was powerless to stop financial reform's most draconian measures, and even worse, to stop his old friends in the Democratic Party from using Wall Street as a punching bag to ram this half-assed bill through Congress.

It is, of course, hard to feel even an ounce of sorrow for Dimon; for all his skill and talent as a banker, it was also his talent for lobbying Big Government that allowed JPMorgan to survive and thrive during the financial crisis. Since then, Dimon has positioned himself as a Wall Street savior—the man who came to the rescue of Bear Stearns at the beginning of the financial melt-down and then guided his own bank successfully through the rough waters of the crisis as the rest of Wall Street teetered on the brink of destruction.

According to his PR team, it was really Dimon who was doing God's work, though unlike Blankfein, both the bank's flacks and Dimon himself were smart enough not to say such a thing in public—even if the PR people constantly reminded reporters that the government had asked JPMorgan to buy the financially impaired Bear Stearns, and that in doing so, the firm "took one for the good of the country," as a spokeswoman told me.

Amid such mythmaking (from one of the savviest PR teams in corporate America, no less) are some inconvenient facts. Dimon, of course, is a great CEO and a tough manager and understands the downside of risk better than any of his peers. But through the bulk of the financial crisis and well into 2010, very few newspaper stories focused on the fact that, despite admirably navigating through the financial crisis, JPMorgan still held billions of dollars in problematic loans on its books or that Dimon had readily accepted federal bailout money during the height of the implosion because he, like the rest of the world, knew the future was uncertain.

Then there was JPMorgan's purchase of Bear Stearns, the first firm to implode as the collapse began in March 2008. Dimon has told people he agreed to buy Bear at least in part out of patriotic duty. His advisers contend the purchase was costly, and if they had to do it again, Dimon would walk away, let the firm collapse, and buy it in bankruptcy court for next to nothing.

Maybe so, yet dig deeper into the deal and you'll quickly notice that there wasn't much charity involved in JPMorgan's bailout of the troubled Wall Street trading house. The charity, if there was any, came from the American taxpayer. The feds arranged the deal, which cost JPMorgan next to nothing: a paltry $10 a share for a major firm (it was initially just $2, but Dimon was forced to up his bid amid outrage from existing shareholders), and the government or, to be more precise, the U.S. taxpayer, picked up nearly all the losses from Bear's holdings of toxic debt.

In other words, a Bear Stearns with one of the best trading and clearing businesses on Wall Street and mostly rid of its toxic assets was virtually given to JPMorgan free of charge.

As pointed out earlier, Dimon was prohibited from officially declaring Obama his favorite candidate, but he directed others, such as the firm's CFO, to carry out the dirty work of fund-raising for Obama. Meanwhile, on the New York Fed board Dimon met Tim Geithner, then the president of the New York office, and their relationship blossomed as Geithner became Obama's Treasury secretary.

Combine strong ties with Geithner, a friendship with Rahm Emanuel, connections to Obama's inner circle from Chicago, and fund-raising for the president, and Dimon became a fixture in the Obama White House for most of the president's first year in office, and JPMorgan did very well during those months. In addition to the lax accounting rules on toxic assets, the Treasury continued to guarantee JPMorgan's long-term debt, giving the bank access to cheap borrowing. Other programs allowed the bank, with the rest of Wall Street, to make a bundle trading bonds to more than make up for any losses on loans given to people unemployed as Obama fiddled with health care and allowed unemployment to remain at an alarming 9.7 percent for most of 2009 and into 2010.

Now, for all the apocalyptic talk about financial reform (which would cut profits on the high end by 15 percent, according to one estimate), JPMorgan and the rest of the Street knew they would survive with most of their immense wealth intact as soon as they figured out how to game the new system, as they had done in the past. "Once we figure this thing out," said a senior JPMorgan executive, "it's going to be a wash. Mark my words."

So why, then, was Dimon so pissed off? Because he not only had to figure out how to adapt to the new regulatory environment, but he also had to figure out how to deal with the new political landscape.

"I don't want to lose my home," screeched a woman seated in the audience as JPMorgan began its 2010 annual meeting at JPMorgan's New York headquarters. The prior year, it had been a love fest, with people thanking Dimon for a job well done and looking to shake hands with the man the *New York Times* described as Obama's favorite banker.

But this time the scene was very different. Security guards roamed the room, which was packed with several hundred people, many of them angry homeowners demanding modifications to mortgages they could no longer afford.

Obamanomics, at least in Dimon's mind, wasn't supposed to be like this. Many of the people in the room were demanding handouts—free mortgages—as if they didn't have any responsibility to figure out if they could afford their homes or not. Obama and the class warriors in Congress looking for cheap political points were now saying they didn't—after all, if the banks could be bailed out, why shouldn't average folk?

Dimon, dressed in his designer suit, was inwardly seething as a group of people representing something called the Neighborhood Assistance Corporation of America demanded what sounded like reparations from his bank because they had taken out loans they couldn't afford.

"When it comes to homeowners, we have to do it one by one," he responded, calmly but coolly. "Do they live there? Can they afford to pay it? Is it the right thing to do? We have experts here. They will go through your situation—what can and can't be done—directly, openly, and honestly."

Dimon also addressed his concerns about financial reform. The company had spent $8 million in the last few years on legal and lobbying fees, he said, to push back on parts of the bill he thought were bad for business. During the meeting it also became clear that the attacks on the banking industry had begun to tarnish Dimon's once-gold-plated reputation. A move by one large investor, in fact one of the world's largest, the California Public Employees' Retirement System, which manages close to $200 billion in assets, to split his job and force the bank to retain a separate chairman was voted down, but not by a wide margin.

Then, adding insult to injury, Evelyn Y. Davis, an octogenarian shareholder activist known to ask CEOs uncomfortably goofy questions (I remember her once asking Dow Jones chairman Peter Kann about his love life) actually asked Dimon a pretty good one: "Are you still the president's favorite banker?"

Dimon replied without missing a beat, "I heard he has a new one."

That new one was Brian Moynihan, the new CEO of Bank of America. Moynihan had just taken over for the ousted Ken Lewis, but he hadn't wasted much time kissing up to his new masters in Washington. After being named CEO in December 2009, he had made it to the White House about six times in the next six months (that's about six more times than Dimon or any other CEO of a major bank had visited during 2010). While Dimon had begun to openly question the president and other politicians about their Wall Street bashing, not to mention aspects of the financial reform legislation (he truly hated the consumer protection agency that seemed to be aimed directly at consumer banks like his), Moynihan had remained noticeably silent, though when he did speak, he actually came out in favor of the consumer agency, despite having a business that was nearly identical to JPMorgan's.

Obama appeared so smitten with his new Wall Street friend that it was Moynihan, not Dimon, who attended the second state dinner of Obama's presidency. Since then, Moynihan has had private dinners and meetings with various administration officials.

Regardless of Moynihan's motives, Bank of America, Dimon reasoned, needed all the help it could get. The bank had been bailed out once, nearly nationalized during the financial crisis over losses in its loan portfolio, not to mention its purchase of Merrill Lynch, which was losing tens of billions of dollars. Its longtime CEO, Ken Lewis, had been ousted because of the ill-fated Merrill purchase, and Moynihan had been chosen as his replacement after a near civil war broke out on BofA's board, with a contingent favoring Moynihan (who had come to BofA after its purchase of Boston-based Fleet Bank) and one favoring a Charlotte-based executive named Greg Curl.

But more than that, what contributed to Dimon's growing anger at Obama, at the entire political atmosphere, was the realization that the whole exercise of "financial reform" was really a colossal waste of time.

Publicly, Dimon would say he agreed with the vast majority of what was being shoveled into the bill despite the haphazard fashion in which many of its components, like Blanche Lincoln's derivatives amendment or Barney Frank's proposed bank tax, seemingly came and went by the day.

But privately Dimon had his doubts, not just about the process but with what was looking like the end product. The consensus, not just at JPMorgan among Dimon's senior staff but across Wall Street, was beginning to emerge that the legislation in its near-final form really accomplished little toward its primary objective—ensuring that another meltdown wouldn't occur somewhere down the road.

To be sure, what was shaping up as "financial reform" was an unprecedented meddling in the financial markets. The risk committees, the consumer protection agency, and the checks and balances meant bureaucrats would have more say in how capital was allocated than at any time in this nation's history. In effect, the same bureaucrats who hadn't seen any of the most recent market collapses coming, including the big one in 2008, would be determining which businesses got loans and which didn't.

But something more fundamental irked Dimon, I am told. As much as he loved to mine Big Government for special favors, the notion that stupidity should be rewarded with a bailout bothered him a lot more than the consumer protection agency ever could. A few months earlier Dimon had given a speech in which he called the nanny state's approach to Wall Street, also known as "too big to fail," "ethically bankrupt" because it allowed the risk takers to avoid consequences and rewarded those, like Citigroup, that screwed up. Even worse, these policies lumped JPMorgan into the same class as Citigroup.

"The term too big to fail must be excised from our vocabulary," Dimon had written in a *Washington Post* op-ed. Dimon had later been assured it would be, by just about every top regulator who walked through JPMorgan's door.

Far from being excised, now the nanny state protection of loser banks was growing, Dimon was told after he received a briefing about the bill. The FDIC was gaining the authority to "wind down" or take over troubled banks before they spread Lehman-like contagion. Sheila Bair, the FDIC chief, described the new oversight as a "powerful" weapon that would prevent banks from getting too big. Dimon saw it as just the opposite: the invisible hand of government once again coming to the rescue of idiots like the guys who ran Citi into the ground.

The more he thought about the bill and the name-calling that surrounded the debate over its dubious merits, the more Dimon seethed. Wall Street had been his whole life (his dad had been a stock broker for Sandy Weill, which had led to Dimon getting an internship and eventually becoming Weill's right hand as he built the now-faltering banking empire known as Citigroup), and for all his liberal bluster and support of Big Government over the years, Dimon was also a businessman, and what he saw happening to the banks, not to mention the economy, was not good for anyone's business.

When I mentioned to Dimon's aides that their boss was soured on the president, they reminded me how much the two really got along. "I know Obama likes Jamie, and Jamie likes the president," a spokesman for JPMorgan said. But friends of Dimon say the JPMorgan CEO had his doubts not about the president as a person but about his approach to the economy. Never before had so much money been printed for so little gain: a stimulus package that failed to stimulate the economy; near-zero interest rates; an unimaginable amount of spending; takeovers of the automobile industry; and GDP barely improved, while unemployment grew to enormous highs.

Dimon, like Fink, believed he was supporting moderation when he put all his bank's resources behind Obama, and like Fink he now felt betrayed, people who know him tell me. Even worse, when it came to the business he worked in, Obama and the Democratic political elite he had supported really didn't distinguish between the firms that "did it right," as he would tell his staff, and those that didn't. It was one thing for Blankfein to be branded a greedy bastard—in Dimon's mind Goldman is nothing short of a greed machine that screwed its clients for years with deals like Abacus and many others.

When Blankfein went before Congress to defend his firm's actions,

Dimon was unconvinced by his excuse. "What they did was wrong, plain and simple," he said.

And yet JPMorgan had become, at least in the rhetoric of the White House and the Democratic Party, a kinder, gentler version of the vampire squid.

That's when Dimon did something that once would have seemed unthinkable: He appeared to take the advice offered to him when he had met with House minority leader John Boehner just a few months earlier to complain about the direction of financial reform, and he and his firm began to support Republicans.

News spread through JPMorgan about fund-raisers being held for Republican candidates. Old friends like New York representative Carolyn Maloney, who represents the Upper East Side of Manhattan, and senators Chuck Schumer and Kirsten Gillibrand of New York felt the chill immediately in terms of a drastic reduction in Wall Street campaign contributions. The firm that had bent over backward for the Democrats in 2008 (62 percent of all JPMorgan campaign money had gone to the Democrats) was now doing the same for the Republicans, plowing just as much money into the campaigns of Republicans running for office as they did for Democrats during the first half of 2010, according campaign records.

Dimon began adding up in his head everything he had done for the administration: The political donations from JPMorgan had helped Obama get elected. His sage advice during the past year had helped an economically inexperienced president understand the markets. Emanuel had even called Dimon and asked him to call key senators and press them to approve Fed chairman Ben Bernanke's reappointment (and his potentially inflationary, albeit Wall Street friendly, policy of keeping interest rates near 0 percent), which he did.

Dimon had already directed his senior staff to begin spreading the wealth around—he may be a lifelong liberal Democrat, but he wasn't going to reward bad behavior—and he wasn't alone. Wall Street was now hedging not just its market bets but also its political bet on Obama and his agenda. By placing all their bets on Obama and his fellow travelers in

Congress, they had helped elect the most liberal governing bodies in years, without a bipartisan check. To be sure, Big Government brought the banks enormous profits, but it had also brought them an uncertain future as banker bashing became the new politics of the Left. Now they began to hedge their bets in an unprecedented fashion. Contributions to key Democratic congressional committees fell by 65 percent. Dimon himself gave nothing to the committees, while making a $2,000 contribution to a Republican congressman. Blankfein, a longtime Democrat, went further: He called for a moratorium on all contributions from the firm until financial reform had been completed. "We don't want to be seen influencing the decision," a firm spokesman said. But people inside the firm say the money was cut off to make a bigger point that the firm was tired of the attacks.

Another practical reason for the hedge was the changing political environment. With unemployment remaining abnormally high, by the late spring of 2010 political analysts like the prescient Charlie Cook and pollster Doug Schoen even began to predict the possibility of a Republican takeover of the House and Senate.

Obama's own poll numbers began to fall, meaning that the class-warfare attacks were not only not working, they were screwing both him and his party out of much-needed campaign cash. But instead of making up with their former contributors, the Democrats were only emboldened to ratchet up their Wall Street attacks. Barney Frank, for years a solid Wall Street vote in Congress despite his social liberalism, had joined the anti–Wall Street parade by introducing a bank tax to pay for the financial regulations few on Wall Street believed would ever work.

On Wall Street, the word back from the administration was that Geithner, Summers, and even Volcker were opposed to the initial amendment proposed by Arkansas Democrat Blanche Lincoln to force banks to spin out their derivatives businesses, even if she used the clause to successfully remind voters back home that she was keeping tabs on the greedy bankers in New York and won a tough primary challenge.

The absurdity of the measure, as the Wall Street firms and their lobbyists tried to point out, was that it would impact far more than just the big Wall Street firms. Of course, everyone on Wall Street had used derivatives to gamble; credit-default swaps—those insurance policies on corporate debt—were traded incessantly during the financial crisis. Short sellers of bank stocks would buy them to panic investors into selling their shares of bank stocks; when investors saw a spike in CDS prices on Wall Street banks, they would sell their shares and the short seller would walk away with a handsome profit through a form of market manipulation.

But the derivatives trading that the financial reform bill came down so hard on wasn't originally developed as a trading tool for financial firms. Instead, its first application was in agriculture, where contracts on the future prices of grain, hogs, and other agricultural products allowed farmers and their customers to lock in prices in the future without worrying that wild swings in the commodities markets might wipe out their profits.

Many other companies use similar financial products as well, to lock in volatile oil prices, for example, to hedge against counterparty risk (the chance that that one's opposite party in a transaction might go bankrupt or be unable to deliver), or to protect against swings in the currency markets.

But Lincoln, with her primary victory in hand and a tough general-election fight about to get under way, stubbornly stuck to her guns, and the amendment remained in the bill with a few modifications.

So the word went out during the spring of 2010, not just at JPMorgan but across Wall Street, that the banks should keep moving. Even Citigroup, run by the ever-malleable Vikram Pandit and still technically owned by the Obama administration (as this book goes to press the Treasury Department is trying to sell its stake in the bank), began holding fund-raisers for Republicans, with 63 percent of all contributions going to Republicans during the first half of the year, compared with just 47 percent for all of 2008. Goldman, after contributing to Obama by a three-to-one margin in terms of campaign cash, began to evenly split its donations.

Tom Nides's friendship with Rahm Emanuel aided Morgan Stanley in landing some plum assignments—including acting as lead adviser on the new stock issued by GM and helping the Obama administration cash out of its bailout stakes in the automaker and Citigroup. But he couldn't stop the fund-raisers held by bankers to support Republicans; 52 percent of all Morgan Stanley contributions went to Republicans, compared with just 47 percent in 2008. Moynihan may have relished his new friendship with the president, but the firm's executives didn't. Bank of America executives split their contributions in favor of Republicans 58 percent to 41 percent, campaign records through June show. This is a near complete reversal from 2008 contributions.

By the middle of 2010, the tally of contributions told the story—more than two-thirds of all Wall Street contributions were now heading to Republican candidates.

But the Republicans didn't necessarily come cheap. In a meeting with Wall Street executives, huddled in a private room at the Peninsula Hotel in Manhattan, two key Republican senators, Mitch McConnell and John Cornyn, basically repeated what Dimon had been told by House minority leader John Boehner a few months earlier: They were willing to forgive past snubs, but Wall Street would have to continue to spread the wealth if Republicans were going to have a fighting chance to reverse the massive intrusion of government into the private sector, not just on Wall Street and in banking but also in the auto industry, health care, or any industry Obama had targeted to expand his leftist agenda. In terms of financial reform, the senators' plan was to fight the most egregious antibusiness parts of the Dodd bill (they hated the too-big-to-fail aspect) and then bide their time until the midterm elections so they could add Republicans to the Senate and kill the most anti–free-market parts of the bill.

But first they needed money. Neither McConnell nor Cornyn was particularly fond of Wall Street's risk taking or the access the Street had enjoyed for so long with the current administration. They were well aware of how Wall Street had gone head over heels for the president, including support from Goldman executives who alone had donated close to $1 million to Obama during the 2008 election cycle (not counting cash given to the party and other soft-money accounts) as the firm earned $13.4 billion in 2009 thanks largely to Obama's policies. That's $13,400 in profits for every dollar the company gave directly to Obama—an extraordinary investment by any measure. Obama as president earned $400,000 in salary in 2009, while Blankfein took a massive pay cut but still walked away with around $9 million and Jamie Dimon earned about $17 million.

Not bad for a year's pay working for the nanny state.

"By my estimate," Jamie Dimon was overheard saying one afternoon in early July as the Dodd bill was starting to take its final shape, "I think we can get the costs of this thing down to 8 percent," from original cost estimates of as high as 15 percent.

After months of bluster, Dimon wasn't exactly celebrating, but he was, according to people who know him, feeling like he and his bank had dodged a major bullet as the most onerous forms of the financial reform legislation—at least in terms of how they would impact the big banks—appeared to have been watered down. Paul Volcker, who had pushed for many of the strict measures that had appeared in earlier drafts, was disappointed, giving the near-final product a B, according to the *New York Times*.

Maybe that's why JPMorgan and its CEO joined the ever-compliant Vikram Pandit in pronouncing the legislation fit for public consumption. "We support the vast majority of what's in this bill," a JPMorgan spokesman assured me in June 2010. According to senior Wall Street executives, the cranked-up lobbying effort by JPMorgan and even Goldman (whose lobbyists had managed to break through the barriers of working for a firm considered toxic), just before President Obama signed the final product into law, had yielded significant benefits.

The Volcker rule in its near-final form didn't appear so ominous after all, which is why its author was so pissed and Goldman was feeling pretty relieved. The activity it was supposed to outlaw, proprietary trading, or trading using the firm's own capital, became more a term of art than a strict definition, and given the way the rule was being written and interpreted by the lawmakers, banks would be able to engage in risky trades as long as the trades involved a customer order, as 90 percent of all trades do.

JPMorgan's nightmare of having to spin out its hedge fund and private

equity businesses, the massive Highbridge Capital and One Equity Partners, also appeared to be watered down—the new and improved Volcker
rule allowed the firm to keep its investment as long as it didn't risk more
than 3 percent of company capital in such investments, which, as Wall
Street had discovered, might not be such a bad thing. The practical effect
was that the firms could pull out their own money and still scoop up hefty
management fees, and if the funds failed, they had no responsibility to bail
out these investments, as Bear Stearns had been forced to do when its hedge
funds imploded in 2007. Even Blanche Lincoln's derivative spin-off proposal failed to live up to its billing: Firms could still buy, sell, and trade
these complex products in house without having to create and finance
separate subsidiaries. "It's not a big change for commodities. It's fine-tuning
more than a material impact," Blythe Masters, the head of JPMorgan's derivatives unit, told the *Financial Times*.

As the contents of the final bill became clearer, Dimon, a self-described
"geek" who loves to quantify every management decision in terms of how
much it will cost and how much it will help make his bank, joined Goldman in believing that the bill, as it was taking shape, had a limited downside for Wall Street and his bank in particular.

While members of Congress and the president congratulated themselves on the bill's progress (by mid-July, Dodd had corralled enough Senate
votes for passage of a very compromised bill, while Barney Frank promised
that the bill would have swift passage in the House before being signed into
law later in the month by President Obama), and Wall Street breathed a
sigh of relief, independent analysts wondered about the bill's effectiveness.

Writing in the *Daily Beast*, former SEC chief Harvey Pitt likened the
bill to the Sarbanes-Oxley Act, the accounting overhaul passed by Congress in the wake of the Enron implosion, which had accomplished very
little in ensuring that Wall Street complied with rules and regulations. "As
it was with Sarbanes-Oxley, we'll be told that our last economic crisis was
someone else's fault (but never Congress') and all we really need is a hefty
dose of legislative medicine," Pitt wrote. "And 'hefty' doesn't even begin to
describe this dose of legislation. In 2,500 pages of dense prose, we're about

to receive legislation that could better be entitled 'The Lawyers' and Lobbyists' Full Employment Act.' Which begs the question, what's the likely impact of Dodd-Frank?"

Pitt's answer: "Congress has labored mightily, and brought forth a mouse!"

Here's why: The banking system will be layered with new costs to pay for all the new mandates, which will be passed on to consumers in one way or another. Fees on ATM card transactions will be capped, but the banks are talking about doing away with free checking accounts. Banks might be forced to hold more capital in reserve to protect against market losses. If you think that's such a good thing, consider the following: Because they have to hold more money, they will make less available to small businesses to expand and begin hiring again.

The SEC's new powers to regulate part of the financial business, like the rating agencies, which ineptly placed triple-A ratings on toxic debt and hid the burgeoning bond debacle, are hardly comforting given that the agency has missed so many other scandals in the past. The Fed may be the best of all regulators, and it receives some added enforcement powers, but this is the same agency that allowed Citigroup to buy and hold all those risky bonds that led to its near bankruptcy.

More than anything, if you read though the bill's 2,500 pages, you will notice that there's not one reference to ending "too big to fail." It's hard to find a serious student of the 2008 financial collapse who doesn't believe that the notion that government will protect, albeit by regulating, the big financial institutions wasn't a major reason for the mindless risk taking by the banks that led to the meltdown. Yet if you read the bill (I haven't, but Harvey Pitt has), it is still alive and well and ready to create the next crisis as traders view the protection of government as license to take risk.

As the *Wall Street Journal* pointed out: "The Democrats who wrote the bill are selling it as new discipline for Wall Street, but Wall Street knows better. The biggest banks support the bill, and the parts they don't like they will lobby furiously to change or water down.

"Big Finance will more than hold its own with Big Government, as it always does, while politicians will have more power to exact even more campaign tribute. The losers are the overall economy, as financial costs rise, and taxpayers when the next bailout arrives."

Even worse, government will be intruding in the financial system more than ever before, based on the false premise that a lack of regulation caused the financial crisis, rather than the nanny state of bailouts over the past three decades (most notably in 2008) that let Wall Street believe consequences did not go hand in hand with risk taking.

The two lawmakers who seem most destined to take credit for the legislation, Senator Chris Dodd, the head of the Senate Banking Committee, and his counterpart in the House, the inimitable Barney Frank, are preparing, I understand, for political stardom. Dodd in particular is viewing the bill as the cornerstone of his long political career, which is now coming to an end. But both have blood on their hands, so to speak; as the *Wall Street Journal* has pointed out, just a few years ago they were "cheerleaders for" the largesse of the government housing-bubble makers, Fannie Mae and Freddie Mac. Ironically, both Fannie and Freddie, now in receivership, remained untouched in all the reforming going on in Washington. In fact, the talk from Frank was to revive them in some way as the cost of their bailout neared $1 trillion.

And what did Vikram Pandit say about financial reform?

"America—and our trading partners—need smart, common-sense government regulation to reduce the risk of more bank failures, mortgage foreclosures, lost GDP and taxpayer bailouts. Citi embraces effective, efficient and fair regulation as an essential element in continued economic stability."

In other words, on Wall Street the nanny state lives, no matter how many times the protection of the financial sector by the federal government has been at the heart of the massive risk taking that has led to thirty years of booms and busts, and ultimately the recent great recession that may not be felt on Wall Street, but continues to squeeze the lives on Main Street.

AFTERWORD:
WHERE DO WE GO FROM HERE?

"We're done with lobbying, finished," explained a senior JPMorgan Chase executive in mid-July 2010, about the firm's and the industry's position on the financial reform bill as it neared completion.

Considering where it began, as nothing more than an exercise in futility, the bill could be seen as a major accomplishment. Wall Street would be forced to give up certain lucrative businesses—namely proprietary trading, even if it represents only a modicum of the risk taken by the banks on a daily basis. There would be greater oversight of the banks, even if lack of oversight was never really a problem in the past.

At nearly the last moment, Republican senator Scott Brown, whose victory in Massachusetts caused the panic that led to the Democratic attacks against the bankers, proved to be a formidable obstacle to getting the bill passed due to his opposition of the bank tax Barney Frank had tried to insert to force Wall Street to clean up costs. But even that could be finagled.

In the end, Frank agreed to forgo the tax and take the money from the government bailout funds known as TARP and Brown agreed to drop his opposition, ensuring the legislation's passage.

Brown's opposition meant the bill missed its July 4 deadline to be signed into law by the president. What a pity. Wall Street used the holiday that celebrates the creation of our country and the vast freedoms endowed upon its people to regroup and figure out how to maneuver around the bill's various edicts, thus influencing the Big Government it has manipulated, and that manipulates them.

"There's nine buckets in this thing and we have to figure how each of those buckets works for us over the next couple of months," one senior banking executive told me on the eve of the bill's passage.

Wall Street, for all its worry over Obama's various reforms and his verbal assaults, has done pretty well under this president, so why shouldn't it expect, once all the smoke has cleared, to do well in the future? In fact, Wall Street hiring is up from last year and for all the alleged costs of the new law, banks continue to hire. Trading profits took a dip during the second quarter of 2010, but with interest rates low, Wall Street and the banks can't help but print money for the foreseeable future, no matter how many "Volcker rules" are thrown at them.

It won't be that easy for the average American worker, or for the men and women who strive to create businesses on their own to keep the American worker employed. Small businesses are the backbone of our economy; every statistic shows that they employ as much as half of the American workforce and are the engine of any recovery. And yet they have no seat at the table when the goodies of Obamanomics are doled out. Meanwhile, Jamie Dimon is so confident he can limit the downside of financial reform because his bank, one of the largest and most powerful in the world, can grease the wheels of Big Government through campaign contributions and the hiring of lobbyists.

Maybe that's why in the midst of all the talk about the increased costs of financial reform, the *New York Times* in mid-July ran a story under the headline "Wall St. Hiring in Anticipation of an Economic Recovery."

Small businesses, as I've pointed out, enjoy no similar benefits because they enjoy no such access to Big Government. As a result, they will be paying higher taxes, will be forced to dole out more benefits through the president's entitlement agenda, and will be hiring fewer people than the crony capitalists who run and ruined our financial system.

Obamanomics, as I've tried to explain in this book, may bode well for the banks, and megacorporations like GE, but it has been an unmitigated disaster for the average American worker by just about every measure available. The *New York Times* may choose to ignore the absurdity of his economic agenda, but I can't; on the eve of Independence Day, unemployment fell from 9.7 percent to 9.5 percent, but only because few Americans are looking for work and the government hired thousands of people as temporary census workers. Businesses are making money; that's a fact that the president keeps harping on as he proclaims the positive GDP numbers as proof his policies are producing results, even as he ignores the high unemployment numbers. But we don't need the president to explain pretty simple economic facts; the reasons for the massive joblessness even as the economy grows were laid out by independent analyst Peter Sidoti in a *New York Post* column I wrote in January: Businesses are hoarding cash because they are afraid of the cost of Obamanomics—the taxes, entitlements, and massive amounts of spending that they will ultimately have to pay for.

Put it all together and the hope and change Obama promised for most of the country has translated into despair and pain. If you don't believe me, talk to a construction worker who faces the unemployment line because no one wants to take a risk and build in this economy, or the single mother who can't find a job in sales because people aren't buying stuff.

Even some of Obama's friends in the media and corporate America (aside from the beaten and bruised Wall Street crowd) are beginning to publicly denounce the folly in his approach to the economy. Writing in the *Washington Post,* journalist Fareed Zakaria reiterated what Peter Sidoti had predicted months earlier when he noted that "America's 500 largest nonfinancial companies have accumulated an astonishing $1.8 trillion of cash on their balance sheets."

In other words, they're not spending money on job creation. The reason, according to Zakaria: "Most of the business leaders I spoke to had voted for Barack Obama. They still admire him. Those who had met him thought he was unusually smart. But all think he is, at his core, anti-business."

Put Jeffrey Immelt in that category. Immelt, GE's CEO, has helped his company feast off of the subsidies of Obamanomics, such as, according to the *Wall Street Journal,* "electric-grid modernization, renewable-energy

generation and health-care technology upgrades." Immelt did this in much
the same way the Wall Street CEOs did: through politics. He's a registered
Republican, but he publicly embraced Obama, sat on some of his advisory
boards, and supported his policies, such as the $800 billion stimulus pack-
age that gave GE tremendous benefits (the stimulus plan subsidized GE
clean-energy projects) but left the rest of the nation with serious debt and
rising unemployment.

Immelt touted his status as a registered Republican when he stated
publicly and infamously among his Republican friends his support of the
president, saying, "We are all Democrats now." His friends tell me that the
reasons Immelt supported Obama came down to the fact that he liked
the president on a personal level and believed he was the moderate that
he sold himself as on the campaign trail. At CNBC, where I worked for
several years, Immelt called a meeting of top talent to discuss coverage of
Obama's economic agenda and whether the heavy criticism by on-air com-
mentators (like me) was fair to the new president.

But in mid-2010, Jeffrey Immelt felt a little like Larry Fink: used and
abused by a president who talked moderate before the election and acted
leftist after. At a meeting with Italian executives in Rome, Immelt lashed out
at Obama's "overregulation" of the economy, said the business mood in the
United States was "terrible," and accused the president of being antibusiness.

When Immelt's handlers back in New York heard the remarks, they
quickly backtracked, calling the quotes, which first appeared in the *Financial Times,* as taken out of context. But people who know Immelt tell me
they pretty accurately describe his soured mood.

Why the change of heart? GE may have benefited from a few government handouts, but with the economy weak, the conglomerate's many
businesses reflect the Obama-induced economic malaise caused by putting
ideology, in the form of socializing health care and imposing higher taxes
on entrepreneurs, before the economic well-being of the American people.

More than that, it appears that Immelt (along with Ivan Seidenberg,
chairman of the Business Roundtable and CEO of Verizon) has come to

the realization that for all the benefits offered by Obamanomics to Big Business, the well-being of the country might just be more important.

As I write this, the Obama administration, worried about losing support from big business and Wall Street, has begun a charm offensive to repair the damage of months of class warfare. They are telling business leaders that the president really isn't antibusiness, that, according to a senior executive at one major New York City–based company, he believes the business community "is really part of the solution, not the problem."

As absurd as all of that might sound to the average reader who knows just a little about what this president stands for, I believe the charm offensive will work. Because in the end, Jamie Dimon, Jeff Immelt, and the rest of the big-business titans will come to realize that the benefits of being bought and paid for far outweigh those of opposing the system that has served these so-called capitalists so well over the years.

One indication of its effectiveness came on the eve of the Senate's passage of financial reform, when the SEC announced that it had settled its high-profile case against Goldman Sachs.

Goldman executives had been convinced that the SEC had brought the case to showcase allegations of Wall Street sleaze in order to drum up public support for financial reform, and that once the reform bill was passed the commission would back down and settle for a relative pittance.

They were right. The SEC's fine was a modest $550 million; to put that into context, it's far less than the market value Goldman gained when its stock soared on news of the deal. Goldman, meanwhile, had to neither admit nor deny wrongdoing (it was, however, forced to admit that it could have done a better job disclosing the bad stuff about the transaction to its clients) nor settle more serious securities fraud charges. Instead, the charge levied by the SEC was brought down several notches to "negligence."

Moreover, CEO Lloyd Blankfein, whose job was thought to be on the line when the case was first filed, is safe, at least for the moment.

As one Wall Street executive told me, "all those campaign contributions Goldman made to Obama finally paid off."

So what happens now? I hope I've convinced you that the deep and twisted ties between Wall Street and Washington have, over the last few decades, resulted in a financial system that, in the ultimate irony, is among the least free markets in America today—a banking system where unbelievable amounts of risk are taken, often by people barely out of college, in the comforting knowledge that the U.S. government has always been there in the past and will be again.

I also hope I've convinced you that this deep and almost unholy bond between America's most powerful industry and its center of government power has reached a level we've never seen before in the election and subsequent presidency of Barack Obama.

Under Obama, as I've tried to show, mere *months* after nearly destroying our financial system, the men and women responsible were rolling in profits that were essentially guaranteed by the American taxpayer.

Nor is that the end of the story. At the same time, the endless handouts that have been thrown Wall Street's way, combined with the Obama administration's other domestic policies, have caused our national debt to skyrocket to a level not seen since World War II. If this sounds like so much abstract jargon, the sort of thing economists blather about at academic meetings, it's not. Because sooner or later our creditors *will* demand to know how we're going to pay them back. The second largest creditor of the United States of America is communist China. And when they come calling for their money, or begin demanding even higher levels of interest to buy our debt, well, let's just say it could make the Great Depression and our own great recession look like mild economic hiccups.

I don't think it's unjustifiable, that it's patriotism run amok, to fairly call the twentieth century the "American century." In the last one hundred years, America has become the most powerful nation in the world because of its tradition of free-market capitalism. The world's media and entertainment industries and technology industries owe their success to America's embrace of the free market, non–welfare state capitalism that our founders put in place, with a Constitution deliberately designed to limit the powers of government and to give individual ingenuity, invention, creativity, and hard work free rein.

But when I think about what lies in store for this country, I look at a world in fear, where investors would rather buy gold for $1,200 an ounce than invest in growth industries as sophisticated investors get nervous about Barack Obama's extraordinary and rapid expansion of the U.S. debt.

And I've come to realize that unless something changes (and soon), unless ordinary American taxpayers—ordinary American voters—act to turn around this unprecedented expansion of government that is turning what used to be the world's bastion of capitalism into a welfare state, the twenty-first century will not be an American century.

Far from it.

It will likely be remembered as the era when, after centuries of extraordinary growth, innovation, and success—in a country whose worst moment was slavery, a stain on our history that we overcame to an extraordinary degree by electing Barack Obama president—it all came crashing down in a tidal wave of debt, debt, and more debt that was sold to China and the public by the government's hand-in-glove partners in crime on Wall Street.

But if all you watch and read is the so-called mainstream media, which is actually far to the left of the majority of this country (and I should know; I've spent my entire career in media in one of the most liberal cities in America, New York), you may never know any of this to be true.

In these pages, I've tried to lay out just how much damage has already been done, just how much Wall Street got for its investment when it bought candidate Obama, and just how much worse it's going to get unless and until ordinary Americans wake up and realize how close we are to destroying so many of the values and institutions that have made this country great.

EPILOGUE

"Goldman Sachs will not support Obama," muttered Lloyd Blankfein to an expressionless Larry Fink during a dinner meeting in late 2011.

Blankfein was closing in on his sixth year as CEO of Goldman, and this last year was possibly his most difficult since the crisis itself, so difficult in fact that many people inside the firm were predicting that 2012 would be his last year at the top.

Fink, meanwhile, continued to keep a tight grip on the firm he created nearly a quarter century ago, BlackRock. But along with running the world's largest money management firms, Fink was widely regarded among his peers for having the best access to the Obama administration, a relationship that began when Obama was still fighting for the nomination before his 2008 presidential election.

It was Fink's goal during this dinner meeting held at his favorite Upper East Side restaurant, Sistina, to see if the mighty Goldman Sachs would be once again supporting the president in his upcoming re-election campaign.

Fink wasn't the only Wall Streeter to support the president that year—as we saw in this book, all the major banks coughed up millions to put the president furthest to the left since FDR into office. But now, four years later, Fink was discovering that he was an outlier. Most others, like Blankfein's Goldman Sachs, had had enough of the president's name-calling and class warfare policies and were putting their money behind Mitt Romney to win the Republican nomination and hopefully the presidency.

Fink wasn't ready to make that same break. Friends tell me that it isn't so much that he's a devotee of Barack Obama's economic policies of massive government programs, regulations on businesses large and small, and of course all that class warfare, than he is keenly aware of his *own* place in history if the president can be re-elected (with his help).

And that place in history, at least in Fink's mind, begins with one of the best stories on Wall Street and ended—at least in his mind—as Treasury Secretary, a post he had to turn down at least once because, he told people, both his wife and BlackRock's board objected.

Obama, of course, could do far worse than have Larry Fink advise him on economic affairs. Fink built BlackRock from scratch in the late 1980s after being fired for bond-trading losses at First Boston. By 2008 he managed more money than anyone in the world.

In the process he had become incredibly rich; he built a business that managed money from some of the world's richest people, including the Kuwaiti government. He also accumulated at least some of his wealth thanks to his connections to big government, the current one in particular. While President Obama was threatening small businesses with higher taxes, new regulations on carbon emissions, and a health care mandate, BlackRock feasted on the myriad bank subsidies and bailouts doled out during the first years of the Obama White House.

With that, BlackRock became a fixture in Washington as well as on Wall Street, and Fink became one of the most powerful people in that incestuous world, and according to people who know him, one with his eye on the ultimate prize for the ultimate Wall Street–Washington insider: seeing his name on a dollar bill as Treasury Secretary.

In that spirit Larry Fink gingerly approached Blankfein about taking another shot with the president. Keep in mind, Goldman under Blankfein's leadership was an even bigger supporter of Obama in 2008 than Larry Fink. Other than the ultra-liberal University of California, no single donor contributed more to Team Obama than Goldman Sachs.

Goldman loves picking winners and the winner it picked in 2008 was supposed to be a moderate in the Bill Clinton mold; as the bank saw it, taxes might go up but largely to pay down the deficit. The housing and financial crisis might mean more regulations, but not the type that would destroy whole businesses, as the Dodd-Frank plan the president ended up adopting has been doing.

Wall Street might be criticized, Goldman figured, but not vilified, as many Democrats and more than a few Republicans were ready to do.

But just the opposite had happened as President Obama led one of the most frighteningly far-left administrations in recent memory. He may have personally liked many of the key players in the Wall Street crowd (Jamie Dimon of JPMorgan Chase chief among them during the president's first two years in office), but now he used them as a punching bag; whenever his poll numbers slipped—and they kept slipping and slipping given the lackluster economy that has left millions of Americans unemployed— Obama seemed never to miss an opportunity to scold "fat cat" bankers and "millionaires and billionaires."

Making matters worse for Goldman was that during the Obama presidency, all the hatred focused at Wall Street appeared to be targeted at the singular face of Goldman Sachs, or to be more precise, Lloyd Blankfein.

Blankfein wasn't just grilled over Goldman's financial crisis business practices during numerous congressional hearings but also ridiculed, mocked, and eventually threatened with perjury charges as the fat-cat bashing from the president and his allies in the media grew. He became so obsessed with the media coverage over Goldman's alleged questionable activities during the financial crisis that he used to Google his name incessantly (his press secretary Lucas van Praag finally prevailed upon him to stop). Known for a dry sense of humor, Blankfein quipped, "The Mob wives start their husbands' cars in the morning; my wife reads the morning papers."

He was only half kidding. (Apparently Blankfein continued to read the *Financial Times*, which had more toned-down coverage of Goldman's post-crisis travails.) But he wasn't kidding when he told Fink that Obama's biggest contributor in 2008 was placing its bets elsewhere in 2012.

It didn't matter that by choosing the firm's preferred candidate, Mitt Romney, the former Massachusetts governor, he was only reinforcing the firm's "fat cat" image. Romney was, of course, the former CEO of the highly successful private equity firm Bain Capital, and had a personal net worth of hundreds of millions of dollars.

As Blankfein chatted with Fink, the onslaught against Romney's Bain record had barely just begun with Republican primary candidate Newt Gingrich soon to be dealing the sharpest blows for Romney's alleged "vulture capitalism" of buying companies, firing employees, and walking away with hefty profits once the pared-down remains were sold.

Romney's Bain exploits were much more complicated: some jobs were lost in his many buyouts and investments; many more were gained. The nature of private equity is to buy floundering businesses in the hopes of salvaging the profitable parts so at least some people keep their jobs.

This subtlety of course would be lost on the alleged free-market Republican candidates and would be lost on Obama as well if Romney won the nomination, as was increasingly likely.

Indeed, Blankfein had already heard through his contacts in Washington that Obama was ready to take the "evils" of private equity to new levels during the campaign. The Obama spin machine was no doubt adding to its arsenal the fact that in addition to being a vulture capitalist, Romney was now the biggest recipient of campaign cash from the hated Goldman Sachs.

And as he sat in Sistina, Blankfein was immediately suspicious of Fink's intentions. He had also heard of Fink's desire to run the Treasury and he knew anything he said would make its way back to Washington not long after he said it.

He also couldn't have cared less. "In the end we're still going to be Goldman Sachs," is what he told Fink, an indication that the firm was tired of the constant public attacks and was going to support the candidate that best supported its own interests.

To be sure, what Romney supported wasn't quite the return to the good old days that Goldman had previously expected from Obama, the days when it would have a firm say in the nation's economic policies. Post–financial crisis politics would make it difficult for any firm, much less

Goldman Sachs, to play anything more than an advisory role in public affairs. Rather Romney was the firm's best bet to change the tone in Washington from banker bashing to at least accepting that banks and brokerages do perform a vital function helping companies raise capital, and that the policies coming from the White House were squeezing both the banks and the economy.

When I confronted both Fink's and Blankfein's advisers with the details of the dinner meeting, they both declined to comment, though I hear the very fact that I had discovered that the two of them had met and what they met about had them seething—and a little scared.

The re-election of Barack Obama is of course no sure thing, and yet he is still considered on Wall Street the odds-on favorite given the tremendous weapons at his disposal, including an unrivaled ability to raise money and his widespread support with most of the mainstream media. With the power granted to the president under Dodd-Frank, Obama had more power to regulate the banks and investment houses in Washington than any other president in modern history.

And yet, Blankfein and the rest of the Wall Street hierarchy continue courting Romney. Jamie Dimon spent a lot of time with Obama early in his first term, but now he's openly disdainful of Obama's economic policies, not to mention the president's Wall Street attacks, calling them a form of "discrimination." He also has no problem being seen with Romney at a public event—an indication of where his firm is placing its bets in 2012. Like Goldman, JPMorgan Chase is also a big Romney contributor. Money is also pouring into Romney from Citigroup and Bank of America, whose CEO, Brian Moynihan, briefly replaced Dimon as the president's favorite banker.

I wrote *Bought and Paid For* to expose the corruption that occurs when big government and big business join forces as they did for years in both Republican and Democratic administrations, and for all its anti-Wall Street rhetoric, the current administration as well.

The pressure will be on Mitt Romney to show that he isn't a captive of the banking machine. If he doesn't, he'll probably lose the election to a president who both bashes Wall Street when he needs to and uses them as he sees fit. Keep in mind, for all his bank bashing as president, Obama was ready to appoint as Treasury Secretary one of Wall Street's biggest bundlers of cash, the infamous Jon Corzine—former head of Goldman Sachs, ex–New Jersey governor, and former U.S. Senator—who, as CEO of MF Global, led a firm that made wild bets in the markets, blew up, and then "misplaced" hundreds of millions of dollars in customers' accounts.

Keep in mind something else: The Obama presidency hasn't been all banker bashing. At times it's been a bonanza for Wall Street thanks in large part to a compliant Federal Reserve keeping interest rates at near zero and to an administration that continues to shower the benefits of "too big to fail" on the banks.

While Wall Street may be tiring of Obama, senior executives at the big firms told me that if Romney wasn't successful they would have eagerly supported the president's re-election for the simple reason that for all his rhetoric and support of financial reform, he is far more preferable to them than the more conservative, Tea Party–inspired Republican candidates who would go much further in ending the cozy relationship between big government and the banks.

In fact, take away the rhetoric and some of the extremes of Dodd-Frank, and you can make the case that Obama is doing his best to keep much of the status quo that the banks love. Under Dodd-Frank, "too big to fail" remains, meaning banks can remain large and powerful and are still government protected. There is more oversight on the banks, but that just means the banking executives can do one of the things they do best—lobby (and lobby and lobby) for better terms.

Yes, the banks want "too-big-to-fail" protection, but the cost of that is an ever more powerful federal government that controls every move they make. Blankfein was concerned that his meeting with Fink was discovered because he knows that Goldman's ultimate masters aren't his shareholders—they're all those newly appointed federal bureaucrats in Washington who answer to Barack Obama. They, too, are Bought and Paid For.

Acknowledgments

I could not have written this book without the support of friends, family, and sources, most of whom don't want to be named. In writing *Bought and Paid For,* I also relied on numerous articles from various publications, which I have cited both directly and in my notes when appropriate. Having been ripped off myself, I hope I've given these writers their due.

I want to begin by thanking my assistant, Maxwell Meyers, who worked long and hard to crash this book out. Despite a full-time job as a TV producer, Max made sure deadlines were met, facts were checked, and my writing was clear. Thanks for a great effort. My editor and co-agent Ethan Friedman made my copy a hell of a lot better within some difficult time constraints. Ethan did something else: He believed in this concept from the beginning, as did my other co-agent, Steve Hanselman, the people at LevelFiveMedia, including Julia Serebrinsky, and the people at Sentinel, most of all Adrian Zackheim and his team, including Brooke Carey, Will Weisser, Amanda Pritzker, Nick Owen, Alex Gigante, Tricia Conley, Jillian Gray, Hilary Roberts, Joe Perez, Roman Genn, Amy Hill, Alissa Amell, Spring Hoteling, and Fabiana Van Arsdell.

I'd like to thank my wife, Virginia Juliano, for giving me the advice and support to do two things in 2010 that took my career in a somewhat different, albeit more fulfilling, direction. One was to do a book about the confluence and corruption of Big Business and Big Government, which is what *Bought and Paid For* is all about, and two was to join the Fox Business Network and work with people who both understand and appreciate what

I do on a daily basis, namely Roger Ailes, Kevin Magee, David Jones, and Ray Hennessey, the people in the Fox public relations department—Brian Lewis, Caley Cronin, Stephanie Kelly, and Irena Briganti—and my friends and colleagues Judge Andrew Napolitano and Neil Cavuto.

I'd also like to thank my brother, Dr. James Gasparino. As many people know, one of the main characters in this book, Goldman Sachs CEO Lloyd Blankfein, once compared what he does in the business of buying and selling stocks and bonds to "God's work." Blankfein should spend a few minutes watching my brother save lives in an inner city hospital to understand the true meaning of that term.

Paul Carlucci, the publisher of the *New York Post* and head of News America Marketing, has been a mentor to me for some time, and I would like thank him for his sage advice, along with my agent, Wayne Kabak, who helped me get to where I want to be.

Speaking about the *New York Post,* I have many friends there who have supported me in my career, including the editor Col Allan and the people on the editorial page: Mark Cunningham, Eve Kessler, Adam Brodsky, and Bob McManus.

Tina Brown and Ed Felsenthal of the *Daily Beast* and Stuart Whatley of the *Huffington Post* have also been friends, supporters, and editors of my columns, and I'd like to thank them as well. Kevin Goldman, Susan Krakower, and Jonathan Wald also deserve to be thanked for their support and guidance as well as Chris Ruddy of Newmax and Mike Flynn of Big Government (part of Andrew Breitbart's Web empire) for taking an interest in my work.

Appendix I

Key People

William "Bill" Ayers: A University of Chicago professor and former member of the Weather Underground, a sixties radical antiwar group that planted bombs in federal buildings in protest of U.S. foreign policy. Years later, Ayers hosted Obama at an informal gathering at his house to raise money for Obama's first run for public office.

Ben Bernanke: Chairman of the Federal Reserve since February 2006 and the architect of the U.S. government's unprecedented bailouts of the private banking system. Bernanke was reappointed by President Obama in 2009 and has been alternately credited with saving the banking system and criticized for responding too slowly to the credit crisis. Either way, he is considered the most powerful Fed chairman since the institution's inception. In 2009 *Time* magazine named him man of the year.

Lloyd Blankfein: Goldman Sachs's chairman and chief executive officer since June 2006 and a director since April 2003. Prior to taking the helm at Goldman, Blankfein had been the company's president and chief operating officer since January 2004. While other firms melted down following their forays into risky subprime loans, under Blankfein's leadership Goldman largely dodged the crisis. Like many of his Goldman colleagues, Blankfein has contributed to Democratic candidates for much of his professional life. But unlike many of his colleagues, Blankfein grew up in government housing in Brooklyn, an experience that undoubtedly shaped his political ideology.

George W. Bush: Forty-third president of the United States. Bush's administration saw not only the terrorist attacks of September 11 but also the subsequent twin tech and housing bubbles that inflated and ultimately destroyed the economy. In the waning days of his presidency, Bush signed off on an unprecedented bailout of the financial system. Though his policies were unpopular at the time, his successor, Barack Obama, has left many of them in place.

James "Jimmy" Cayne: Former Bear Stearns chairman and CEO. Cayne joined Bear in 1969 as a retail broker, rising through the ranks to become one of the wealthiest CEOs on Wall Street. Though he is a staunch Republican, his firm was the chief beneficiary of the government housing policies, which fueled Bear's enormous mortgage business. Some question Cayne's financial knowledge, but few question his smarts. Under Cayne's leadership, Bear's stock jumped from $16 a share to a high of $172. Backed by a government bailout, JPMorgan Chase ultimately purchased the company for $10 a share in 2008; Cayne lost most of his vast fortune.

Robert Citron: Longtime treasurer of Orange County who was at the center of the county's bankruptcy, the largest municipal bankruptcy ever, in 1994. A popular Democrat in a largely Republican district, Citron was responsible for investing Orange County's tax revenue. But instead of following a conservative investment strategy, Citron rolled the dice and invested in risky derivatives at the urging of Michael Stamenson and others, a move that would have fateful results.

William Jefferson "Bill" Clinton: Forty-second president of the United States. Clinton presided over a period of unprecedented economic prosperity by following a somewhat conservative approach of reducing deficits and cutting government spending. But at the heart of his economic plan was the expansion of homeownership, a move that would ultimately lay the foundation for America's credit crisis.

Gary Cohn: Goldman Sachs's president since 2006 and sole chief operating officer since April 2009. Cohn had a front-row seat to both the extreme highs and the lows that Goldman witnessed in the later part of the last decade. Cohn played a crucial role in devising a scheme to help the Greek government disguise its true debt levels, a transaction that ultimately unraveled as the country's finances deteriorated.

John Cornyn: Republican senator from Texas. Cornyn counts JPMorgan Chase among his largest campaign contributors. When Obama ratcheted up his anti–Wall Street rhetoric, Cornyn supported less stringent financial reform in an effort to court Wall Street and its massive campaign dollars.

Andrew Cuomo: New York attorney general. At the time of this writing in spring 2010, Cuomo has decided to run for the same office his father once held: governor of New York State. As New York's AG, Cuomo has rightfully earned praise for his relentless war on Wall Street's abusive practices. But his role as housing secretary in the Clinton administration, where he pushed for an increase in the nation's rate of homeownership, has earned him an equal amount of scorn from critics.

Jamie Dimon: Chairman and CEO of JPMorgan Chase since December 2005. Dimon joined JPMorgan when it purchased Bank One, where he had been chairman and chief executive officer since March 2000. Although Dimon did not contribute directly to Obama's presidential campaign, he has been a powerhouse for the Democratic Party and supported Obama when he ran for Senate in 2004. Since 1989, Dimon and his wife have donated over half a million dollars to Democratic candidates and causes. Although he has said his firm didn't need the money, JPMorgan Chase received $25 billion in bailout funds.

Chris Dodd: Longest-serving senator in the history of Connecticut. Dodd sits atop the powerful Senate Banking Committee and is one of the most influential Democrats in Congress. The financial collapse occurred under his watch, but that didn't stop Wall Street from funneling him a ton of cash. Since 2005 he has received just over $1.2 million in campaign contributions from the securities industry.

Rahm Emanuel: Obama's chief of staff and top enforcer. Emanuel's ties to Wall Street run deep. A former member of the House of Representatives from Illinois, Emanuel briefly worked at Goldman Sachs and in 1999 managed Wasserstein Perella's Chicago office, earning $16 million for just two years of work. When Emanuel returned to public life, he relied more than ever on his Wall Street friends for fund-raising; in 2008 Emanuel received more money from the financial services industry than any other House member.

Larry Fink: Chairman, chief executive officer, and founder of money-management firm BlackRock. Fink is considered a pioneer in the mortgage-backed securities market, an industry whose growth depended on government-assisted housing programs. Fink was an early supporter of Obama's candidacy and in the last several years has personally contributed only to candidates from the Democratic Party.

Greg Fleming: Former president and chief operating officer of Merrill Lynch. From 2003 to 2007, Fleming was the head of Merrill's investment-banking unit. A cool operator, Fleming played an integral role in the government's orchestrated takeover of Merrill Lynch by Bank of America.

Barney Frank: Powerful chair of the House Financial Services Committee. Frank, a Democrat from Massachusetts, is also the first openly gay member of Congress. Elected to the House in 1982, Frank enjoys great support from Wall Street: His two top campaign contributors are the American Bankers Association and JPMorgan Chase.

Richard "Dick" Fuld: Former chairman and CEO of Lehman Brothers. Prior to the firm's bankruptcy, Fuld's fourteen-year reign at the helm of Lehman was the longest of any Wall Street CEO. While not terribly political, Fuld's firm was quick to profit from the government's expansion of existing housing policies. Ultimately, it was that push into real estate that led to the firm's collapse.

Mark Gallogly: Managing principal of Centerbridge Partners, a private-equity firm. The consummate Wall Street insider, Gallogly was one of Obama's earliest and biggest supporters, introducing Obama to some of his biggest supporters in the financial service industry. After a long and successful career at Blackstone, Gallogly struck out on his own and created Centerbridge Partners. He sits on Obama's Economic Recovery Advisory Board.

Timothy "Tim" Geithner: Current Treasury secretary and former president of the New York Federal Reserve Bank. Geithner played a key role in the unprecedented government bailout of the U.S. banking system. While he has never worked on Wall Street, he remains very close with the people he is charged with monitoring. At one point, Sandy Weill offered him the top job at Citigroup.

James Gorman: Morgan Stanley's CEO since January 2010. Gorman replaced Wall Street legend John Mack. Gorman came to Morgan Stanley from Merrill Lynch, where he held a number of top management positions.

Alan Greenspan: Chairman of the Federal Reserve from 1987 to 2006. Some economists have pointed to his aggressive lowering of interest rates following the attacks of September 11 as the fuel that lit the housing crisis. Greenspan had openly supported the use of derivatives as risk-mitigating tools and had even advocated for adjustable-rate mortgages.

John McCain: Longtime Republican senator from Arizona. McCain is a self-described "maverick" and has often been a voice of criticism of Wall Street. That dislike could have cost the senator his best shot at being president, as McCain's campaign contributions from the securities industry trailed those of his chief rival by a nearly two-to-one margin.

Mitch McConnell: Republican Senate minority leader from Kentucky. Although McConnell publicly claims to be no fan of Wall Street, he counts the securities industry as one of his leading sources of campaign contributions.

John Mack: Former CEO of Morgan Stanley. Mack's career at Morgan Stanley spanned nearly thirty years. He left the company in 2001 amid a power struggle with then CEO Phil Purcell, eventually taking the helm at Credit Suisse First Boston. He returned to Morgan Stanley in 2005. Mack's sharp focus on cost cutting earned him the nickname "Mack the Knife." But his parsimonious reputation did not stop him from taking $10 billion in taxpayer bailouts. Mack stepped down as CEO after he directed the firm's trading units to scale back on risk taking following the financial crisis of 2008.

Angelo Mozilo: Deeply tanned former CEO of Countrywide Financial. Mozilo rose from being the son of a Bronx butcher to lead one of the world's biggest mortgage lenders, where he was an enthusiastic advocate of subprime mortgages. Mozilo's meteoric rise and fall became a symbol of the excesses of the real estate market. The growth of his firm was a direct result of the government's efforts to increase home affordability.

Barack Obama: Forty-fourth president of the United States. Though he comes from humble origins and is only a few years removed from being a community organizer, with a relatively brief political career in the Illinois State Senate and the U.S. Senate, Obama's ties to Wall Street run deep. His cabinet is littered with Goldman alums, and during his campaign, Wall Street's contributions to Obama nearly doubled those the industry made to his rival, Senator John McCain.

Stanley "Stan" O'Neal: Former CEO of Merrill Lynch. O'Neal led Merrill's fatal push into subprime mortgages while simultaneously working to destroy the firm's clubby insider culture, known as "Mother Merrill." The grandson of a former slave, O'Neal is the highest-serving African American to have worked on Wall Street. Though not outwardly political, O'Neal did contribute to Obama's campaign. However, unlike many other Wall Street firms, during O'Neal's reign as CEO Merrill actually contributed more to the Republican party.

Vikram Pandit: CEO of Citigroup. Pandit joined Citigroup after the bank purchased his hedge fund, Old Lane Partners, for $800 million in 2007. Prior to running his hedge fund, Pandit ran Morgan Stanley's investment-banking business, where he oversaw sales and trading. With over $50 billion in TARP money, no bank has benefited more from government bailouts than Citigroup.

Henry "Hank" Paulson: Former Treasury secretary (serving during the heart of the financial crisis) and CEO and chairman of Goldman Sachs from 1999 to 2006. Few straddle the intersection of Wall Street and Washington as Paulson does. He was CEO of Goldman at the same time Jimmy Cayne, Stan O'Neal, and Dick Fuld ran their respective firms, and in 2008 he engineered the federal bailout of America's financial institutions. Despite his financial support of Republican candidates through the years, Paulson is a committed environmentalist who has a number of close relationships with key House Democrats, including House Speaker Nancy Pelosi and Barney Frank.

Nancy Pelosi: First female Speaker of the House of Representatives. Pelosi is one of the most powerful and liberal Democrats in the House. Though she has publicly rebuked Wall Street for its risky behavior, she played a key role in approving the government's massive bailout of the financial system.

Charles "Chuck" Prince: Former CEO and chairman of Citigroup. In 2003 Prince inherited Sandy Weill's far-flung financial kingdom, which was created after the Clinton administration lobbied for the repeal of the Glass-Steagall Act. A former attorney with no background in trading mortgages, Prince stepped down from both positions due to heavy losses in the mortgage market.

Harry Reid: Senate majority leader and the four-term Democratic senator from Nevada. Reid played a key role in crafting the government's massive bailouts of the U.S. financial system. Though his home state is thousands of miles from Wall Street, Reid has received more campaign contributions from the financial services industry than he has from the gaming industry, which is based in his backyard.

Robert Rubin: Treasury secretary under Clinton and cochairman and co–senior partner at Goldman Sachs in the nineties. Rubin went on to become a director and senior adviser at Citigroup before stepping down in January 2009. As Treasury secretary, Rubin was the chief architect of the Mexican bailouts and a driving force behind the Street-led bailout of Long-Term Capital Management. Though Rubin has repeatedly claimed he had no operational authority at Citigroup, many credit (or blame) him for the firm's push into the mortgage arena. Rubin enjoys a close personal relationship with both the Clintons and the Obamas.

Warren Spector: Former co-president of Bear Stearns. Spector's twenty-four-year career at Bear came to a crashing halt after the implosion of the company's two subprime hedge funds. Spector headed Bear's mighty mortgage business, rising through the ranks at a young age to the top of the firm. Although some colleagues considered him aloof, and his left-leaning political views put him at odds with his boss, Jimmy Cayne, few doubted his financial prowess. After being ousted in the summer of 2007, Specter found part-time work as a volunteer for the Obama campaign. He was an early Wall Street supporter of the future president.

Michael Stamenson: Former Merrill Lynch bond broker. Stamenson sold millions of dollars' worth of risky derivatives to the Orange County treasurer, Robert Citron. Those bets ultimately failed and led to the largest municipal bankruptcy in U.S history. Orange County filed suit against Merrill Lynch, and the case was ultimately settled for $400 million.

Larry Summers: Treasury secretary under Bill Clinton. Robert Rubin's protégé, Summers's professional life has straddled academia, Washington, and Wall Street. As Treasury secretary, Summers championed the deregulation of Wall Street, arguing that the repeal of the Glass-Steagall Act would "better enable American companies to compete in the new economy."

After serving in the Treasury, Summers returned to Harvard to become the university's first Jewish president. He resigned after questioning women's aptitude for math.

Paul Volcker: Chairman of the Federal Reserve from 1979 to 1987. Volcker currently chairs Obama's Economic Recovery Advisory Board. Many economists credit Volcker with ending rampant inflation in the late seventies. Volcker was an early supporter of Obama and led the administration's efforts to reform the banks.

Sandy Weill: Former CEO and chairman of Citigroup. Weill created the idea of the one-stop shopping megaconglomerate, engineering a series of mergers that eventually brought Citicorp and Travelers under the same roof and in the process created the world's largest financial company. The combination was only made possible through years of lobbying Congress to repeal the Glass-Steagall Act. During the financial crisis, only AIG took more in government bailouts than Citi did. But over the years, few firms have given more to the Democrats than Citigroup. In fact, since 1990 Citigroup has given nearly $14 million to the Democratic Party.

Reverend Jeremiah Wright: Obama's former pastor. Wright's fiery and invective-filled sermons almost cost Obama the presidential election. Wright's ties to Obama run deep; he officiated Obama's wedding and baptized his two daughters. After initially trying to distance himself from Wright's comments, Obama eventually resigned from the Trinity United Church of Christ, where Wright had been a pastor.

Appendix II

Key Firms, Government Departments, and Organizations

ACORN: The Association of Community Organizations for Reform Now is a left-wing organization that advocates on behalf of low- and moderate-income families. The organization has been accused in the press of helping in voter registration fraud in the last election. Additionally, ACORN found itself in the midst of a national controversy when a tape surfaced that appeared to show a low-level employee advising people how to hide prostitutes and avoid taxes. The incident led to a collapse in fundraising, and the organization went bankrupt in 2010.

AIG: American International Group is the largest insurer in the world, whose collapse threatened to take down the entire financial industry. Founded in 1919 and built into a colossus by Hank Greenberg, AIG's troubles began when it moved away from offering standard insurance products and started insuring complex mortgage securities, which left it vulnerable to the housing market. Since AIG's collapse, the U.S. government has bailed out the company to the tune of some $182 billion.

Bank of America: One of the largest U.S. banks by revenue and deposits, Bank of America (known as BofA for short) was founded as the Bank of Italy by immigrant Amadeo Giannini in 1904. It has been subject to a series of government bailouts following its purchases of Countrywide Financial and Merrill Lynch.

Bear Stearns: Founded by Joseph Bear, Robert Stearns, and Harold Mayer in 1923, Bear was traditionally a bond house. The first major victim of the credit crisis, Bear's heavy focus on mortgage-backed securities and use of leverage eventually led to its collapse in March 2008. Prior to the subprime crisis, Bear had never posted an unprofitable quarter.

BlackRock: Founded in 1988 by Larry Fink as Blackstone Financial Management, BlackRock changed to its current name in 1992 and emerged as one of the few winners in the financial crisis, garnering key contracts from both private and government players to manage beaten mortgage portfolios. With $3.36 trillion under management, BlackRock is one of the world's largest asset-management companies. Made in the image of its founder, BlackRock is renowned for its expertise in risk management.

Citigroup: At one point the largest financial services company in the world, Citigroup was formed by Sandy Weill through the merger of Citicorp and Travelers Group in 1998. The combined company endured massive losses following the credit crisis and had to be bailed out by the government to the tune of $50 billion in direct taxpayer-financed aid and hundreds of billions more in loan guarantees.

Countrywide Financial: The nation's largest mortgage lender, Countrywide was a leader in offering subprime loans to home buyers. Led by its charismatic CEO, Angelo Mozilo, Countrywide became the corporate face of the housing bubble.

Department of the Treasury: Established by Alexander Hamilton in 1789, the Treasury Department prints all U.S. currency and collects taxes. Additionally, the department supervises U.S banks and thrifts. Under former secretary Hank Paulson, the Treasury was often the first line of defense against the global financial meltdown. The current Treasury secretary is Tim Geithner.

FDIC: Created by the Glass-Steagall Act of 1933, the Federal Deposit Insurance Corporation insures its member banks' deposits in the amount of $250,000 dollars per account. The agency was created to prevent widespread panic that might cause people to withdrawal their funds all at once (known as a "run on the bank").

Federal Reserve: Created in 1913 as part of the Federal Reserve Act, the Fed, as it is often called, is the nation's central bank. It is responsible for controlling the amount of money flowing through the economy and for regulating banking institutions. The Fed is also charged with maintaining the stability of the financial system, a mandate that was put to the test during the credit crisis.

Federal Reserve Bank of New York: One of twelve member Federal Reserve Banks, the Federal Reserve Bank of New York is chiefly responsible for implementing monetary policy that comes out of the Federal Reserve. Tim Geithner was the bank's president prior to running Obama's Treasury Department.

Goldman Sachs: The gold standard of investment banks, founded by Marcus Goldman in 1869, Goldman largely sidestepped the subprime crisis. Still, at the height of the financial market, Goldman converted to a bank holding company, signaling the end of the modern investment bank. The last of the major investment banks to go public, in 1999, Goldman remains unrivaled for its risk management. Former senior Goldman executives have held a number of high-level positions in government, and since 1990 two-thirds of all the firm's campaign contributions have gone to the Democratic Party. Despite repeated claims that the firm did not need any taxpayer assistance, Goldman received $10 billion in bailout funds during the collapse of 2008.

JPMorgan Chase: Formed in 2000 when Chase Manhattan Bank purchased J.P. Morgan, JPMorgan Chase is one of the largest commercial banks in the world. With the Fed's backing, it purchased Bear Stearns for the paltry sum of $2 a share following the broker's collapse. The final price was later raised to $10. In 2008 the firm received $25 billion in bailout funds following the collapse of the financial system. That same year, 62 percent of its campaign contributions went to the Democratic Party, the highest percentage for the company since 1990.

Lehman Brothers: One of the oldest of Wall Street's investment banks, dating back to 1850, Lehman was spun off from American Express in 1993. Despite its heavy presence in fixed income, after 2000 Lehman made significant progress in diversifying its business model, buying asset manager Neuberger Berman in 2003 for $2.6 billion. Still, the company's fateful push into risky mortgages would spell its doom, and in September 2008 the firm filed for bankruptcy, setting off a global financial meltdown.

Long-Term Capital Management: Founded by former Salomon head of fixed income trading John Meriwether, LTCM used heavy leverage to employ a number of complex fixed-income strategies. While initially successful, bad bets in the credit markets ultimately meant huge losses, and because of the systemic risk that an LTCM failure posed, the hedge fund was ultimately bailed out by a consortium of other Wall Street firms.

Merrill Lynch: Known for its "thundering herd" of brokers, Merrill was a relative latecomer to the subprime arena. But under CEO Stan O'Neal the company made an aggressive push into the sector, a move that ultimately caused its failure and merger with Bank of America in September of 2008.

Morgan Stanley: One of the most storied and celebrated investment banks in the United States, Morgan Stanley was able to weather the financial storm as an independent company, but not without changing its charter and becoming a bank holding company, and not without receiving $10 billion in TARP funds.

Securities and Exchange Commission: Created in the wake of the crash of 1929, the SEC is the Street's top cop. It regulates the exchanges and its member firms, in addition to stamping out corporate abuse. However, over the last couple of years, the agency's reputation has suffered as it not only missed a number of high-profile frauds (most famously that of Ponzi schemer Bernie Madoff) but also failed to prevent the financial meltdown of 2008.

Weather Underground: A radical sixties left-wing group whose membership included Obama confidant William Ayers. The group was responsible for a number of planned bombings of government buildings, including one on the Pentagon in protest of the Vietnam War.

A Few Key Financial Terms and Concepts

Bailout: The act of saving an institution from imminent failure through an injection of funds. During the financial crisis, the government had to bail out many financial firms that were on the cusp of bankruptcy to prevent a total collapse of the financial system. (Contrast this with other forms of government support, such as the discount window.)

Bond: A debt investment where investors lend money to either a corporation or a government for a set period of time at a fixed interest rate. A bond's "coupon" is the interest-rate payment that is made over the life of the bond. The "principal" is the face value of the bond and the amount on which the creditor receives interest. Fixed income is an extremely lucrative business for Wall Street, as both federal and local governments need to tap the credit markets to fund their fiscal obligations.

Carry trade: An investment strategy where investors borrow at a low short-term rate and then proceed to invest in higher-yielding longer-term debt. Investors make money by pocketing the difference between the short-term rate at which they borrow and the long-term rate at which they invest. The carry trade was at the heart of the investment banks' strategy to generate profits during the mortgage boom. Following the bailouts, the remaining big firms were designated "commercial banks" instead of investment banks; the implicit support this gave them from the U.S. Treasury allowed them to make unprecedented profits following the bailouts by borrowing money cheaply from the U.S. government and then investing it in bonds that paid higher rates of interest.

CDO (collateralized debt obligation): A security backed by a pool of other debt securities, such as, but not limited to, mortgages. Car loans and credit card debt are examples of other types of debt that might be packed into a CDO. A CDO is typically divided into various risk categories, or tranches, which are then sold to investors. The higher-rated (more senior) tranches are considered less risky, while the lower-rated, or junior, ones pay higher interest. A CDO squared is a CDO that is backed by other CDOs. The big banks' purchases of tens of billions of dollars' worth of CDOs that went bad lay at the heart of the crisis.

Commercial bank: A financial institution that accepts customer deposits and makes commercial loans. Commercial banks are regulated by the Federal Reserve and, in exchange for being able to access their customers' deposits, are required to take less risk than investment banks. Since the repeal of the Glass-Steagall Act, however, the difference between a commercial and investment bank has decreased.

Credit-default swap: A credit-default swap is a form of a swap, or derivative, whose underlying value is determined by another security. In its simplest form, a CDS is an insurance contract against the default of a bond. While CDSs are often used for hedging purposes, many investors use them to speculate on the health of a company or even a country.

Derivative: A financial instrument whose value is derived from the price of another financial asset. Derivatives are contracts that can refer to a vast array of financial products, from standard equity options like puts or calls to much more complex instruments like credit-default swaps (see entry above), which are linked to the value of an underlying debt instrument. Derivatives are typically used for hedging or speculative purposes. Investors like them for their leverage, but as Orange County found out, leverage can work well on the way up and wipe institutions out on the way down.

Discount window: The discount window is the primary lending mechanism by which financial institutions can borrow from the Federal Reserve. The rate they pay on the loan is called the discount rate. The discount window exists to ease liquidity concerns that may arise in times of trouble. When Goldman Sachs was reclassified a commercial bank, it had the same access to funding as regular banks that take and hold deposits.

Fannie Mae and Freddie Mac: The most prominent of the government-sponsored enterprises, Fannie Mae and its smaller sibling, Freddie Mac, played a crucial role in the expansion of the housing bubble. Fannie Mae, or the Federal National Mortgage Association, was created during the Depression to increase the availability of mortgage lending. It was charted as a public company in 1968. Freddie Mac, the Federal Home Loan Mortgage Corporation, was created two years later. Fannie and Freddie buy mortgages from various lenders and then either hold those mortgages in their portfolios as investments or repackage them with other loans to create mortgage-backed securities, which are then sold to various investors. At one point these two companies owned or insured half of America's $12 trillion in mortgages. Both the Clinton and Bush administrations were unsuccessful in their attempts to rein in the influence of the GSEs. In September 2008, both companies were taken over by the government due to massive losses from risky loans.

Glass-Steagall Act: Enacted in response to the collapse of the banking system during the Great Depression, the Glass-Steagall Act, or Banking Act of 1933, prohibited commercial banks from engaging in investment-banking activities, such as the trading or underwriting of securities. It established the FDIC, which insured commercial bank deposits, but it also divided the banking industry into two distinct houses: the banks, which took in deposits and made loans, and the brokers, which engaged in the riskier parts of the capital markets. Glass-Steagall was changed in 1999 by the Gramm-Leach-Bliley Act, which relaxed many of the restrictions on commercial banking activities. Many have pointed to the watering down of Glass-Steagall as the starting point of the financial crisis that ensued a decade later.

Government-sponsored enterprises (GSE): A group of government-chartered companies whose purpose is to increase the availability of credit for everything from home borrowing to student loans. These corporations include Freddie Mae, Fannie Mac, Sallie Mae, and Ginnie Mae.

Hedge fund: A lightly regulated investment fund that is typically only available to wealthy investors. Unlike mutual funds, which must follow investment mandates, hedge funds can use a wider range of investment and trading techniques to generate profits. Contrary to their name, oftentimes they are most exposed to risk due to their heavy use of leverage.

Hedging: Any investment strategy designed to hedge, or offset, risk against an existing position or investment.

Investment bank: A financial institution that is primarily engaged in the riskier aspects of the capital markets, such as the underwriting and trading and selling of securities. Investment banks offer an array of financial services, from merger advice to back-office services for other financial institutions. The key distinction between commercial and investment banks is that an investment bank does not handle customer deposits. Investment banks are regulated by the Securities and Exchange Commission.

Leverage: The use of borrowed money to enhance investment returns. Leverage was at the heart of the financial crisis, as many firms borrowed at enormous levels, in some cases $30 or more for every dollar they owned, to make speculative bets on the markets. Leverage can work both ways. On the way up it increases returns, but on the way down it can magnify losses. For example, if a trader has $10 and leverages at ten to one, he now has $100 to invest. If his bet goes up 50 percent, he's made $50—or 500 percent of his initial stake of $10. But if his bet goes down 50 percent, he's now in the hole $40—four times the amount of money he has on hand.

Moral hazard: The fear that insulating a person or party from the results of risk taking will encourage more risky behavior. This was the primary argument against bailing out the financial institutions, who all made risky bets only to be saved in the end through taxpayer-financed bailouts.

Mortgage-backed security: A type of bond that is backed by the underlying cash flow of various mortgages.

Municipal bond: A type of bond that is issued by a state or local government. The interest is tax free, making it an attractive investment for wealthy people looking to shelter their income. "Muni" bonds are considered among the safest of all investments, but as Orange County illustrated, there is no such thing as a sure bet when it comes to investing.

Run on the bank: The unexpected and rapid exit of deposits or cash balances from a financial institution. Bank runs occur when individuals lose confidence in the solvency of a particular financial institution. The most historically famous instances of runs on the bank occurred during the Great Depression, when rumors of insolvency at a bank would lead to long lines of customers waiting to withdraw their deposits—leading to just such an insolvency. Runs on investment banks are similar, except that the creditors are hedge funds and other large investors as opposed to ordinary individuals.

Savings and loan (S&L): Savings and loans are commonly called thrifts and are federally insured financial institutions that take in deposits for the purpose of making real estate or other consumer loans. In the eighties and early nineties, lax lending standards and a slowdown in real estate cause the failure of a number of federally insured S&Ls.

Securitization: The process of structuring and redirecting the cash flow of an asset to create multiple securities. Securitization is at the heart of the credit industry, as bankers look to capture the cash flow of any type of receivable, be it a mortgage, credit card loan, or something else, and structure it into a separate security that can be bought or sold by investors.

Systemic risk: The threat of a collapse of the entire financial system, as opposed to the failure of a single company or financial entity. It was the threat of systemic risk that drove the Fed and Treasury to take extraordinary steps in the midst of the financial crisis.

"Too big to fail": The notion that some institutions are so vital to the overall health of the economy that their failure would lead to a collapse of the entire financial system. Some would argue that "too big to fail" coddles banks and tacitly endorses risk taking. Others feel that following this approach saved the U.S. financial system from a complete meltdown. Few argue that, as things stand, in the event of a new crisis the U.S. government would still consider most of the major financial firms too big to fail.

Underwriting: The process by which Wall Street firms bring to market either a debt or an equity security. Underwriters allow companies and governments to access public capital, either in the form of direct ownership or through structuring loans. Underwriting fees used to be the lifeblood of the securities industry, but they have since taken a distant back seat to trading revenues.

Notes

Introduction

3   "$13.4" billion figure for Goldman Sach's annual earnings report.

5   "God's Work" from "Meet Mr. Goldman Sachs," *Times* (London), November 8, 2009.

5   "10 percent unemployment" from the Bureau of Labor Statistics.

5   "vampire squid" from "The Great American Bubble Machine," *Rolling Stone,* July 9, 2009.

6   "Fat Cats" from "Obama Slams Wall Street Bankers," *Wall Street Journal,* December 14, 2009.

6   Description of Blankfein's upbringing from "Lloyd Blankfein, A Profile," *Forbes,* December 16, 2009.

7   ShoreBank's ties to members of the Obama administration from "Wall Street Scrambles to Save ShoreBank," *Wall Street Journal,* May 17, 2010.

7   "Valerie Jarrett sat on the board of Chicago Metropolis 2020" from chicagometropolis2020.org.

8   Eugene Ludwig's role in saving ShoreBank from "Goldman Joins Race to Save Chicago Bank," *Wall Street Journal,* May 13, 2010.

8   "Greg Craig" from "Goldman Taps ex-White House Counsel," *Politico,* April 19, 2010.

8   Various contributions to ShoreBank from "ShoreBank Close to Raising $125 Million in Private Capital," *Wall Street Journal,* May 19, 2010.

9   Rahm Emanuel's ties to Goldman Sachs from "Goldman Will Be Sitting Pretty with Emanuel in the Obama White House," *Washington Examiner,* April 21, 2010.

Chapter 1: A Secretive Meeting

17 Description of meeting between Wall Street bankers and Obama from author's interviews with people who were present and confirmed by members who were there.

18 Description of Wall Street's financial support on Bush/Kerry election from OpenSecrets.org.

19 "Dimon's own 2009 compensation of more than $17 million" from "JPMorgan's Dimon Gets $17 Million Bonus," *New York Times,* February 5, 2010.

20 Description of McCain's relationship with Wall Street from author's interviews with people close to the matter.

20 McCain's description of Wall Street as a "villain" and pledge to "change the way Washington and Wall Street" do business from McCain campaign statement, September 17, 2008.

21 Lawrence Summers's description of females' aptitude for math from "Summers's Remarks on Women Draws Fire," *Boston Globe,* January 17, 2005.

23 Description of Obama's activities as a community organizer from "What Did Obama Do as a Community Organizer," *National Review,* September 8, 2008.

23 "Other states vote; New York invests" from "How Barack Obama Struck Fund-Raising Gold," *New York* magazine, April 15, 2007.

24 Gallogly's relationship with Obama from author's interviews with people close to the matter.

27 Number of meetings between Gallogly and Obama from POTUS Tracker, *Washington Post,* July 14, 2010.

27 Gallogly fund-raising totals from Opensecrets.org.

32 "Exceeded $300 million" from "As Bear Stearns Implodes, Warren Spector Keeps $382 Million," Bloomberg, March 19, 2008.

33 "Impressed immediately" from author's interviews with people familiar with Spector's meeting with Obama.

34 Description of Gallogly's relationship with Volcker from author's interviews with people close to the matter.

34 "Rezko became literally" from "Obama and His Rezko Ties," *Chicago Sun Times,* April 23, 2007.

37 "Cayne had publicly chastised" from "A Top Official at Bear Ousted Over Funds Implosion," *New York Times,* August 6, 2008.

37   "Current scourge of Wall Street" from author's interviews with people in the meeting.

38   "Paid an ACORN Affiliate $800,000" from "Obama and ACORN," *Wall Street Journal*, October 14, 2008.

38   "Mickey Mouse" from "ACORN Charged in Voter Fraud," MSNBC, May 4, 2009.

38   "Most liberal U.S. Senator" from "Why Obama Was the Most Liberal," *National Journal*, August 25, 2008.

38   "Obama had voted against" from "Obama's Record Shows Caution, Nuance in Iraq," *Boston Globe*, March 20, 2007.

39   Reverend Wright's phrase "God damn America" from "Obama's Pastor Disaster," *Orange County Register*, March 15, 2008.

39   "Jewish vote" from *The Daily Press of Newport News*, June 10, 2009.

39   Wright's comments on 9/11 from "Obama's Pastor: God Damn America, U.S. to Blame for 9/11," ABC News, March 13, 2008.

39   Greg Fleming's recollection of Obama's dinner from author's interviews with people familiar with the meeting.

40   Obama and McCain campaign totals from Opensecrets.org.

41   Cavanaugh's contributions to Obama from author's interviews with executives at JPMorgan.

41   Description of Tom Nides's Democratic fund-raisers from author's interviews with people close to the matter.

Chapter 2: The Left Side of Wall Street

44   "Obama rewarded these generous" from "How Barack Obama Struck Fund-raising Gold," *New York* magazine, April 15, 2007.

45   Goldman, JPMorgan, and Bank of America not experiencing a single negative day of trading losses from "'Perfect Quarter' at Four U.S. Banks Shows Fed-Fueled Revival," *Bloomberg Businessweek*, July 19, 2010.

46   Steve Schwarzman's comments on McCain's lack of interest in hearing from Wall Street executives from author's interviews with people close to the matter.

46   Description of McCain's dislike of Wall Street from author's interviews with people familiar with the matter.

47   Account of former Merrill Lynch CEO John Thain's support of McCain from "Thain Is Good for McCain," *Politico*, November 14, 2007.

48   Description of McCain screaming at former Treasury secretary Hank Paulson from author's interviews with people close to the matter.

50   Dimon's directing his senior staff to contribute to Obama from author's interviews with people close to the matter.

50   Goldman and JPMorgan Chase's campaign contributions for September 2008 from Opensecrets.org.

52   John Mack's endorsement of Hillary Clinton from "John Mack Backs Clinton," *Bloomberg Businessweek*, April 27, 2007.

52   "Nanny-state paternalism" from "The Break-Up, Did Obama Just Dump His Best Friend on Wall Street?," *New Republic*, June 17, 2010.

53   "well exceeds the already enormous $89 billion" from "This Bailout Is a Bargain? Think Again," *New York Times*, April 16, 2010.

54   Average salary of financial CEOs in 2006 from "Is Goldman, Lehman Pay Set in Smoke-Filled Room?," *Bloomberg Businessweek,* April 4, 2007.

54   Goldman, trading profits, and quarterly profit breakdown for Bank of America, Citigroup from SNL Financial.

56   "Helped repeal the Glass-Steagall Act" from "Congress Passes Wide-Ranging Bill Easing Bank Laws," *New York Times,* November 5, 1999.

56   Larry Summers's total earnings from work at D.E. Shaw and subsequent speeches from "Hedge Fund Paid Summers $5.2 Million in Past Year," *Wall Street Journal,* April 5, 2009.

61   "Citigroup was forced to sell Phibro" from "Citigroup Sells Phibro Unit to Occidental Petroleum," Bloomberg, October 8, 2009.

63   Consumer loan statistics and banks' quarterly profit breakdowns provided by SNL Financial.

65   "$7,000 for every citizen in the city" from "Your Share of City's Sky-High Debt Is $7,153," *Daily News,* January 23, 2009.

65   Michael Stamenson's "rattlesnake" quote and description of lavish lifestyle from "The Master of Orange County, a Merrill Lynch Broker Survives Municipal Bankruptcy," *New York Times,* June 22, 1998.

66   "I would say Stamenson is" from ibid.

66   Description of Robert Citron including patronage of the Elks Club from "Ill-Fated Fund Manager: Mr. Main St., Not Wall St.," *New York Times,* December 11, 1994.

67   Description of Wall Street consortium that financed Orange County from "Orange County, Calif., Makes Bankruptcy Filing," *New York Times,* December 7, 1994.

67 Robert Citron's purchase of $100 million in swaps from "Market Place; in Orange County, Strategies Sour," *New York Time,* December 5, 1994.

68 "$6.3 billion" in derivatives from ibid.

68 "Misappropriating public funds" from "Citron Pleads Guilty to Felonies," *Los Angeles Times,* April 28, 1995.

68 "Joke" comment form Securities and Exchange Commission official from author's interviews with people close to the matter.

69 Merrill fine of $470 million from "The Master of Orange County, a Merrill Lynch Broker Survives Municipal Bankruptcy," *New York Times,* June 22, 1998.

70 Stamenson's description of Citron as a "highly unsophisticated" investor from "Ill-Fated Fund Manager: Mr. Main St., Not Wall St.," *New York Times,* December 11, 1994.

70 "Stamenson had donated $4,000" from "The Master of Orange County, a Merrill Lynch Broker Survives Municipal Bankruptcy," *New York Times,* June 22, 1998.

Chapter 3: Deep, Deep Roots

71 "Where's Sandy, where's Sandy" and description of Reverend Jackson's relationship with Sandy Weill from author's interviews with people close to the matter.

76 "He donated $1 million" from "Dimons Give $1 Million to University of Chicago," *Chicago Business, Crains,* June 1, 2005.

76 "$3,000 per month" from "Goldman Sachs Will Be Sitting Pretty with Emanuel in Obama White House," *Washington Examiner,* November 21, 2008.

76 $450 trillion estimated outstanding national amount of derivative contracts provided by the International Swaps and Derivatives Association (ISDA).

77 Account of Robert Rubin pestering colleagues during the Super Bowl and description of office from "An Old Wall Street Pro's Voice in the Campaign," *New York Times,* September 22, 1996.

79 "The objective of promoting United States exports" from "Mexican Bailout Defended Amid G.O.P. Criticism," *New York Times,* July 15, 1995.

80 Robert Rubin's role in crafting Mexican bailouts from "A Struggle to Deal with a $20 Billion Precedent," *New York Times,* February 23, 1995.

81 Senator Alfonse D'Amato accusing Lawrence Summers of misleading Congress about true state of Mexican economy from "D'Amato Seeks to Limit Foreign Bailouts," *New York Times,* July 22, 1995.

81   "The looting of America" and Pat Buchanan's subsequent accusation that the Mexican bailout benefited Goldman Sachs from "Mexican Rescue Plan: Washington; Rescue; Durable or Brief," *New York Times,* February 2, 1995, and "Mexico: Who Was Right?," *New York Times,* August 25, 1995.

83   "There is a point to that!" and joke between Summers and Rubin from "Mexico Repays Bailout by U.S. Ahead of Time," *New York Times,* January 16, 1997.

84   Description of conversation between Rubin and Gary Gensler from *An Uncertain World, Tough Choices from Wall Street to Washington,* New York: Random House, 2003.

87   Rubin's quote that "Citigroup was the best" offer from author's interviews with people close to the matter.

87   Greenberg's refusal to pay Rubin "$8 million a year to fly around the world" from author's interviews with people close to the matter.

88   "Fish, read books, and play tennis" from "Former Treasury Secretary Joins Leadership Triangle at Citigroup," *New York Times,* October 27, 1999.

89   Clinton administration's efforts to increase homeownership rates from "Fannie Mae Eases Credit to Aid Mortgage Lending," *New York Times,* September 30, 1999.

Chapter 4: "So, Do You Want to Come to the Administration?"

91   Description of Warren Spector's fund-raising activities for Obama from author's interviews with people close to the matter.

93   "$145.9 billion" cost for Fannie and Freddie bailout from "Cost of Seizing Fannie and Freddie Surges for Taxpayers," *New York Times,* June 19, 2010.

94   Cayne's description of Spector as "Lord Fauntleroy" from author's interviews with Jimmy Cayne.

94   "Tight shorts" from author's interview with Jimmy Cayne.

95   Fink's description of Obama as a "moderate" from author's interviews with people close to the matter.

95   "Dimon's personal donations" from "JPMorgan CEO Jamie Dimon Donates Serious Cash to Democrats," OpenSecrets.org, July 21, 2009.

96   Description of Spector's first meeting with Obama and subsequent reaction from author's interviews with people close to the matter.

98   Poll data showing Obama was leading McCain from "Obama Seen as More Likely to Beat McCain," *New York Times,* February 26, 2008.

99   John Mack's membership in an exclusive country club from "A Path to a Seat on the Board? Try the Fairway," *New York Times,* March 11, 2006.

100   Rubin's prodding of Citigroup traders to take more risks from author's interviews with people close to the matter.

100   Description of "Barack's Bundlers" from "Money Chooses Sides," *New York* magazine, April 15, 2007.

100   "It's Rahm" comment from Tom Nides to John Mack from author's interviews with people present during the conversation.

101   Details of Nides's and Emanuel's relationship from author's interviews with people close to the matter.

101   Account of Emanuel plunging a knife into a piece of steak from "Life Imitates West Wing for Obama's Attack Dog, Rahm Emanuel," *Sunday Times* (London), November 7, 2008.

102   Rahm Emanuel's $16 million salary from "In Banking, Emanuel Made Money and Connections," *New York Times,* December 3, 2008.

105   Account of McCain and Paulson heated dispute from author's interviews with people in the room.

107   Buffett's $5 billion investment in Goldman Sachs from "Buffett to Invest $5 Billion in Goldman," *Wall Street Journal,* September 24, 2008.

107   Dimon's recognition that bailout money helped prevent a possible collapse of JPMorgan from author's interviews with people close to the matter.

107   Nides's invitation to work for the Obama administration from author's interviews with Morgan Stanley executives.

109   Account of Nides's first speech as head of SIFMA from transcript of speech given at SIFMA 2009 annual meeting.

110   Geithner appointment sends Dow up nearly 500 points from "Stox Soar After Treasury Pick," *New York Post,* November 22, 2008.

110   "No one here would ever hire Tim" from "Obama Is from Mars, Wall Street Is from Venus," *New York* magazine, May 22, 2010.

Chapter 5: "We Know Each Other from Chicago"

113   Account of Perella celebrating at San Pietro from author's interviews with people close to the matter.

114   Description of Dimon's relationship with Bill Daley from "In Washington, One Bank Chief Still Holds Sway," *New York Times,* July 19, 2009.

115 Reverend Wright's sermon in which he claimed "God damn America" from "Obama's Pastor: God Damn America, U.S. to Blame for 9/11," ABC News, March 13, 2008.

115 Wright's description of Italian Americans as "garlic noses" from "Rev. Jeremiah Wright and Them 'Jews,'" *San Francisco Examiner*, June 21, 2009.

115 Wright's prediction that the "Jews" would drive Obama from his church from "Rev. Jeremiah Wright Says 'Jews' Are Keeping Him from President Obama," *Daily Press*, June 10, 2009.

115 Wright's description of Louis Farrakhan as a leader who "truly epitomized greatness" from "Obama's Farrakhan Test," *Washington Post*, January 15, 2008.

115 "Perella soon discovered" from author's interviews with people close to the matter.

117 Peter Sidoti's estimation of small business hiring from Sidoti & Company Research.

120 "Total bullshit" and FBR's Paul Miller's reaction to the news that Citigroup would turn profitable from author's interview with Miller.

122 Goldman's claim that the company was forced to take government money from "Banker: Take Your TARP Money Back," CNNMoney.com, March 27, 2009, and from "Goldman Sachs Would Like to Repay Treasury, CFO Says," Bloomberg, February 4, 2009.

123 "He came to Wall Street" and profile of Pandit from "The Most Powerless Powerful Man on Wall Street," *New York* magazine, March 1, 2009.

124 Dimon's remarks to CNBC's Melissa Francis from February 18, 2009.

124 Ken Lewis's comments about Bank of America's business from "Bank of America Soars after CEO Says Bank Was Profitable," *USA Today*, March 12, 2009.

126 John Edwards investment in Fortress from "Edwards Says He Didn't Know About Subprime Push," *Washington Post*, May 11, 2007.

127 Lack of bank lending from "Regulators Urge Banks to Lend to Small Businesses," *Wall Street Journal*, February 6, 2010.

128 Citigroup's profit analysis provided by SNL Financial.

128 Bank of America's and Goldman's profit analysis provided by SNL Financial.

131 Lucas van Praag's account of Goldman's business from author's interview with van Praag.

131 Morgan Stanley's $8 billion loss from "$9.4 Billion Write-Down at Morgan Stanley," *New York Times,* December 20, 2007.

131 John Mack's decision to alter Morgan Stanley's business plan from author's interview with Mack.

132 "vampire squid" from "The Great American Bubble Machine," *Rolling Stone,* July 23, 2009.

133 "Someone making $100 million" and description of Andrew Hall's trading activities from author's interview with Kenneth Feinberg.

136 Description of Mack's meeting with Lawrence Summers from author's interviews with people close to the matter.

Chapter 6: Doing God's Work

138 "Now's not that time" from "Obama Pressures Wall Street Over Pay," *New York Times,* January 29, 2009.

140 "Let me get this straight" from Jonathan Alter's *The Promise,* New York, Simon & Schuster, 2010.

140 AIG's obligations and payout to Goldman Sachs from "Goldman Sachs Still Has $6 Billion in AIG Exposure," Bloomberg, March 20, 2009.

140 Goldman's bonus pool from "Bank Set for Record Pay," *Wall Street Journal,* January 14, 2010.

140 "$67 million bonus in 2007" from "Goldman Awards Blankfein a Record $67.9 Million Bonus," Bloomberg, December 21, 2007.

141 Buffett's $5 billion investment in Goldman Sachs from "Buffett to Invest $5 Billion in Goldman," *Wall Street Journal,* September 24, 2008.

141 Account of Senate majority leader Harry Reid and Goldman president Gary Cohn from author's interviews with people close to the matter.

142 Hate mail to John Mack and Lloyd Blankfein from author's interviews with people close to the matter.

143 "God's Work" from "Meet Mr. Goldman Sachs," *Times* (London), November 8, 2009.

145 Description of Blankfein's upbringing from "Lloyd Blankfein, a Profile," *Forbes,* December 16, 2009.

146 2008 Wall Street compensation figures from "Wall Street on Track to Award Record Pay," *Wall Street Journal,* October 14, 2009.

153 Internal e-mails from Goldman executives describing its inventory of CDOs as "shitty" from "Sachs and the Shitty," *The Economist,* April 29, 2010.

153 Goldman's role in Greek financial crisis from "Wall St. Helped to Mask Debt Fueling Europe's Crisis," *New York Times,* February 13, 2010.

Chapter 7: Fat Cats and Fat Bonuses

158 Account of discussion between Rubin and Obama regarding Valerie Jarrett from author's interviews with people familiar with the conversation.

159 BlackRock's fees for managing Maiden Lane assignments from www.new yorkfed.org/aboutthe fed/Blackrock.

159 "Being in the flow of information" from "BlackRock to Earn $71 Million to Oversee Maiden Lane," Bloomberg, July 14, 2009.

163 "We're the only thing separating you guys from the pitchforks" from author's interviews with people close to the matter.

163 Obama's comments that Blankfein and Dimon were "savvy businessmen" from "Obama Doesn't 'Begrudge' Bonuses for Blankfein, Dimon," Bloomberg, February 10, 2010.

165 Description of Ken Langone's exchange with Lawrence Fink from author's interviews with people familiar with the discussion.

165 Account of Perella's exchange with Fink from author's interviews with people familiar with the discussion.

166 Account of Steve Croft interview from *60 Minutes,* March 23, 2009.

168 Account of discussion between Mack and Blankfein from author's interviews with people familiar with the discussion.

171 Description of Dimon's trip to Washington and use of private plane from author's interviews with people close to the matter and "Blankfein, Mack Flub Making Obama Meeting; Dimon Cozies Up," *Wall Street Journal,* December 14, 2009.

173 Spencer Bachus's comments about "a pet rattlesnake" from author's interview with Bachus.

174 Account of Spitzer's use of a prostitute from "Spitzer Is Linked to Prostitution Ring," *New York Times,* March, 10, 2008.

175 Account of Congressman John Boehner's meeting with Dimon from author's interviews with people close to the matter.

176 Senator Kirsten Gillibrand's claim that "70 percent of New Yorkers hate Wall Street" from author's interviews with people familiar with the matter.

176 Account of Goldman lobbyist pressuring Congresswoman Carolyn Maloney to not investigate the firm's activities from author's interviews with people familiar with the discussion.

177   "16 percent of the economy" from "Record Share of the Economy Spent on Healthcare," *Washington Post,* January 10, 2006.

178   Report that Moody's Investor Service might downgrade rating of U.S. debt from "Moody's: U.S. Rating Could Be Pressured in Long Term," Reuters, January 10, 2009.

Chapter 8: Money Well Spent

181   "There's no guarantee" from author's interview with Lucas van Praag.

181   Goldman's "$23 billion" in bonuses from "With Bigger Bonuses, Another Upside for Banks," *New York Times,* December 31, 2009.

182   James Gorman's salary from "Morgan Chief Sees $15 Million Pay Day," *New York Times,* April 5, 2010.

183   2009 compensation statistics for Bank of America, JPMorgan, Citigroup, and Morgan Stanley from "Banks Set for Record Pay," *Wall Street Journal,* January 14, 2010.

186   Treasury's claim that the government would make $8 billion in profit from its investment in Citigroup from "U.S. Will Begin Selling Citigroup Shares, Could Make Almost $8 Billion," *USA Today,* March, 29, 2010.

187   "I hear about all these wonderful innovations" from "Paul Volcker: Think More Boldly," *Wall Street Journal,* December 14, 2009.

192   Blankfein's 2010 $9 million annual compensation from "Blankfein's $9 Million Bonus Is PR Genius," *Wall Street Journal,* February 5, 2010.

194   "Volcker is crazy" from author's interviews with people close to the conversation.

197   "Goldman will surely deny" from "A Tale of Two Bailouts," *Wall Street Journal,* July16, 2009.

199   Account of Treasury official who orchestrated AIG bailout while owning Goldman Sachs stock from "In U.S. Bailout of A.I.G., Forgiveness for Big Banks," *New York Times,* June 29, 2010.

202   Description of Buffett and Goldman's program to empower small businesses from "Goldman Sachs, Buffett Team to Empower Small Businesses," *Washington Post,* November 18, 2009.

202   "By the end of 2009" from Goldman Sachs Letter to Shareholders, Goldman Sachs 2009 annual report.

204   Details of Mary Schapiro's compensation from "Starting Public-Sector Jobs with Parting Gifts in Hand," *Washington Post,* February 10, 2009.

206   Account of Dimon's conversation with Senator Gillibrand from author's interviews with people familiar with the matter.

210   "Vikram will survive" from author's conversations with people close to the discussion.

212   "We're all Democrats" from "General Electric Pursues Pot of Government Stimulus Gold," *Wall Street Journal*, November, 17, 2009.

212   "$1 in compensation" from "Citi's Pandit Vows to Take $1 Salary and No Bonus," *New York Post*, February 12, 2009.

213   Account of Vikram Pandit's and Sheila Bair's mutual disdain from author's conversations with people close to the matter.

214   Pandit's heated conversation with Sheila Bair from author's interviews with people close to the matter and confirmed by Bair's spokesman.

215   Account of Michael Paese's comments to Nides from author's interviews with people familiar with the discussion.

218   Details of SEC charge against Goldman from "SEC Charges Goldman Sachs with Fraud," *Wall Street Journal*, April 17, 2010.

219   Bear Stearns's refusal to package Paulson's CDOs from Gregory Zuckerman's *The Greatest Trade Ever: The Behind-the-Scenes Story of How John Paulson Defied Wall Street and Made Financial History*, New York, Broadway Books, 2009.

221   Account of Census Bureau hiring practices from "Census Workers Share Their Horror Stories," *New York Post*, June 1, 2010.

222   Account of Dimon nearly punching a senior executive while at Citigroup from author's interviews with people close to the matter.

222   JPMorgan executives claim that they would not go through with the purchase of Bear Stearns again from author's interviews with people close to the matter.

224   Dimon's reactions to criticisms made during JPMorgan's annual meeting from "Mood Sours in a Year at JPM: Dimon Keeps a Title," *American Banker*, May 19, 2010.

226   Account of Obama inviting Bank of America's Brian Moynihan and not Jamie Dimon to a state dinner from "President Obama Has Party, Does Not Invite Former Best Banker," *New York* magazine, May 20, 2010.

227   "The term too big to fail" from "No More 'Too Big to Fail,'" *Washington Post*, November 13, 2009.

229   Dimon's directive to senior JPMorgan staff to begin contributing to the Republican Party from author's interviews and "Irked, Wall St. Hedges Its Bet on Democrats," *New York Times*, February 8, 2010.

232 Citigroup's, Goldman Sachs's, and Morgan Stanley's contributions to the Republican Party from Opensecrets.org.

231 Account of meeting between Wall Street executives and Republican senators Mitch McConnell and John Cornyn from author's interviews with people present during the meeting.

233 Paul Volcker's grading of financial reform from "Volcker Pushes for Reform, Regretting Past Silence," *New York Times,* July 9, 2010.

234 "As it was with Sarbanes-Oxley" from "The Ugly Truth About Financial Reform," *Daily Beast,* July 14, 2010.

235 "The Democrats who wrote the bill" from "The New Lords of Finance: Why Wall Street and Washington Both Like 'Reform,'" *Wall Street Journal,* May 24, 2010.

236 "Cheerleaders for" from "Triumph of the Regulators: The Dodd-Frank Financial Reform Bill Doubles Down on the Same System It Failed," *Wall Street Journal,* June 28, 2010.

236 "America—and our trading partners—need smart" from prepared testimony of Vikram S. Pandit, chief executive officer, Citigroup Inc., before the Congressional Oversight Panel, March 4, 2010.

Afterword

238 "Wall St. Hiring in Anticipation of an Economic Recovery," *New York Times,* July 10, 2010.

239 "An astonishing $1.8 trillion of cash" from "Obama's CEO Problem—and Ours," *Washington Post,* July 5, 2010.

240 Immelt's description of the business environment in the U.S. as "terrible" from "Immelt Hits Out at China and Obama," *Financial Times,* July 1, 2010.

INDEX